THE JOHNS HOPKINS UNIVERSITY STUDIES IN HISTORICAL AND POLITICAL SCIENCE

Under the Direction of the Departments of History,
Political Economy, and Political Science

SERIES LXXIII   NUMBER 1
(1955)

THE PARIS COMMUNE IN FRENCH POLITICS

1871–1880

THE PARIS COMMUNE IN FRENCH POLITICS, 1871-1880

THE HISTORY OF THE AMNESTY OF 1880

VOLUME I

THE PARTIAL AMNESTY

BY

JEAN T. JOUGHIN

BALTIMORE

THE JOHNS HOPKINS PRESS

1955

TO CELIA,
who co-operated.

PREFACE

The Third Republic in France was born in defeat and died seventy years later in decay and collapse. It was the longest lived regime France had had since 1789, although in 1871 the odds were against its even surviving. At the beginning it was saddled not only with the humiliation of defeat at the hands of Bismarck's new German Empire but also by the equally humiliating fratricide that was the Paris Commune, when Frenchman slaughtered Frenchman in full view of the victorious Germans. In addition, power in the Republic lay in the hands of men dedicated to the destruction of republican government.

Even when the Republican forces got control, the pattern of democratic government in France as it evolved during the first decade of the Third Republic seemed to be marked by weakness, confusion, and instability, by contradiction and compromise. These characteristics were in evidence throughout the life of the Third Republic and are present in the Fourth Republic as well. But in the early years of the Third Republic, when its mere survival was in doubt, these qualities can be seen as the reflection of necessary day-to-day tests of strength, reshufflings, and adjustments. In the formative years of the Third Republic, a number of controversial questions strained the solidarity of the Republican forces almost unbearably, often forcing the champions of the Republic to sacrifice principle to the mere staying in power through a middle-of-the-road coalition.

Understanding of how the political practices of modern France developed can be helped by tracing in detail the history of one of the major controversies in the first ten years of the Third Republic. This was the problem of what was ultimately to become of the men who had supported the Paris Commune, a sharp thorn in the side of the Republic from 1871, when the physical destruction of the Commune was accomplished, to 1880, when the last of its political and social consequences were obliterated—by law, at any rate. The events of these years and their effect on the political life of the young Republic made the Commune, after its defeat, more of a force to be

9

reckoned with than it had ever been during the ten weeks the red flag flew over Paris.

The Paris Commune also exercised an influence which outreached the event itself in the area of the labor problem. The France of the Third and Fourth Republics has been and continues to be a land of acute and unabating class struggle, not a hypothetical and ideological class struggle, but a desperately real one, rooted deep in history. Much has been written describing the evolution of the innate class-consciousness of the French workingman prior to 1871. The June Days of 1848 set a wedge between the worker and the State, and the Second Empire drove it deeper, in spite of Louis Napoleon's professions of sympathy for the laboring masses. During these dreary years, workingclass leaders had idealized republican government as the necessary prerequisite for any improvement in conditions. The time, then, for the French worker to have been integrated in the French State was at the very outset of the Third Republic. In Paris at the end of the 1860's there was an articulate artisanate, enlightened as to its own interests and hostile to Empire and Monarchy alike. In 1871, therefore, when the workers and the lower middle class rose in exasperation against a Monarchist-dominated Assembly, their action had the declared aim of saving the Republic. But their effort to defy the Assembly was drowned in blood, and its authors were labeled enemies of society.

If the Third Republic had given positive evidence from its beginning that the old days of preferential treatment among citizens were ended, a reconciliation might have taken place between the workingman and society. This was not done. For one thing, the Paris Commune had inevitably acquired overtones of a class uprising. For another, the Republicans of the 1870's were in far too precarious a position to risk jeopardizing the regime for the sake of the so-called " Communards." By therefore putting off an amnesty for the Paris Commune until for political reasons it could not be postponed any longer, the Republicans deprived the amnesty of any meaning as an act of social reconciliation.

Finally, the class struggle in France was transmitted to the Third Republic strengthened with a powerful new myth, the myth of the Paris Commune as a great proletarian bid for power. The hardening of a small core of actuality from the Paris of 1871 into a fundamental tenet of a powerful ideology was intimately related to the agitation for an amnesty during the first decade of the Third Republic. Indeed, it is the proletarian legend of the Commune which has most often been assessed as its prime—if not only—historical significance. Frank Jellinek, for example, states categorically that " The ultimate historical importance of the Commune is to be found, not in French social or political relationships, but in the domain of revolutionary theory." [1] Similarly, E. S. Mason finds that the Commune, " vanished, leaving hardly a trace on the economic, social, or political life of France," [2] and only subsequently acquired significance " by the activity of the Socialists and the Communists." [3]

There are other writers, however, who hold that the Commune did have an effect upon developments within modern France. At the extreme end of the scale, François Goguel gives the Commune a sweeping role, declaring it a powerful factor not only in the rebirth of conservative interest in imperialism and in the prestige enjoyed by the Republic of Thiers, but also in the radicalism of workingclass movements, in antiparliamentary Boulangism, and, later, in anti-Dreyfusard nationalism.[4] The Commune's broader influence is probably best suggested by David Thomson in his *Democracy in France*, where he writes that, " The Commune of 1871 caught up, fused and projected forward into the new Republic every main strand in the revolutionary tradition. . . . Confused and short-lived though it was, the experience of the Commune provided the lurid and violent background against which the institutions of the Republic were devised and consolidated." [5]

Whatever his view, each of the writers cited above agrees that what was of importance came after the Commune itself, in the way the fact and fiction of that event blended into the

[1] Frank Jellinek, *The Paris Commune of 1870* (*sic*) (London, 1937), 418.
[2] E. S. Mason, *The Paris Commune* (New York, 1930), 296.
[3] *Ibid.*, viii.
[4] François Goguel, *La politique des partis sous la IIIe République* (Paris, 1946), I, 40.
[5] David Thomson, *Democracy in France* (London, 1946), 24.

main currents of life in the last quarter of the nineteenth century. Yet not much study has been devoted to the question of how the defunct Paris Commune figured either in French politics of the 1870's or in contemporary radical movements. And the amnesty of 1880 has been written on only as an argument, in the name of practical politics, for an amnesty covering those convicted by the liberation tribunals following World War II.[6] The present study, *The Paris Commune in French Politics, 1871-1880*, is therefore an examination of the history of the amnesty of 1880 in order to indicate selected possible influences of the Commune and to show how the heritage of the Commune in its several aspects was transmitted to the Third and Fourth Republics.

Any consideration of the amnesty of 1880 and of the politics behind it must of course rest upon the history of the partial amnesty of 1879, to which measure of fractional clemency it was the inevitable sequel. In voting an inconclusive amnesty, the Deputies and Senators committed themselves by irrevocable logic to the enactment of a much broader law. But nothing could have been farther from their intentions in 1879. Seldom has the majority in a representative assembly more dogmatically stated it regarded an issue as definitively closed. Seldom has more political oratory been spilled than on the subject of the impossibility of going any farther than the law of 1879. Yet less than a year and a half later, the Chamber of Deputies voted for a complete, absolute, and unrestricted amnesty for the Commune. Thus the history of the amnesty of 1880 falls sharply into two parts: one, the eight-year period which saw majority sentiment change from a categorical rejection of any kind of amnesty to the acceptance of a carefully delimited measure; and the other, the sixteen-month period which encompassed the dramatic reversal of sentiment from refusal to consider a general forgiveness to the adoption of an almost full amnesty.

In the present study, a separate volume has been devoted to each of these two periods of the amnesty controversy, unequal in length though these spans were. The first volume, *The*

---

[6] Bâtonnier Charpentier, "L'amnistie de 1880," *La Revue* (successor to *Revue des deux mondes*), August 15, 1950, 577-94.

Partial Amnesty, takes into account the fundamental changes which occurred in the Third Republic's political life between 1871 and 1879, and relates to them the changing character of the demands for an amnesty. The effect of these two sets of developments was such that by 1879 the Republican leadership had to recognize that some kind of amnesty law was necessary. It is thus against the broad canvas of the establishment of the Third Republic in fact as well as in name that the events of the first phase of the amnesty controversy are worked out. In contrast, the second volume, *The Final Amnesty*, is characterized by a detailed examination of the swiftly accumulating pressures which culminated in an abrupt about-face on the question of the amnesty. Between the partial amnesty of 1879 and the final amnesty of 1880 there were no important shifts in political strength; there was no change in the elected representatives of the nation. Most of the men who had held a full amnesty to be forever impossible in 1879 deemed it imperative in 1880. The events of the second phase of the amnesty controversy are therefore considered in terms of the almost day-to-day happenings which rendered life embarrassing for the Republican leadership.

One specific limitation of the study should be noted. The influence of the Commune, and particularly the amnesty controversy, in the foreign relations of the Third Republic has not been included. This would be a rich and probably revealing area of investigation. Part of the story has been treated by Georges Bourgin, in " La lutte du gouvernement française contre la première Internationale: Contribution à l'histoire de l'après-Commune." [7] To have dealt with this aspect of the problem in the present volumes, however would have carried them beyond manageable limits, and would have been only peripheral to my main interest, which is domestic politics in the early Third Republic.

The reader should remember at all times that the substance of this book is practical politics. Hence he should not be disturbed by obvious misstatements of facts in some of the quoted material. I have liberally drawn from newspapers, parlia-

[7] In *International review for social history*, IV (1939), 39-138.

mentary debates, and party brochures. The emphasis throughout is not so much upon what was, as it is upon what was said,
what was put before the public, what may or may not have been
believed, for these were the instruments of the agitation for
or against an amnesty.

Since all civil wars—or rebellions—have a common denomi-
nator, a facile comparison could be made between the aftermath of the Paris Commune and the Reconstruction which
followed the American Civil War. The temptation to draw
parallels has been avoided, although the champions of an
amnesty for the Paris Commune succumbed. Ironically enough,
they praised the liberality of the American federal government
and called upon the French Republic to emulate the United
States; their interpretation of developments on the other side
of the Atlantic was strictly confined to President Johnson's 1865
Proclamation of Amnesty, and they neglected to mention the
subsequent punitive control by Congress.

The most meaningful comparison that can be made between
the two civil wars is in terms of the conflict between centraliza-
tion and decentralization in government. Just as the Con-
federacy represented an obsolescent concept of the relationship
between the state and the federal government, so the Paris
Commune had an antique view of the role of the municipality
vis-à-vis the national government. Both "lost causes" were
victims of the swing toward concentration of political power
at the top which has been characteristic of the late nineteenth
and the twentieth centuries.

The emergence of the unitary state as the dominant form of
political organization was reflected in a fundamental shift that
took place in the ideology of French Republicans during the
course of the amnesty controversy. At the end of the Empire,
universal suffrage was the keystone of the Republican creed;
the virtues claimed for it figured prominently in the agitation
for an amnesty. By the end of the decade, however, the slogans
and symbols of nationalism were tending to displace universal
suffrage in the thinking of the Republican leadership.

To conclude, I wish to express my sincere thanks to those
who have contributed in one way or another to this study. I
am deeply indebted to Professors David Thomson, Georges

Bourgin, and Henry Ehrmann, all of whom were kind enough to discuss with me the general concept of the book. None of them, however, should be held responsible for the opinions and interpretations found herein. To my mother, for her genuine encouragement and support, I am profoundly grateful. My friends Beatrice F. Hyslop and Emma C. Llewellyn have generously provided me with suitable places to work, when these were a prime necessity. Finally, to the officials and staffs of libraries both here and in Paris and Geneva I owe appreciation for unfailing courtesy and co-operation.

JEAN T. JOUGHIN

Hastings-on-Hudson
September 1, 1955

TABLE OF CONTENTS

VOLUME I

THE PARTIAL AMNESTY

CHAPTER I

THE PARIS COMMUNE: THE EVENT

From March 18 to May 24, 1871, the red flag of revolution flew over Paris. And even after the remnants of the insurgent government abandoned the burning Hôtel de Ville, four more days of brutal street fighting were necessary before the last defenders of the Paris Commune were crushed by the armies of Versailles. Months more—years even—were necessary before the legal authority was satisfied that it had made France safe from the revolutionary rabble of Paris.

What was the Paris Commune? Gambetta, some time after the event, was to characterize it as a " convulsion of misery, famine, and despair." But to the National Assembly, which ruled France in 1871, the Commune was an attempt to subvert the whole order of decency and civilization, and the violence of the Commune's final agony only more firmly coupled to the restoration of order a desire for revenge.

The " Commune " in its simplest aspect meant merely the municipal council of Paris. Historically, the strength of the communal idea derived from the powerful Commune of 1793, which had in many ways been the heart and soul of the revolutionary movement. Deprived of its municipal freedoms under the Second Empire and in September 1870 cut off from the rest of France by encircling Prussian armies, the Paris of the radical clubs and the National Guard began to think about a magic Commune. The Government of National Defense, which had taken over the power lost by Napoleon III, was regarded with distrust and suspicion; Paris was by no means sure its interests were in good hands. Efforts to lift the siege did not seem to be pushed vigorously, and the open distrust of the National Guard manifested by the regular commanders was galling.[1] When announcement of a possible negotiated armistice, coupled

---

[1] See especially Gustave Flourens, *Paris livré*, 3e édition (Paris, 1871), 101 ff, particularly 102, on the " ardor " of the National Guard and its relations with the regular commanders.

21

with news of the fall of Metz, was made at the end of October, discontent erupted into an invasion of the Hôtel de Ville. Shouting "*Vive la Commune*," the mob of National Guardsmen demanded immediate municipal elections. Troops loyal to the Defense, however, rescued the Government, and in a plebiscite held a few days later, almost ninety per cent of the voters endorsed the Government of National Defense. Similarly, in the municipal elections of November 5—held as a concession —the majority of the mayors-elect belonged to the forces of order; the moderate Jules Ferry replaced the moderate Arago at the Hôtel de Ville. But in the clubs and in the left-wing press, the attacks on the Government were unabated.

The siege continued, and so did the unrest in Paris. As privations increased, the Government had to deal with sporadic riots over food distribution. A far more serious cause of irritation, however, was the fact that after the middle of January feeling was growing in official circles that further resistance was senseless, although the people of Paris—despite hunger and cold and the bombardment which had begun on January 5—still had a firm will to hold out. In this atmosphere of mutual suspicion and annoyance, a group of National Guardsmen early on January 22 forced the prison of Mazas and freed its political prisoners. Later the same day a mob once more formed around the Hôtel de Ville, demanding a Commune. Talk accomplished nothing, and soon shots were being exchanged. This kept up for half an hour, until the demonstrators —who had lost around thirty men—were dispersed. The Government remained unshaken. As a result of the abortive insurrection, the radical clubs of Paris were closed and over eighty suspected instigators of the affair were arrested.

Four days later Paris learned that the Defense had agreed on armistice terms, calling for the immediate election of a National Assembly to treat with the victor and the disarming of all French troops except for one division. The siege officially ended at midnight, January 27. Paris felt betrayed, humiliated by the Government's coming to terms. "History will have a hard time understanding something like this, which is unique in its annales. It will ask in astonishment how a people could fall to this degree of degradation, could consent to its ruin with such cowardice," wrote Gustave Flourens, a fire-eating journalist, on January 28.[2] Paris found small consolation in the fact that the armistice allowed the National Guard to keep its arms, when the flags of the newly-created German Empire rose over the forts of the city on January 29.

Paris was still more deeply disturbed when the results of the general election held February 8 were known. Although the city had voted overwhelmingly in favor of the Republic and of continuing the war, rural France had given the National Assembly, which met at Bordeaux on February 12, a strong monarchist-clerical majority with but one thought on the issue of peace or war—peace seemingly at any price. Paris was blamed for having caused the war's prolonging. The most powerful figure in the new Assembly, moreover, was Adolphe Thiers. Returned from over twenty Departments, the former Minister to Louis Philippe was named, on February 17, Chief of the Executive Power in the Third Republic. Much of Thiers' reputation rested upon his vanquishing of Paris in 1848; his power in 1871 could only be interpreted as a mandate against Paris.

In the capital city itself the lead in organizing defense against whatever the National Assembly might do came from members of the National Guard. During the siege they had got in the habit of working independently of their officers through special committees, and now they took steps, at a mass meeting on February 15, to make this independence complete by giving a federal form of organization to the battalions of the National Guard and placing them under the control of an elected command.

Before the proposed federation was actually brought into being, several more developments had widened the gap between Paris and Bordeaux. For one thing, there was the Assembly's requirement that henceforth no National Guardsman would receive his daily allowance of 1 franc 50 except upon written declaration of indigence. Also there was Bordeaux's appointment of Vinoy, the general who had signed the capitulation, as Commander-in-Chief of the National Guard, replacing

[2] *Op. cit.*, 1 (from the Preface, dated Paris, January 28, 1871).

General Clément Thomas, who had resigned after the February 15 meeting. In Paris, three days of spontaneous patriotic demonstrations began on February 24 with a " pilgrimage " of National Guardsmen to the Place de Bastille, where a red flag was displayed for the first time in Paris since 1848.[3] At this very moment, the Government of Thiers signed a preliminary peace treaty with Bismarck, and Paris learned that the Germans were to enter the city—specifically that 30,000 German troops were to encamp in the Champs-Elysées on March 1. The immediate response of the National Guardsmen to this news was to move their cannon from the gunparks at Passy and the Place Wagram into Paris, to Montmartre, Belleville, the Place des Vosges, and other popular quarters. There was also much talk of attacking the Germans upon their entering the city. The provisional committee elected by the National Guard at the February 15 meeting put an end to this wild idea, but only by promising to isolate the Germans from the rest of Paris by barricades.

The Germans entered Paris on schedule, March 1, to find a dead city. The stillness of deep mourning was everywhere. No one saw, no one spoke to the conqueror. No shop was open to do business with him. " Paris of her own free will suspended her life," reported the next day's *Journal officiel*, adding, " [Paris] . . . understands that it is incumbent upon her not to add more terrible and perhaps irreparable misfortunes to [those] which [already] crush our country, . . . that she owes it to herself . . . to endure this new test with proud dignity. . . . Paris is calm." [4] Patronizing at worst, these remarks, taken as insults, created more bad feeling between the harrassed, exhausted people of Paris and the Government. But far more real causes of resentment and fear were to come. It was only too plain where the National Assembly was heading: a bill had just been passed in committee for fixing the seat of power elsewhere than Paris; final peace terms had been accepted— the loss of Alsace-Lorraine, the five-billion franc indemnity, the occupation of the eastern forts—which seemed extraordi-

---

[3] [Prosper-Olivier] Lissagaray, *Histoire de la Commune de 1871*, Nouvelle édition (Paris, 1947), 70.

[4] *Journal officiel de la République française*, March 2, 1871, 128:2.

narily harsh; a Bonapartist with an unsavoury record, Aurelles de Paladine, had been named the new Commander-in-Chief of the National Guard; and a bill had been introduced on overdue commercial paper which portended bankruptcy for many thousands. Finally, it was impossible to escape the impression that the National Assembly intended to re-establish monarchy in France.

Inevitably, therefore, when the Federation of the National Guard was formally established on March 3, its statutes emphasized loyalty to the Republic. More than that, the delegates present at this meeting resolved that " The Department of Seine constitutes itself an independent Republic in the event that the Assembly should take the capital away from Paris." [5] It was further provided that the governing body of the National Guard was to be a committee, made up of three delegates from each arrondissement, elected without reference to rank.

Two weeks later, the Central Committee of the National Guard held Paris. Its advent to power had not been the result of any conscious plan, and it was conspicuously embarrassed by and reluctant to assume the responsibility that had almost accidentally fallen upon it. The Central Committee, it should be pointed out, had no political or social program. Many of the men elected to it were political unknowns, and as a group it had no ideological homogeneity. Besides preserving the Republic, its view of its function was to defend the rights of the people in case of aggression. Despite its inexperience and its rather vaguely defined goals, however, the Central Committee was the one effective organization on the scene when the National Assembly, disregarding the black mood that Paris was in, indulged in several measures which made popular anger erupt.

The Bordeaux Assembly had obviously wanted to believe Paris in a state of insurrection from the federating of the National Guard on. Assurances by the Deputies sitting from Paris that all was calm had been contemptuously dismissed. Far from any thought of placating the troublesome city, the Assembly now proceeded to enact measures designed to restore the country

[5] Lissagaray, *Histoire de la Commune de 1871*, 74.

rapidly to business as usual, but guaranteed to infuriate the majority of the Parisian population. March 10 was the fatal day. The moratorium on commercial paper which had gone into effect the past August was rescinded; under the new law, repayment—including interest—was to begin in three days.[6] At the same time, the Assembly resolutely refused to consider any measure of relief for the thousands of tenants unable to pay their rent because the war had wiped out their means of livelihood.[7] The ultimate blow against Paris came when Versailles, the traditional home of monarchy, was designated as the capital, instead of the city which was the traditional home of Republican France.[8] The National Assembly then adjourned for ten days.

The National Guard Takes Paris

Before the Assembly resumed, Paris was to be in open revolt. Grievance continued to be added to grievance. Just when Paris was learning of the Assembly's menacing actions, it also was stunned by the news that six Republican newspapers had been suppressed,[9] and that the death sentence—*in absentia*, however—had been passed upon the old revolutionary Blanqui and the popular Flourens for their parts in the October 31 riots.[10] Then there was an attempt by Aurelles to take away the Montmartre cannon. The Guardsmen of the XVIIIth refused to surrender these pieces and dragged them, without any real interference, up the Butte to a commanding position.

On March 15 the acting Central Committee of the National Guard gave way to a permanent body which was the product of elections in the arrondissements. On March 15 also, Thiers

---

[6] See *Journal officiel de la République française*, March 12, 1871, 159:3-4, and March 13, 1871, 167:1.

[7] See *ibid.*, March 12, 1871, 163:2, for the bill introduced by Millière, Deputy from Paris, providing that persons unable to pay their rent should not be required to pay if they could prove that their loss of livelihood had been caused by the war.

[8] See *ibid.*, March 11, 1871, 157:2, and March 13, 1871, 172:2.

[9] *Ibid.*, March 12, 159:3. In addition, all future periodical publications dealing with politics or economics were forbidden for as long as martial law continued in Paris.

[10] And upon two other men as well. Also, Jules Vallès got six months in jail, and Goupil got two years. See *ibid.*, March 13, 1871, 172:2.

arrived in Paris determined to assert the authority of Versailles in the worsening situation. By now the cannon of the National Guard had become symbolic of the test of strength between Paris and Versailles, and Thiers' first move was to order their seizure. In a placard announcing his intentions, which was posted the night of March 17, he called upon the people of Paris to endorse his use of force.

Before dawn on March 18 a band of soldiers, led by General Lecomte, climbed the narrow path of the Butte Montmartre and surprised the sentinels guarding the cannon. Getting possession of the cannon was easy but getting them away was another matter, for the troops had brought no horses with them. Only by around eight o'clock in the morning had they begun to move a few pieces. But by that hour Montmartre was awake. First came the women, going about their errands. The commotion they raised when they saw the troops halted further movement of the cannon and brought out the rest of the quarter to see what was happening. The National Guard was alerted and soon commanded the scene. Lecomte and his officers were arrested and imprisoned.

That afternoon another general fell into the hands of the Guardsmen. This was Clément Thomas, detested by many for his role in the Revolution of 1848. Although having no part in the operation against the cannon and not even in uniform, he was recognized as he wandered about and was immediately seized. The fury of the XVIIIth arrondissement, now that the cannon had been saved, turned against the generals. Before their improvised prison on the Rue des Rosiers a mob of soldiers was demanding their blood. The National Guard officers stationed to protect the prisoners were forced aside—one was killed—and Clément Thomas and Lecomte were thrown into the garden behind the house and shot.

Elsewhere in the city the alerted National Guard had saved the rest of the cannon. Gathering revolutionary momentum as the day went on, they began the occupation of public buildings. Little or no resistance was offered. When the Hôtel de Ville was surrounded at seven-thirty in the evening, the police troops guarding it fled. An hour later Ferry, the Mayor, and his assistant, having no orders, no instructions from the Government, left the dark and deserted building. Soon after, the National Guard moved in. The gas was brightly lit, and a red flag was hoisted on the belfry.

In the face of this spontaneous and successful uprising, and lacking strength within the city, Thiers decided to abandon Paris to the insurgents, at least temporarily.[11] That very afternoon he instructed all the regular troops to withdraw to Versailles. At the same time he ordered the evacuation of the forts to the south of the city, as well as the commanding heights of Mount Valerian. These movements were carried out the night of March 18-19 without interference from the National Guard.

While the troops were withdrawing, the first emissary from Versailles was talking to the Central Committee. He was Langlois, a Lieutenant-Colonel in the National Guard and formerly a Proudhonian member of the International, with whom the Government had hastily replaced the unpopular Aurelles as Commander-in-Chief of the National Guard. It was hoped Langlois would be *persona grata* to both sides and so be able to induce the Central Committee to recognize his authority. Accompanied by the Radical Deputy Lockroy, he presented himself at the Hôtel de Ville. The Central Committee would not give up the Federation's asserted right to elect its own officers, and Langlois would not recognize the possibility of any authority except that of the National Assembly at Versailles.

The next unsuccessful attempt to conciliate the Central Committee was made the night of March 19, and was on the initiative of the Deputies sitting in the National Assembly from Paris and the Mayors of the twenty arrondissements. To the latter, Thiers had turned over whatever remained of the legal authority when he had ordered the withdrawal from the city. This group of men—the Mayors and the Deputies—was the elite of the Republican, radical, and socially-oriented politicians in France: Clemenceau, Tolain, Lockroy, Millière—these were the most conspicuous figures. Their plea to the Central Committee was to return within the bounds of legality, give up the

[11] *Journal officiel de la République française*, March 20, 1871, 189:1, carries the Government's statement on the departure from Paris.

Hôtel de Ville, accept the authority of the National Assembly, and above all relinquish the illegal idea of conducting elections for an independent Paris municipal council. In return, the Deputies promised to do everything within their power to get redress of Paris's very legitimate grievances. It was perfectly plain, they argued, that no concessions could be got from the Assembly so long as the Central Committee held on to the power it had not only usurped but had murdered two generals in the doing. The Central Committee was unmoved. Pointing out the minority impotence of the Republican and radical Deputies in the National Assembly, it questioned that the would-be conciliators could even make themselves heard in that body, much less obtain what Paris wanted. Warnings that the Central Committee was preparing a repetition of the June Days of 1848 had no effect. The new men of the Hôtel de Ville insisted that their loyalty to those who had elected them required the Central Committee to defend the freedom of Paris and the Republic against the reactionary Assembly. Talk went on until after midnight and ended with the defeated conciliators heart-sick or exasperated or both.

Even before this meeting the Central Committee, once it had recovered from the surprise at finding itself the *de facto* power in Paris, had begun to carry out its role of revolutionary government. It had taken over the functions of the various Ministries and public services. It had ended martial law and abolished military tribunals. It had announced amnesty for all political offenses. And it had issued a call for municipal elections on Wednesday, March 22. Now that there was to be no conciliation, the Central Committee sought—and got—a million francs from the Bank of France against the city's credit, sent its own troops to occupy the forts (but Versailles beat them to Mount Valerian), and enacted measures to ease the economic straits of the populace: sale of objects in the national pawnshops was forbidden; payments due on commercial paper were put off for a month; landlords were forbidden to evict tenants until further notice. Finally, on March 22, it put down with force an attempt by some of the city's outraged conservatives to seize the Place Vendôme.

The Election of the Paris Commune

The announced municipal elections, twice postponed because of disorder in the city, were finally held on March 26. There had been only a week for anything resembling a campaign, and as a result no strong parties or factions with clear-cut platforms had had time to emerge. In the lower and middle-class arrondissements, various *ad hoc* committees had put forward men of known revolutionary backgrounds; the Central Committee itself had warned against professional politicians and urged the election of "men of the people"; [12] and the Paris section of the International Workingmen's Association had issued a proclamation in which the emancipation of the worker was equated with freedom of the municipality.[13] As was to be expected, the conservative quarters put forth more moderate candidates. The voting took place in a comparatively quiet atmosphere. The election boards sent out by the Central Committee to set up polls in the local town halls met some opposition from the staffs of the incumbent administration, but the polls opened on schedule. During the day, thirty armed National Guardsmen stood duty at each poll to maintain order. When the votes were counted, however, it was found that only 47 percent of the registered voters, or around 230,000 men, had taken part in the balloting for Paris's new Commune.

For whom had their ballots been cast? [14] Of the ninety places to be filled, sixteen went to moderates or conservatives, for the most part mayors and assistant mayors. As was to be

[12] Georges Bourgin, *Les premières journées de la Commune* (Paris, 1928), 116-7, gives the text of this proclamation.

[13] See *Réimpression du Journal officiel de la République française sous La Commune*, Victor Bunel, L'Editeur (Paris, n. d.), March 27, 1871, 66:1-2–67:1, for text of the proclamation by the Federal Council of the Parisian Sections of the International Workingmen's Association and the Federal Chamber of Workers' Societies.

For the dates March 20 to March 22, this publication bears the title *Réimpression du Journal officiel de La Commune*; the former title applies from March 22 through May 24, the final issue.

[14] The following analysis of the composition of the Commune has been derived from *Réimpression du Journal officiel de la République française sous La Commune*, March 31, 1871, 101:1-108:2; Georges Bourgin and Gabriel Henriot, *Procès-verbaux de la Commune de 1871* (Paris, 1924), I, 28-30, 64-8; Lissagaray, *Histoire de la Commune de 1871*, 136-6; and Bourgin, *Les premières journées de la Commune*, 125-7.

expected, the Ist, IInd, and XVIth arrondissements elected slates solidly opposed to everything that had happened on March 18 and subsequently. In the IXth three out of five members-elect of the Commune were moderates, while in the deputations elected for the IIrd, the VIth, and the XIIth, a moderate formed a minority of one in each instance. The best-known names that figured on the right of the Commune were Méline, Tirard, and Marmottan.[15] At the other extreme, fifteen members of the International, of whom five—Pindy, Varlin, Avrial, Theisz, and Langevin—were also members of the Federal Chamber of Workers' Societies, were elected. Of these men, Varlin was chosen in three arrondissements, and Theisz in two.[16] The largest group to win seats in the Commune—nineteen in all—was recruited from men who had won followings as popular orators in the dozens of so-called " red clubs " which had flourished in Paris during the siege, and whose views on political and social matters covered a wide range, although all had some kind of revolutionary orientation.[17] Of the forty-two men who had made up the Central Committee,[18] thirteen found seats on the Communal council.[19] Jourde, Billioray, and Eudes (later named by the Commune as one of its generals) —these were the members of the Central Committee who were going to figure prominently in the affairs of the Commune.

[15] The sixteen moderates were as follows: A. Adam, Rochard, Méline, Barré (Ist, Louvre) ; Brelay, Tirard, Chéron, Loiseau-Pinson (IInd, Bourse) ; Murat (IIIrd, Temple) ; Leroy (VIth, Luxembourg) ; Desmarest, E. Ferry, Nast (IXth, Opéra) ; Fruneau (XIIth, Reuilly) ; Dr. Marmottan, Bouteiller (XVIth, Passy).

[16] Other members of the International elected to the Commune were: Lefrançais, A. Clémence, E. Gérardin (IVth, Hôtel de Ville) ; Vaillant (VIIIth, Elysée) ; Assi (XIth, Popincourt) ; Duval (XIIIth, Gobelins) ; V. Clément (XVth, Vaugirard) ; Chalain, Malon (XVII, Batignolles). Pindy was elected from the IIIrd, Varlin from the VIth, XIIth, and XVIIth, Avrial from the XIth, Theisz from the XIIth and the XVIII (Buttes-Montmartre).

[17] Representatives of the " red clubs " were: Demay (IIIrd) ; Amouroux (IVth) ; Régère, Ledroit (Vth, Panthéon) ; Goupil (VIth) ; Parisel, Lefèvre, Urbain (VIIth, Palais Bourbon) ; Allix (VIIIth) ; U. Parent (IXth) ; Champy, Rastoul (Xth, Enclos St. Laurent) ; L. Melliet (XIIIth) ; Martelet, Decamp (XIVth, Observatoire) ; E. Clément, Charles Gérardin (XVIIth) ; Puget, Ostyn (XIXth, Buttes-Chaumont).

[18] On the difficulty in determining the exact membership of the Central Committee, see Lissagaray, 109, fn (1).

[19] Not counting Varlin, Pindy, and Duval, who—though members of the Central Committee—have been given above as members of the International.

Among the thorough-going revolutionaries elected numbered six Blanquists—Raoul Rigault, Chardon, Ferré, Tridon, Ranvier, and Protot. Blanqui himself, whom Thiers had had arrested in the provinces on March 17 as a precautionary measure and against whom the *in absentia* death sentence was not carried out, was elected from the XVIIIth and XXth arrondissements. Most of the remaining members-elect of the Commune were journalists. Young firebrands of the opposition such as J. B. Clément, Jules Vallès, Paschal Grousset, Gustave Flourens, and Auguste Vermorel, rubbed shoulders with veterans of 1848 and the Empire such as Charles Delescluze, Ferdinand Gambon, Arthur Arnould, Dr. Robinet, and the irrascible Félix Pyat. Another veteran of 1848 was Jules Miot. Then there was Gambettta's friend Arthur Ranc. And finally, one Icarian socialist—the aged Charles Beslay—completed the membership of the Commune as elected on March 26. A more motley crew would be difficult to imagine. As Georges Bourgin sums it up: ". . . on one hand, grey beards of 'forty-eight or would be politicians, radical revolutionaries enamoured of the Jacobinism of history, puffed up with the high-flown language of the ' Mountain,' theoretical republicans, ferocious anticlericals, pure Blanquists . . . , dissident Blanquists, newspapermen of '48 or of '67 and opponents of E. Ollivier and of the National Defense, . . . the elect of the ' red clubs,' . . . —on the other hand the members and friends of the International. . . ." [20]

The Paris Commune of 1871 was officially installed on March 28, amid great spectacle. While bands played the *Marseillaise* and the *Chant du départ*, while cannon thundered a salute, the members of the retiring Central Committee turned over their power to the Commune-elect in front of an enthusiastic crowd massed before the Hôtel de Ville. " In the name of the people, the Commune is proclaimed," Ranvier shouted, and the National Guard filed in review past the red-draped platform.

Paris now had its independent municipal government. It had cut itself off from the rest of France administratively, and in the next few days it was to be cut off from the rest of France physically to a certain extent, but not so completely as during the siege. Isolation had not been the intent of those men who had invoked the idea of a Commune as the device for restoring Paris to her freedom. The Central Committee had been explicit on this point. " Paris has no intention in the least of separating herself from France," it had proclaimed on March 21.[21] Again, at the first sitting of the Commune, Beslay, presiding as eldest member, had addressed his colleagues as follows. " The enfranchising of the Commune is therefore, I repeat, the enfranchising of the Republic herself; each social group is going to find again its full independence and complete freedom of action.

" The Commune will be concerned with what is local.

" The Department will be concerned with what is regional.

" The Government will be concerned with what is national." [22]

But there was no place in the France of the National Assembly for an autonomous Paris. Furthermore, the Commune's hope of being supported by similar moves in the other major cities was short-lived. Attempts at municipal revolution in half a dozen towns of the Center and South were put down in a few days; on March 28 the Minister of Interior was able to report that the Assembly had only Paris to deal with.[23] Through a circular to the Prefects, the Government had already called upon the Departments for aid against Paris.[24] Finally, at the end of March, private as well as public communication between Paris and the nation at large was cut off by the disruption of the postal service. The once capital city now stood alone.

The Start of Hostilities

Fighting began almost at once. On March 28 Thiers, in a telegram to the Prefects, gave ample warning of what was to come. " If the Government," he wired, " in order to avoid the shedding of blood as long as possible, has temporized, it has not remained idle, and the means of re-establishing order will only be the better prepared and the more certain because

---

[21] *Réimpression du Journal officiel de la Commune*, March 21, 1871, 15:1.

[22] Bourgin and Henriot, *Procès-verbaux de la Commune de 1871*, I, 46.

[23] National Assembly, *Annales*, II, 154-5.

[24] *Journal officiel de la République française*, March 28, 1871, 297:1; the dispatch is dated Versailles, March 23.

of this." [25] A few days later, April 2, the batteries of Versailles opened fire against the outskirts of Paris.

In the first skirmishing the Federals, badly outnumbered, lost the village of Courbevoie, which commanded the approach to Versailles. Their losses were not great—a dozen dead and a few taken prisoner. But the summary execution of five of these prisoners served notice to the Commune that this was a civil conflict in which no quarter would be given. Immediately the Commune's military chiefs urged an attack on Versailles, a suicidal plan opposed by the majority. Nevertheless, on April 3 the forces of the Commune were led forth on their only major venture outside Paris. Duval, Eudes, Bergeret, and Flourens—these were the men behind the ill-fated expedition. With no functioning military organization—no system of command, no plan of communication, no quartermaster services, no ammunition for many of the Federals' guns—they thought to take Versailles. The sally was very soon turned into a retreat. Shells from Mount Valerian broke up the column headed via Rueil, and during the next two days the troops of Versailles checked the Federals proceeding via Châtillon and Sèvres. Advance units of Federals vainly tried to hold back the enemy, but in the end, the troops of the Commune were forced back into Paris. The Commune was badly shaken by the events of April 3 to 5. Two of its most popular leaders—Flourens and Duval—had been killed, not in the fighting, but in brutal, on-the-spot executions. Nor were they the only ones; from the ranks of Federals surrendering under promise of life to be spared, all regular soldiers found fighting on the side of the Commune were taken and shot. Prisoners taken to Versailles alive numbered over two thousand,[26] and included the eminent geographer Elisée Réclus.

Paris and Versailles were at war, and the sally of April 3 demonstrated how poorly organized the Commune was to utilize the resources of manpower and equipment it possessed. Its first response to the disaster was to pass a law of hostages, designed to forestall further massacring of prisoners. Intro-

[25] *Les murailles politiques françaises* (Paris, 1873-4), II, 131.
[26] *Journal officiel de la République française*, April 5, 1871, 405:2.

duced by Delescluze, the law provided for arrest and judgment within three days of persons accused of aiding Versailles; if found guilty, they were to become "hostages of the people of Paris"; finally, for each execution of a prisoner of war or any supporter of the Commune, three hostages would immediately be put to death.[27]

For its part, the Central Committee, which had by no means disappeared from the picture when the Commune was installed, responded to the beginning of hostilities by a declaration which sought to transform the civil war into a class war. The Central Committee had already, even before the election of the Commune, characterized the uprising of March 18 as the work of the proletariat, "those who produce everything and enjoy nothing."[28] Now, on April 5, it summoned the people of Paris, "Workers, don't deceive yourselves . . . ; this is the great fight. Parasitism and work, exploitation and production are in the lists."[29] Since the Commune itself was not committed to any social or economic program, to any revolutionary ideology, proclamations such as this could not fail to be embarrassing to it—as indeed was the whole continuing existence of the Central Committee as a powerful separate entity.

Weaknesses of the Commune

One of the fatal flaws of the Commune was its ever more apparent inability to deal firmly with the challenge presented to its authority by the Central Committee. Formally and officially, the Central Committee had stepped out of political and administrative affairs with the installation of the Commune. The following day its delegates had appeared before that body to pledge loyalty, saying that they would not cease "to be always in accord with the Commune."[30] In fact, however, the Central Committee continued to issue public proclamations, defied a subsequent order to disband, arrogated to itself a large

[27] Bourgin and Henriot, *Procès-verbaux de la Commune*, I, 125. The public announcement of this decree, however, stated that hostages would be put to death in equal number, or at the ratio of two hostages for every supporter of the Commune (*ibid.*, 129).

[28] Lissagaray, *Histoire de la Commune de 1871*, 104.

[29] Bourgin and Henriot, *Procès-verbaux de la Commune*, I, 131.

[30] *Ibid.*, I, 36.

part of the direction of military affairs, set up a system of sub-committees which issued orders on their own authority, and toward the very end, when the Commune was disintegrating, came to regard itself once again as the sole revolutionary authority.

Nor was the Commune more conspicuously successful in regulating its own affairs. Throughout its nine-week existence, the revolutionary municipal council was the victim of confusion and ineptness, arising largely from the diversity of views and personalties within its membership. The defense of Paris, in the hands of the Commune, became one misfortune after another. Disputes over military commanders were frequent, and changes in command correspondingly frequent. Troop movements were unco-ordinated, so that some battalions remained unrelieved at their posts, while others saw little action. Communiqués from the front lines were ignored. And while construction of stronger defenses was ordered, the work remained largely unexecuted for lack of a vigorous follow-up. Similarly the ninety-man Commune failed to solve its problems of effective executive leadership (it experimented first with an elected executive committee and then with the heads of the various services, grouped in council), and of internal security.

Inevitably, confronted by the multiple difficulties of its situations and apparently incapable of solving them, the Commune lost rapidly in prestige. So rapidly, in fact, did popular interest decline that few citizens bothered to vote in the supplementary elections held on April 16. Thirty-one places in the Commune were vacant, through resignations, death, or the fact of representatives' having been elected from more than one arrondissement.[31] Only 12½ per cent of the registered voters cast their ballots, and even though the Commune—doing violence, many

---

[31] The conservative members-elect of the Commune had resigned almost immediately: Tirard on March 28; Rochat on March 29; Méline, Robinet, E. Adam, and Leroy on March 30; Fruneau, Loiseau-Pinson, and Brelay on March 31; Marmottan on April 1; and Murat on April 2. After the fatal sally, U. Parent resigned on April 5; Ernest Lefèvre and Arthur Ranc on April 6; and Goupil on April 11. In addition, Flourens and Duval were dead, and Blanqui—held prisoner—was unable to assume his place. Of those elected in more than one arrondissement, Varlin had opted for the VIth, Delescluze for the XIXth; A. Arnould for the IVth, and Theisz for the XVIIIth.

thought, to the principle of universal suffrage—declared a simple majority of votes cast sufficient to elect, only twenty-one of the vacancies were filled.[32] These elections of April 16 were, in their way, almost as disastrous for the Commune as the military misadventure of April 3 had been. The apathy toward the elections showed the Hôtel de Ville that it was no longer supported by the revolutionary *élan* of a month before. The unfilled vacancies remaining in the municipal council and the insignificant vote which had brought in such replacements as there were denied the Commune its character as the true creation of universal suffrage. Finally, both the violent disputes and the petty bickerings which took place in the communal council on the question of validating the elections tended still further to destroy its public support.

Provincial Communes

Nor was the Commune able, despite repeated attempts, to win effective support in the provinces. Reference has already been made to the several unsuccessful movements in the Center and in the South. At Lyons, as soon as news arrived of what had happened in Paris on March 18, a large section of opinion had urged the same pursuit of municipal freedom for Lyons. After the Mayor had refused to yield an inch, units of the National Guard had invaded the Hôtel de Ville, arrested the Prefect, set up a five-man executive committee, and raised the red flag. This had been on March 22. But the opposition had easily gathered its forces, and two days later the insurrection at Lyons had melted away. At Saint Etienne, on March 23, delegates of the local revolutionary club had called upon the Municipal Council to demand a Commune. This had been followed by promises of new municipal elections, and several days of disorder during which an angry mob had milled around in front of the Hôtel de Ville, where National Guardsmen, dissatisfied with the scant concessions offered, had forced entry and set up an executive committee. Both sides had been put in a rage—the populace by the shooting of a workingman in the

[32] Two of the men thus validated—Briosne from the IXth and Rogeard from the XIth—refused to sit because of the light vote.

mob, and the forces of order by the killing of the unpopular Prefect while he was held prisoner. But the insurrectionary council of the National Guard had not been able to hold its followers, and the importation of regular troops had forced it out of the Hôtel de Ville on March 28. Numerous arrests had then been made. There had been similar unsuccessful movements toward a Commune at Le Creusot, Toulouse, Cette and Perpignan. At Marseilles, an ardent Republican, Gaston Crémieux, had taken the lead in urging the radical clubs to support Paris. On March 23, National Guard units had seized power and set up a six-man committee for the purpose, it was said, of preventing civil war and of watching over the Republic. But the revolution at Marseilles had not picked up support, and on April 4, regular troops had bottled up its leaders in the Prefecture, which had then been subjected to an eight-hour bombardment. The repression that followed the Commune at Marseilles had been heavy-handed; hundreds of prisoners had been shut up in the Chateau d'If, and months later—after Paris itself had been crushed—Crémieux and other members of the local Commune were to be executed. The Commune at Narbonne had seemed the most likely to endure, because it had had competent leadership in the person of Emile Digeon, an old radical, hardened by exile under the Empire. Promptly, however, Narbonne had been surrounded by regular troops, and the barricades that Digeon had had erected had been worthless against the threat of a bombardment that would have razed everything. The town hall had been evacuated, while Digeon had sought his own arrest. The last of the provincial Communes, Limoges, had been touched off by Paris's defeat in the sally of April 3. But although the Prefecture had been occupied by National Guardsmen, they had not held it overnight.

What had the Paris Commune been doing to support its sister movements in the provinces? It had sent delegates—notably Landeck and Amouroux—to spur on the revolutionary spirit in the South.[33] Its executive commission had issued a proclamation to the provinces on April 6, denying the character given to the Paris Commune by the Versailles press and insisting that the

[33] Bourgin and Henriot, *Procès-verbaux de la Commune*, I, 133 (sitting of April 6).

Commune was fighting for municipal autonomy and the salvation of the Republic.[34]

The Commune's biggest bid for support from the provinces, however, was its " Declaration to the French People," issued on April 19. This document was the Commune's summing up of its program. Largely from the pen of the old Jacobin Delescluze, it represented Paris as once more suffering for the whole of France, " for which, by its combats and its sacrifices, it is preparing intellectual, moral, administrative, and economic regeneration, glory and prosperity." [35] It closed by summoning France " to disarm Versailles by the solemn manifestation of its irresistable will." [36] As an appeal for aid, the declaration's vagueness and doctrinaire quality made it wholly ineffective.

Despite these fine words, the Commune continued to argue within itself as to what its practical relations with the provinces should be. Some wanted to send delegates to rouse the provinces to arms, others felt that hard-pressed Paris could not afford to dispense with a single one of its revolutionary leaders. The subject was warmly discussed on April 22, but the debate was closed without anything's being decided.[37] At no time in its short life did the Paris Commune consolidate it position with sympathetic elements in the provinces. An occasional emissary, without instructions, without authority, was sent out, but that was all. On May 15, it is true, Paris issued a call to arms to the provinces, but then it was too late.

Government by the Commune

Nor did the Commune in its administration of internal affairs within the city of Paris consolidate its position with potential supporters of the lower middle and the working classes by a program of bold social and economic reform, such as might have been expected from a government which claimed to be revolutionary as well as insurrectionary. Again, on this subject of reforms, it was demonstrated how much the Commune was the accidental product of a set of discrete circumstances and lacked a formulation of either the techniques or the objectives

[34] *Ibid.*, I, 140, fn (4).   [36] *Ibid.*, I, 284.
[35] *Ibid.*, I, 282.   [37] *Ibid.*, I, 363-4.

of its role, as well as any real spirit of cohesion among its membership. In areas such as the judicial and the educational systems where left-wing demands for reform had long been raised, existing arrangements were left comparatively intact. A few innovations, it is true, were introduced in the sphere of labor—the suppression of night work in bakeries, the opening of public employment exchanges, and the prohibiting of hold-backs on wages. There was even a project for converting *ateliers* abandoned by their proprietors into workers' co-opera-tives. But none of these were fundamentally revolutionary acts, compared with what the Commune might have done and did not do: specifically, it might have seized the Bank of France. Although the Paris Commune of 1871 did institute some ameli-orative measures, it made no changes so fundamental as to commit the Parisian population to its " revolution."

As the month of April progressed, it became more and more evident that the communal council was not hanging together. Progressively fewer members attended its meetings, and the line was becoming more sharply drawn between the majority—those who looked upon themselves as the direct heirs of the Jacobins of 1793—and the minority—those who represented some sort of socialist-collectivist orientation. It was the Jacobin majority, incidentally, which had been strengthened by the April 16 elections.[38] The open break between majority and minority came at the beginning of May, and with it came the virtual disintegration of the Commune as a governing body. The immediate issue was the creation by the majority of a Committee of Public Safety, on the model of that of 1793. Such a drastic step was the direct outcome of the flurry of panic when the fort of Issy fell to Versailles. The minority, bitterly opposed to what it regarded as the senseless invocation of a name and the unwarranted establishment of a plural dictatorship, denounced the majority in the public press and declared it would no longer sit in the Commune. Issy was recaptured and lost again a week later; the initial Committee of Public Safety was scrapped, but

[38] New additions to the Jacobin majority by the April 16 election were as follows: Cluseret, Pillot, Pottier, Johannard, Sicard, Philippe, Lonclas, Dupont, Viard, and Trinquet. The Socialist minority gained: Andrieu, Serrailler, Courbet, Longuet, and Arnold.

a new one was set up almost at once; the minority failed to carry out its threat and did continue its presence at the Hôtel de Ville. Sessions of the Commune bogged down in recriminations between the two factions.

This point was reached by the middle of May. While the Commune had disputed, Versailles had almost daily been making important military gains The result was that as the final, definitive bombardment of the gates of Paris began, the Commune was in a state of disruption, confusion, and inertia. The end was near.

Versailles' Successful Offensive

On April 27 Thiers had praised before the National Assembly the excellent army assembled by Versailles. Lamenting the necessary use of arms against Paris, he had sought consolation in the hope for a speedy finish.[39] Ten days later, he had summoned the honest people of Paris, "a hundred times more numerous than the sectarians of the Commune," to open their gates to this powerful army.[40] But the only answer had been an order by the Committee of Public Safety for the demolition of Thiers' house, and the work had been started on May 13. Meanwhile the troops of Versailles were continuing their steady penetration of the city's outskirts, more and more enraged by its obstinate resistance.

The smouldering fury of the Versailles commanders was fanned to a blaze on May 16 by the Commune's ceremonial destruction of the Vendôme column, that military memorial to the Grande Armée of 1805. "Soldiers!" exhorted Marshall MacMahon in indignation, "if the memories which this column recalls are no longer graven in its bronze, they . . . still live in our hearts, and . . . we can give France a new gauge of bravery, devotion, and patriotism."[41] Even later, after the Versailles troops had entered Paris, the destruction of the Vendôme column was rankling the Government; Thiers denounced the men of the Commune as "scoundrels . . . who have done

[39] National Assembly, *Annales*, II, 734.
[40] *Réimpression du Journal officiel de la République française sous La Commune*, May 9, 1871, 511:2.
[41] Quoted in Auguste Le Page, *Histoire de la Commune* (Paris, 1871), 251.

what no savage people would—torn down the monuments of our national glory." [42] The attackers were further enraged on May 17, when the church of Notre-Dame-des-Victoires was sacked by a police commissioner of the Commune, and on May 18, when two dozen Dominicans charged with aiding the enemy from their College of Albert the Great at Arcueil were arrested. By the time the Versaillese did enter Paris, they had become avenging crusaders in a holy war against sub-human infidels entitled to no quarter.

On Sunday, May 21, the troops of Versailles were within the ramparts. The gate of St. Cloud, shattered by heavy bombardment, had been left unguarded. Although the Commune—or at least some of its members—was fully aware of this, nothing had been done to stop the hole in the city's defenses, such was the weary torpor of its leaders as the Commune's final agony approached. So it was that at the welcoming all-clear signal of a Versailles sympathizer, a road-gang foreman named Ducatel, the enemy poured unobserved into the once capital city. Their presence was hardly believed until the next morning, when their shells began to fall on the Legion of Honor. From now on, in the defense of Paris, it was virtually every barricade for itself, each man, even, for himself.

Collapse of the Commune

The next day, in a burst of lyrical sentimentalism, Delescluze, the Commune's Delegate for War, called on the irresistable *élan* of the *bras nus.* Two proclamations by the Committee of Public Safety breathed the same spirit; ". . . behind its barricades, Paris is impregnable," concluded the second proclamation.[43] But Versailles' advance was little impeded by ill-fortified, hastily thrown up barricades. In rapid succession, the Arc de Triomphe, the Place de la Concorde, the Elysée, the Parc Monceau, and the Ecole Militaire were occupied. By the end of the day, the forces of the National Assembly held a line from the Gare des Batignolles to the Gare Montparnasse. Many Communards were already being herded away as prisoners.

[42] National Assembly, *Annales,* III, 110.
[43] Lissagaray, *Histoire de la Commune de 1871,* 261.

Flames from the Ministry of Finance, the Tuilleries, and the barracks of the Champ-de-Mars, all ignited by heavy shells, leaped into the sky, while the defenders of Paris worked feverishly to throw up more and better barricades.

Their optimism, their almost gaiety after this first day's engagement soon turned to frantic desperation, as the Versailles troops pushed ruthlessly forward against the stiffened resistance. Batignolles fell, and soon after Montmartre as well. Hopeless appeals to proletarian solidarity were directed to the rank and file of the invading army by both the Committee of Public Safety and the Central Committee, but the fury of the fighting did not slack. With the taking of Montmartre, in fact, the Versailles troops had begun mass executions of prisoners at the spot where Generals Lecomte and Thomas had been killed on March 18. These were continued throughout the day, not only in the Rue des Rosiers, but in every quarter of the city where the forces of order had established themselves. And by the end of the day, Versailles held over half of Paris. In a last-ditch attempt to stem the advance, the Committee of Public Safety now ordered the burning of every house from which a shot was fired against the Federals.[44]

Nothing remained of any directing authority or discipline on the side of Commune. The old Delescluze, it was true, still nominally functioned at the Hôtel de Ville as the Delegate for War, but he was soon to find death on the barricades, as other members of the communal council were doing. The general chaos now combined with the no quarter shown by the enemy to create a situation in which the hostages held by the Commune were doomed. The executions began when the fanatically single-minded Procurator of the Commune, Raoul Rigault, shot—on his own authority and to satisfy his own grudge—the venerable Republican Gustave Chaudey, who had long before been arrested on charges of being responsible for the fatal firing on the demonstrators of January 22. With Chaudey were shot three gendarmes arrested on March 18. Meanwhile the defenders of the barricades were still having to fall back. More and more stories of massacres of prisoners by

[44] See *Réimpression du Journal officiel de la République française sous La Commune*, May 24, 1871, 649:1.

the Versaillese were circulating in the popular quarters. There-fore, by evening a mob of Federals had formed around the prison of La Roquette, where the main body of hostages were now being held. Soon the Commune's decree of April 5 was recalled, and reprisals against the hostages were demanded. From the list of captives were selected the names of the six most eminent—the Archbishop of Paris, for whom Thiers had refused to exchange his prize prisoner Auguste Blanqui, the President of the Supreme Court, three Jesuits, and the *curé* of the Madeleine. There was lively competition among the Federals to win a place on the firing squad.

The execution of these hostages gave vent to some of the Federals' feeling of exasperation, but it could neither stop the slaughter of their own nor save Paris for the Commune. From the Place de la Concorde to the Hôtel de Ville the city was in flames, and the wind was rapidly spreading the fire. The blazing Hôtel de Ville was abandoned the night of the 24th. From the heights of Montmartre, Versailles' artillery was bombarding the remaining Federal positions. The Panthéon had been taken, and the Place d'Enfer; the Faubourg Saint-Germain was occupied. So lost was the Communards' cause that the Govern-ment looked upon the engagement as ended. Early on the 25th Thiers wired to the Prefects, "We are masters of Paris, with the exception of a small portion, which will be occupied this morning." [45]

Thiers was unduly optimistic. The Communards, their num-bers ever diminishing, their barricades systematically reduced, opposed the armies of Versailles for four more days. Each successive day doubled and redoubled the avenging rage of the victorious troops, who—fed on atrocity stories—made a clean sweep of all suspected of sympathy for the Commune. For their part, the Federals, encumbered by the hostages whom they carried with them as they retreated toward the northeast, also turned to execution *en masse*. The Dominican friars, taken from Fort Bicêtre when it fell to the prison on the Avenue d'Italie, were forced out of the prison when shells began to fall on it too. The fleeing cassocks made inviting targets for the infuriated Federals. In the Rue Haxo, whence the prisoners from La Roquette were taken after its capture, the street mob claimed forty more hostages.

The Finish of the Fighting

But soon the Federals themselves were reduced to only a few desperate bands. Long lines of their fellows—those who had been spared—were being marched as prisoners through a Paris on which a pouring rain fell. The overwhelming majority of the Versailles troops were massed before the remaining defenders of the Commune, who were confined in a semi-circle, with the Buttes Chaumont on the left and Père Lachaise on the right. Their bottling-up was complete when the regulars threw a line around the outer wall of the quarter and attacked from the rear as well. The retreat soon brought the main body of defenders into the cemetery of Père Lachaise itself. Even there, little defense was possible, since shells for Communard artillery had been lacking since noon. Then the Versaillese forced the main gate, and after hand to hand fighting amid the tombs, under a lowering sky, established themselves as masters of Père Lachaise. Only small parts of the XIth and XXth arrondissements now remained in Federal hands.

By noon on Sunday, May 28, the last Federal gun was silenced. Early that morning the Versailles troops had begun their final attack. Belleville had bristled with barricades, but the ammunition to defend them had been low. By ten o'clock the town hall of the XXth had been occupied. By eleven o'clock, only four barricades had been left. The last—the barricade of the Rue Ramponneau—fell at mid-day.[46]

The firing had ceased, but Versailles' reprisals had hardly begun. Thousands of Communards who had survived the final fighting were herded before firing squads, which soon were wading in blood. These were mass executions without the pretense of a trial. Elsewhere in the city, military tribunals were making a farce of interrogating their victims before sending them to the slaughter. Versailles' mission of revenge, moreover, was given a helping hand by the " loyal " citizens

[46] Lissagaray, *Histoire de la Commune de 1871*, 307.

of Paris, who now came forth with a stream of denunciations. Suspected Communards—and this covered everyone shabbily dressed, or with a " wrong " attitude, or with a face that " looked " guilty—who were not shot at once were tied together and marched toward Versailles, amid the hoots and jeers of the respectable elements. From to time the lines of march were interrupted for further executions. Some prisoners who reached their destinations found themselves thrown into the camp of Satory, an old artillery park and cavalry stable, where the great crowding compelled most of the captives to stand in the open, ankle-deep in mud, penned in by ropes, and surrounded by sentries who kept their rifles aimed. Similarly brutal conditions were to be found in the stables of Saint-Cyr, in the cellars of the Grandes-Ecuries, and in the Orangerie, where other prisoners were held.

The forces of order, the conservatives of the National Assembly, had sought to effect a cure for the dangerous disease of Parisian radicalism by the letting of blood. But the patient came near to dying in the process. In combat or by firing squad, no fewer than 20,000 citizens of Paris were exterminated. Double this number filled the improvised prison camps of Versailles to overflowing, awaiting in their turn death or deportation.

Definition of the Paris Commune

Large areas of Paris were in ruins; the city, divided into four administrative districts, was again under martial law; many thousands were dead; and additional thousands of its people were held prisoner in the rude camps at Versailles. Countless others, including many leaders of the Commune, had fled into exile. Few persons still alive and free in Paris felt safe from sudden seizure and peremptory judgment as the military courts of Versailles continued to lay hands on all suspects. The question was how long this state of affairs would continue. To the Government and the respectable world in general, the Paris Commune had been nothing but a large-scale criminal riot by discontented elements, and the repression should continue until all participants had been exterminated or otherwise punished as befitted their crimes against persons and property.

The time was to come when those who favored halting the repression were to characterize the Paris Commune as a civil war. If it had achieved this stature, then the "Communards," although temporarily suffering the disabilities of defeat, would eventually have to be reincorporated in the French state. Under such an interpretation of the Commune, the deeds of its defenders would belong to the domain of justifiable acts of war. Was there any warrant for regarding the Commune as a civil war? First, the Commune failed to find a place in the community of nations. Its belligerency was never recognized by any foreign power. As early as April 3, the question was raised of the Commune's notifying other countries of its existence. This idea was barely considered and dismissed as unnecessary.[47] When, toward the end of April, the further question of the Commune's seeking recognition of its belligerency was introduced,[48] Paschal Grousset, head of External Relations, rejected all thought of this, demanding, "As for the title of 'belligerents,' wouldn't it be . . . puerile to ask for it officially when we have it in fact?"[49] Holding itself aloof from the powers, the Commune was content to claim a *de facto* belligerency based on moral grounds.

Second, in terms of scope of the conflict, the struggle was between a portion of the population of Paris and the rest of France as represented by the National Assembly. Certainly Paris under the Commune did in fact withdraw from the French body politic, despite initial protestations of not separating from France. It also dreamed of broadening the revolt by rousing the provinces against Versailles and by taking the lead in a drastic reorganization of France. Most members of the Commune subscribed to the idea of a social and political organization based upon a system of loosely federated autonomous communes, or, as Gustave Lefrançais, one of the minority members of the Commune, later explained it, ". . . a succession of pacts or freely debated and consented to contracts, going from the individual to the nation and guaranteeing to each his full freedom of action, strengthened by the collective power

[47] Bourgin and Henriot, *Procès-verbaux de la Commune de 1871*, I, 113.
[48] *Ibid.*, I, 517-8.
[49] *Ibid.*, I, 530.

of the group with which he shall be voluntarily associated." [50]
But the Paris Commune did not succeed in enlisting the provinces
on its side, and it remained a city alone rather than the leader
of a segment of the French nation.

Finally, with respect to the Commune's control of Paris, the
communal council looked upon itself as the emergency but
nevertheless legally functioning government of an independent
Paris. It had in fact come into being through elections in which
every adult male had been eligible to vote. But in neither the
initial election of March 26 nor the supplementary election of
April 16 had so many as half the registered voters gone to the
polls. The Commune, however, aspiring to the role of responsible revolutionary government, did carry on, more or less
competently, the various administrative services.

Only a thin case can be made for the view that the Paris
Commune was a civil war. Obviously, then, how the Commune
was going to be defined after the event would depend not on
what had actually happened, but on the interplay of political
forces in the early Third Republic.

What Versailles Had Promised

In the spring of 1871, the Government of Thiers and the
overwhelming majority of the National Assembly were in
complete accord that the Commune was a criminal insurrection.
The only important concern at Versailles was that an end be
made of the affair as quickly as possible. There was no question as to what conditions must be made to prevail in Paris.
" The factious men who have dealt the Republic such a grave
blow will be forced back to the shadows . . . ," [51] proclaimed the
Journal officiel in the first few days of the Commune. Five
weeks later, Dufaure, Minister of Justice, insisted that before
there could be any talk of conciliation, there must be, " First
of all, order established, that is, the Commune reduced and
disappearing, then free elections, as we have promised . . .
will take place in a Paris returned to the empire of the law,

[50] Article, " Communalisme," from Revue socialiste (originally, La Commune:
Revue socialiste, No. 1, April 1874), issues of June, July, and August, 1874,
reprinted in G. Lefrançais, La Commune et la Révolution (Paris, 1896), 33.
[51] Journal officiel de la République française, March 20, 1871, 189:3.

in a calm, laborious, honest Paris, and not in a Paris insurgent under a frightful dictatorship." He praised the idea of conciliation as " an angel which appears after the storm," but insisted that it could come only " after order is re-established, and force belongs to law." [52]

Above all else, France—through the National Assembly—must once again be master of Paris. From the beginning to the end of the Commune, this thought was uppermost at Versailles. Toward the last, as Versailles prepared its final attack, a proclamation to the people of Paris declared, " We have listened to all the delegations which were sent to us, and not one offered us terms which did not mean the abasement of the national sovereignty before the revolt." [53]

Versailles's sole condition of peace was total and complete submission, and the idea of anything resembling coming to terms with Paris was anathema. On March 21, the National Assembly in an address to the people had announced, " Do not fear to find in us those moral weaknesses which aggravate the evil by compounding with the guilty." [54] To a delegation of would-be conciliators from the League of Republican Union for the Rights of Paris, Thiers pointed out that " as head of the sole legal government existing in France, he was not called upon to discuss the bases of a treaty . . . ," and further, that " not in any way recognizing as belligerents the persons engaged in the fight against the National Assembly, he neither could nor would take up the subject of an armistice." [55] When a minority Deputy introduced in the National Assembly on April 20 a bill on " the pacification of Paris," which provided that ". . . the Assembly declares it is ready to treat with Paris," he was violently interrupted by his colleagues, who hastily refused even to consider his proposal.[56] Again, to a delegation

[52] National Assembly, *Annales*, II, 715.
[53] *Journal officiel de la République française*, May 8, 1871, 917:3, and *Réimpression du Journal officiel de la République française sous La Commune,* May 9, 1871, 511:2.
[54] *Journal officiel de la République française*, March 22, 1871, 205:1.
[55] *Réimpression du Journal officiel de la République française sous La Commune*, April 14, 1871, 261:1, report of the delegation.
[56] National Assembly, *Annales*, II, 627-8. The Deputy was Brunet, who a week before had tried to interpellate Thiers as to his intentions toward peace

from the Masonic lodges, Thiers insisted, "not regarding the fighters of Paris as belligerents, he neither could nor would admit the principle of an armistice." [57] The majority of Deputies in the National Assembly were even more blunt than Thiers: "There's only one way to end the civil war—that's to vanquish the factious." [58] "No conciliation is possible between justice and iniquity, between the murderer and his victim." [59] Such remarks were frequent. The most explicit statement of the National Assembly's view came in a committee report presented on May 9. "Peace, like war, supposes the belligerents placed in a certain equality from the point of view of public law; but the fight of the legal power against an insurrection is not called war, and the only happening which can end it is not peace, but submission." [60]

What assurances, if any, did Versailles offer to Paris as inducement to submit? On two of the specific issues which had brought the Parisian kettle to the boiling point, Thiers pleaded his good faith. With reference to the alleged threat to the Republic, Thiers categorically guaranteed the preservation of the regime, pledging on his honor, "that never, so long as he lived and was in power, would the Republic succumb." [61] On the question of municipal freedoms, Thiers insisted that Paris would have exactly the same autonomous rights as were to be given to other cities under the municipal reorganization laws then being worked on by the National Assembly. "Paris will get satisfaction; it will be represented the way all the communes of France [will be]. We are not pretending to be doing it a favor in according this point; we

or war. The National Assembly had killed this move by postponing for a month debate on the demand to interpellate. See *ibid.*, II, 1871, 454-6.
   [57] *Murailles politiques françaises*, II, 330:1.
   [58] *Ibid.*, II, 535.
   [59] *Ibid.*, II, 796.
   [60] National Assembly, *Annèxes*, II, 885 (*Annèxe* No. 215, printed in with the text of the *Annales*, II).
   [61] *Réimpression du Journal officiel de la République française sous La Commune*, April 12, 1871, 242:2, report of the delegation sent by the National Union of Syndical Chambers of Commerce and Industry. See also, *ibid.*, April 14, 1871, 261:1, report of the delegation from the League of Republican Union for the Rights of Paris; *Murailles politiques françaises*, II, 330:3, report of delegation from Free Masons, dated April 22, 1871; and National Assembly, *Annales*, II, 735, Thiers to the National Assembly on April 27, 1871.

recognize its right." [62] He said this to the National Assembly on March 21. On April 8, he told a delegation from the National Union of Syndical Chambers that " Paris has nothing to expect from the Government, nothing more than the application of the ordinary law, which will come out of the municipal statute which the Chamber [sic] is going to vote." [63] And he repeated this to all comers. In time, Thiers grew openly weary of demands for Paris's freedom, particularly after a new municipal law had been voted and failed to satisfy Paris. He vaunted his love of freedom as stronger than that of those who petitioned on behalf of Paris; he held that it was for freedom and freedom alone that the National Assembly was fighting, fighting for freedom against " that odious despotism, that despotism without mandate, born of the disorder of the war, born from all excesses of license, against that despotism without restraint, without principle, without conscience, which knows not what it is doing, and which does evil with disasterous ignorance." [64]

A more personal and more immediate concern than the Republic or even Paris's freedom in the matter of inducing the Commune to submit to Versailles was what treatment those who had revolted could expect. While the Government assured the country at large that the fight against Paris would be vigorously prosecuted, it was assuring Paris that the city could freely return to the fold. On March 21, Thiers told the National Assembly that when Paris came to its senses, " it will find us with open arms, but it must first of all open its own." [65] Soon after the fighting had begun in earnest, he changed to a call to Paris to lay down its arms. In mid-April he told the representatives of the League of Republican Union for the Rights of Paris that " whosoever renounces armed struggle, that is, whosoever goes back to his home, giving up all hostile attitude, will be beyond the reach of any investigation." Excepted

[62] *Journal officiel de la République française*, March 22, 1871, 217:1.
[63] *Réimpression du Journal officiel de la République française sous La Commune*, April 12, 1871, 243:1, report of the delegation. See also *ibid.*, April 14, 1871, 261:1, report of delegation from the League of Republican Union for the Rights of Paris.
[64] National Assembly, *Annales*, II, 735.
[65] *Journal officiel de la République française*, March 22, 1871, 219:1.

from this pledge, however, were the murderers of Lecomte and Clément Thomas, "who will be judged, if they are found." Finally, he promised that the daily payment to members of the National Guard would be kept up until business had recovered and jobs were again available.[66] A week later he said substantially the same thing to the delegates of the Free Masons, insisting that, " in conformity with his earlier promises, all combattants who laid down arms would have their lives spared . . ." [67] To the National Assembly, at the end of April, Thiers exclaimed, " I have repeated to satiety, hoping that you would not disavow me: let these impious weapons fall from the hands which hold them, and the chastising will halt on the spot . . . , except with reference to criminals, who—happily— are not very numerous." [68] Subsequently he added, " as for those who lay down their arms, they will have their life spared; as for the workingmen whom . . . [the Commune] leads astray and against whom it uses the stimulant of poverty to make soldiers of sedition, you . . . can temporarily give them relief." [69] These promises were made again in the May 8 proclamation urging the people of Paris to open their gates. " We have promised . . . ," said the Government, " and we promise again, but this insurrection must cease, for it cannot be prolonged without France's perishing of it." [70]

Each passing day showed how vain was Versailles's hope that the Commune would surrender, and the longer the fighting continued, the more conspicuously the idea of meting out justice figured in official thinking. At the beginning of the Commune, the Government had announced, " The day of justice is near," [71] and on March 21, Jules Favre, Minister of Foreign Affairs, had called upon the rank and file of the National Guard to " bring

[66] Réimpression du Journal officiel de la République française sous La Commune, April 14, 1871, 261:1-2.

[67] Murailles politiques françaises, II, 330:3.

[68] National Assembly, Annales, II, 736. Sitting of April 27. The Right was very disturbed when Thiers made this last statement.

[69] Ibid., II, 738.

[70] Journal officiel de la République française, May 8, 1871, 918:1, and Réimpression du Journal officiel de la République française sous La Commune, May 9, 1871, 511:2.

[71] Journal officiel de la République française, March 20, 1871, 189:3.

to justice . . . the wretches who oppress the capital." [72] But near the end of the Commune, the tone was much firmer and much harder. Dufaure, Minister of Justice, unequivocally announced on May 11, "When France has become again master of Paris, when the insurrection has been vanquished, justice will do its duty in seeking out the guilty, all [of them], whoever they may be, and in punishing them." [73] Finally, on May 22, when Thiers informed a jubilant National Assembly that their troops had entered Paris, he devoted a large part of his message to the kind of punishment the Government would impose. "Gentlemen, we are honorable men. . . . Only the law will step in, but . . . [the law] will be executed in its full rigor." Before a wildly applauding Assembly, he concluded, "Expiation will be complete, but it will be, I repeat, expiation such as honorable men ought to inflict when justice requires it, expiation in the name of the law and by the law." [74]

During the entire lifetime of the Commune, therefore, not one word was said at Versailles which could have led the Commune to expect any rights as a defeated belligerent. The Government's promises, to summarize, were few: the Republic would be preserved, Paris would have the same rights as other cities, anyone laying down arms would have his life spared, and the National Guard would continue to get its daily pay for a few weeks. On the other side of the ledger was an insistence that everyone guilty would be punished to the full extent of the law.

The only suggestion that a different course might be possible had come out of the conversation on April 8 between Thiers and the delegation of conciliators sent by the National Union of Syndical Chambers. One of the points in the delegation's draft of a settlement had called for a general political amnesty. Thiers had gone over this draft without challenging any of its proposals and the delegation had optimistically reported, ". . . explanations which were exchanged à propos of such and such a paragraph, notably on the subject of the amnesty, left us all under the impression that the terms of the note in question

[72] *Ibid.*, March 22, 1871, 221:3.
[73] National Assembly, *Annales*, II, 912.
[74] *Ibid.*, III, 109-10.

could . . . serve as the base for a subsequent discussion of an arrangement." [75] No impression could have been further from the truth, as the continued hostilities and Thiers's absolute refusal to discuss terms demonstrated. Between April 8 and May 28, moreover, lay fifty days of bitter fighting, culminating in the massacres of the Bloody Week. As the end drew near, only on the side of the Commune, only in the Central Committee of the National Guard, did thoughts turn to an amnesty. In a manifesto of the sheerest bravado, posted on the night of May 25, the Central Committee announced armistice terms, which included a reciprocal amnesty.

The Meaning of Amnesty

In the months and years to come the word "amnesty" was to be used more and more often in statements of what ought to be done to restore affairs to normal following the Paris Commune. It is important, therefore, to establish exactly what this word meant in France in the 1870's. Those who used the term "amnesty" gave the Commune the implied status of a civil war, for the forgiveness that followed civil war went by the name of amnesty. It belonged primarily to the political sphere, not to criminal offenses or civil suits, and was regarded as being—and here European usage differs from the American —of an order far superior to pardon. Amnesty, under this interpretation, was more than pardon because it wiped the record clean; it conjured the rebellious act into the realm of non-existence. And it left—by law, at any rate—no lingering taint. Persons freed from prison or exile under an amnesty were restored to the full enjoyment of their civil and political rights. Finally, one of the most important distinguishing characteristics of an amnesty was the fact that it treated not of special cases but of whole categories, for it was in effect the deed itself which was being amnestied, not the doers. Such was the pure theory of amnesty. In practice there had been amnesties which affected only the individuals specifically named; there had also been amnesties which set up varying degrees of exclusion; and there had been amnesties which provided for

[75] Réimpression du Journal officiel de la République française sous La Commune, April 12, 1871, 243:1.

certain continuing limitations on personal freedom. Despite these exceptions it was the concept of amnesty as a device obliterating an unpleasant past event which gave the idea of a general amnesty its potency.

On the practical side, too, pardon alone was not regarded as capable of giving a satisfactory solution to the problems created by a civic upheaval. First was the problem of what was to become of persons not yet apprehended and tried for their role—real or alleged—on the defeated side. Until the statute of limitations should come into play—a dreary ten years later—their lives would be those of fugitives, while informers for gain or personal revenge would have ready victims. On the other side, the state would not only have to bear the cost of continuing prosecutions but also risk unpopularity for convictions made long after the event, should public opinion in the interval have become inclined toward leniency. Pardon could not be given prior to conviction, so that the absence of an amnesty would mean an untold number of citizens whose freedom had not legally been taken away, but who nevertheless were not free because they lived in fear. Secondly, even if the pardoning power were broadly used, it would not reintegrate the participants on the losing side in the life of the nation. The fact of the conviction would remain, and if the sentence had been a heavy enough one, the pardoned individual would not enjoy full citizenship rights. For any regime with pretensions of being a democracy, these two problems could lead to grave difficulties.

The Constitutional History of Amnesty in France

For obvious reasons, therefore, the historical evolution in France of the meaning of amnesty to the special definition current at the time of the Paris Commune was largely tied up with the development of liberal and democratic ideology, particularly the doctrine of separation of powers. Under the Old Regime, amnesty, or at any rate the power to wipe out both the penalties of a conviction and its consequences, belonged to the King, who exercised this power through his "letters of abolition." But these were suppressed by the Legislative Assembly of 1791, along with other royal devices for arbitrary interference with justice. It was not, however, until the Constitution of 1848 that the concept of amnesty was written into the organic law of France. Nevertheless, during the intervening regimes, amnesties of one sort or another had been enacted. But the very variety of these measures indicated a lack of precision in the meaning of amnesty. Royal ordinances amnestying violations of the forest and hunting laws were fairly common, as were ones for desertion from the Army or the Navy. Charles X early in his reign did accord a general amnesty applying to all persons convicted of political offenses under the press laws,[76] but another of his amnesties applied only to the some hundred thirty men named therein, and provided that each should be under police surveillance for five years.[77] After the July Days, Louis Philippe inaugurated his reign with a broad political amnesty; the royal ordinance of August 26-September 10, 1830, set aside without distinction all political convictions imposed since the second restoration of Louis XVIII.[78] At the same time, the parliament passed a law—not called amnesty, however—which restored all civil and political rights to those banished by the restored Bourbons in 1816.[79] Seven years later another amnesty by royal ordinance freed all persons held in prison for political reasons, but imposed police surveillance on those convicted of serious crimes.[80] Then came the Revolution of 1848. The Provisional Government of February used its power to amnesty by decree on a few occasions, but only for small, local or military matters. Next came the June Days, with the largest mass indictment as well as the bloodiest street fighting France had yet experienced. Consequently, the power to amnesty became a prized prerogative, to be entrusted only to the safest representatives of the nation.

Written into the Constitution of 1848 was the careful distinc-

[76] Jean-Baptiste Duvergier, *Collection complète des lois, décrets d'intérêt général, traités internationaux, arrêtés circulaires, instructions, etc.* (Paris, 1824 and following), XXV, 227.

[77] *Idem.*

[78] July 7, 1815. *Ibid.*, XXX, 212.

[79] *Ibid.*, XXX, 235.

[80] *Ibid.*, XXXVII, 117. One of the political prisoners freed by this amnesty was Auguste Blanqui. In 1840 this ordinance was extended to cover all persons convicted of political offenses whether or not they were actually held in prison at the time of the 1837 ordinance.

tion between pardon and amnesty and between the executive and the legislative powers in these matters which was to be basic to Republican thought in France. Article 55 of Chapter 5, " The Executive Power," provided that the President should have the power to pardon, but only upon the advice of the council. It stated explicitly that " Amnesties cannot be accorded except by a law." [81] In the Constituent Assembly's debates on this clause it had been urged that amnesties, because of their political seriousness, should be enacted only when introduced by the President of the Republic. The Deputy who had proposed an amendment to this effect had argued that in the case of amnesties, the right of legislative initiative had no advantages and many disadvantages. As he explained it, " If . . . [the President] does not believe that the amnesty ought to be accorded, . . . in what situation will you be placing him? You will place him in the presence of a minority (for if the majority, in agreement with the President of the Republic, wants the amnesty, it will be realized). You will place him in the presence of a minority which will incessantly, on the subject of amnesty, reawaken political passions [and] stir up irritating debates to no avail. And what will come of that? You will have brought disfavor upon the President of the Republic." [82] But the majority in the Assembly had been more devoted to separation of powers than to considerations of practical politics. The amendment had been voted down as endangering, ". . . the fundamental and essential right belonging to each member of the Assembly, which is none other than the right of the Assembly itself." [83] The exclusive prerogative of the legislative branch in a republic to enact an amnesty was thus established.

A genuine division of powers is the negation of an authoritarian regime, and Louis Napoleon hurriedly restored the amnestying power to the sovereign. Article 1 of the *Senatus Consultum* of December 25, 1852, provided that, " The Emperor has the power to grant pardons and to accord amnesties." [84] As the Government explained, in putting this text before the

[81] National Assembly, *Compte rendu*, V, 285.
[82] *Ibid.*, IV, 823.
[83] Duvergier, *Collection complète*, XLVIII, 587, fn (1).
[84] Senate, *Procès-verbaux des séances*, 1852, II, 113.

Senate, " All the monarchic governments which have followed
one another in France have considered the right to accord
amnesties an attribute of the sovereign power. . . . It cannot,
without serious political inconveniences, be contested or denied
to the Head of the State." [85]

In 1859, on the verge of the " liberal Empire," Napoleon III
used this power to decree full amnesty for " all persons who
have been convicted of political crimes or offenses, or who have
been the object of measures of general security." [86] Despite
its broad terms, the act failed to enhance the Emperor's popularity, seeming instead only to furnish new opportunities to the
opposition for attack. Victor Hugo, Edgar Quinet, Schoelcher,
Louis Blanc, and other celebrated exiles remained abroad,
heaping scorn upon the " little Napoleon." [87]

With the fall of the Empire, followed within the year by
the Paris Commune, France was both lacking any fundamental
law on the subject of amnesty and pardon and at the same time
confronted by thousands of potential cases in which demands
for clemency, either individual or general, were going inevitably
to be formulated. At once the National Assembly remedied
this situation. The law of June 17, 1871, introduced on May 26,
reasserted that no amnesty could be accorded except by a law.
As for pardon, a specific delegation of this power was made
to the Chief of the Executive Power, but his use of it was
limited in all criminal cases relating to the Commune. In such
cases, pardon was to be exercised jointly by the executive head
and the National Assembly, as represented by a fifteen-man
committee. In the event of disagreement between the two
branches of government thus represented, the conviction was
to stand.[88] Originally the bill had given the committee only
consultative status, but the National Assembly, jealous of its
prerogatives, had voted an amendment strengthening the Com-

[85] *Ibid.*, 1852, II, 99.
[86] Duvergier, *Collection complète*, LIX, 298.
[87] Also refusing to be amnestied were Barbès, Charras, and Ledru-Rollin. But
Proudhon, Emile Deschanel, Challemel-Lacour, and " many others " did come
back. " Soon, only stubborn and strong-willed intransigeants remained abroad.
. . ." (Octave Aubry, *The Second Empire*, translated by Arthur Livingston
[Philadelphia, 1940], 161.)
[88] National Assembly, *Annales*, III, 486.

mission on Pardons, on the grounds that the Chief of the Executive Power had, after all, only the powers delegated to him by the National Assembly, and that this body, " the only sovereign [power]," must not have less authority than its delegate.[89] This restriction, however, on the executive right to pardon, was understood to apply solely to cases arising from the Commune.

Under the constitutional law of February 25-28, 1875, on the relative powers of the legislative and executive branches, no restrictions were placed on the right to pardon enjoyed by the President of the Republic. For one thing, the conservatives now felt sure of their man; MacMahon, elected for a seven-year term in 1873, was not likely to pardon Communards promiscuously. Furthermore, the majority in the National Assembly was satisfied in 1875 that its Commission on Pardons had virtually disposed of the aftermath of the Commune. Finally, the Deputies were reassured by the fact that the new law would not under any circumstances go into effect until the National Assembly should dissolve; until that time, the Commission on Pardons would continue its work. As for amnesty, the new constitution specified merely that it could be given only by a law.[90]

The two laws of 1871 and 1875 established the legal framework within which the agitation for a general amnesty for the Paris Commune was to take place.

An Earlier Amnesty Question: After the Revolution of 1848

Whether or not there would ever be an amnesty for the Paris Commune was going to depend on a great many more complex factors than a mere constitutional provision. France, regardless of the form of government, had no strong tradition of forgiveness for its civil enemies, particularly for Parisians at the barricades. Following the Revolution of 1848, for example, there were wholesale arrests and mass deportations, but there never was an amnesty. Amnesty bills were introduced

[89] *Ibid.*, III, 485-6.
[90] *Ibid.*, XXXVII, 647. The language of this clause had been taken over by the committee on the bill from an amendment proposed by Marcel Barthe. See *ibid.*, V, 317.

in the National Assembly, but the mounting tide of reaction, culminating in the Second Empire, made them still-born. On October 14, 1848, Emile Ollivier brought in a bill amnestying all political crimes and lesser offenses since the previous February 24. Co-sponsors of the bill were Ledru-Rollin, Félix Pyat, Eugène Raspail, Pelletier, and fifty-four other convinced Republicans.[91] Any thought of an amnesty at this time was effectively damned by a committee report which was heavily loaded with inflammatory statements. "Murder, devastation, [and] pillage were the means by which the fomenters of anarchy expected to achieve the annihilation of family and property, the sacred bases of every social order," was a typical observation.[92] The guilty, it was maintained, either had criminal records or had been led astray by " detestable doctrines," and pardon or commutation of sentence would serve adequately to take care of cases deserving consideration.[93] The champions of an amnesty found it impossible to get debate of the report put on the calendar. Their repeated pleas were often interrupted with disorderly remarks ("We don't want the amnesty," said Champvans, on December 18. "You aren't giving life back to our friends who were killed!").[94] Many Deputies were hoping, however, that once the new President of the Second Republic—Louis Napoleon Bonaparte—was inaugurated, he would take the initiative and sponsor an amnesty bill, but no hope could have been more futile. On December 30, his Orleanist Minister of Justice, Odilon Barrot, appeared before the National Assembly to explain that the President's most sincere wish was " that the French Republic should be sufficiently strongly established, that public security should be sufficiently deeply guaranteed for it to be possible to give ear to the voice of generosity without danger." [95] But alas, an amnesty was out of the question at present.

Two months later the National Assembly finally debated whether it would take up the question of amnesty. The Left

[91] National Assembly, Compte rendu, V, 317.
[92] Ibid., V, 315.
[93] Ibid., V, 316.
[94] Ibid., VI, 319.
[95] Ibid., VI, 475.

spoke earnestly ("Political reconciliation," said Schoelcher,
" means peace with everyone "),[96] but the Deputies voted overwhelmingly against consideration.[97] Other attempts were made
to bring amnesty before the National Assembly: It was proposed that for the celebration of the February Revolution all
dossiers be examined and amnesty given to those whose character had been vouched for by "honorable witnesses"; [98]
another amendment to the bill on the February 24 holiday
asked a general amnesty for all political offenses during the
past year except for persons who had also been prosecuted for
murder, theft, or pillage.[99] Neither proposal was considered.
Early in June 1849 two more amnesty bills were introduced: one
by Pascal Duprat, giving "full and complete amnesty to all
citizens convicted of political crimes or lesser offenses since the
February Revolution"; the other, by Colonel Laborde, amnestying, "those convicted of political charges from May 1848
to the present." Both bills were unanimously turned down in
committee.[100]

Almost two years later a final effort was made to get an
amnesty for participants in the Revolution of 1848. The bill,
introduced on February 14, 1851, called for " full and complete
amnesty for all citizens convicted of political acts since February
24, 1848." Its sponsors, numbering 188 and headed by Pascal
Duprat, rested on their previous arguments for an amnesty.
But the committee on the bill preferred, in any event, to listen
to the Ministers of Interior and of Justice, who painted a black
picture of subversive activity, strengthened by the machinations
of the exiles in Switzerland and England. The Government,
for its part, promised to pardon as generously as was compatible

[96] Ibid., VII, 609.
[97] Ibid., VII, 614.
[98] Ibid., VIII, 96.
[99] Ibid., VIII, 95.
[100] Ibid., 2e série, I, 431. Debate on the committee report on the Pascal
Duprat, Charras, and Latrade bill was scheduled for July 16. When the time
came, Charras withdrew the bill, because of, as he said, "events which have
taken place" since it was introduced. He was obviously referring to the
happenings of June 13, 1849, when the abortive revolt engineered by Ledru-
Rollin caused the conservatives to take extremely severe measures against the
Republicans—numerous arrests, the forbidding of banquets, the dissolution of
mutual aid societies, and so forth.

with security. The committee therefore concluded that to enact
a general amnesty would be " to turn upside down all notions
of justice, [and] to strike a serious blow at the security of
society. . . ." [101] Its report was ordered printed and distributed.
This was the last heard of the question of an amnesty for the
Revolution of 1848.

The report was never debated, and Louis Napoleon's *coup
d'état* of December 2 swept away any possibility that the Republicans, who endorsed the idea of an amnesty, might ever come
to have a majority in the legislative body of the Second Republic.
Soon, thereafter, as has been shown, the so-called legislative
branch lost even the power to enact an amnesty. Meanwhile,
a new set of political proscripts had gone into exile. The Second
Republic had not been strong enough or endured long enough
for there to have been an amnesty.

Alignment of Political Forces in the Early Third Republic

The Third Republic in 1871 was not strong and certainly
did not seem likely to endure. This was pertinent to the general
problem of what was ultimately to become of the so-called
Communards because, by common view, an amnesty can be
granted only when the government in power feels securely
established in its position. And at the beginning of the 1870's
France had a Republic in name, a strong body of convinced
Monarchists, and an uneasy bloc of convinced Republicans. A
brief examination of the prevailing political alignments following the defeat of the Paris Commune is therefore basic to the
study of the amnesty controversy which subsequently developed.

Because of the Republicans' inherent weakness in the 1870's,
the idea of making the regime a Republic in actuality dominated
their thoughts and actions. An amnesty, when the issue was
raised, became something to be put off—in their own words—
until the Republic had been further " republicanized." The
difficulty was the Republicans' lack of fundamental agreement
on the meaning of " republican."

The source of their differences lay in conflicting interpretations of the nature of the state, a heritage from the days of

[101] *Ibid.*, 2e série, XII, 290.

the French Revolution of 1789. Did "Republic" mean a liberal republic, with its laissez-faire, neutral-state connotations, or did it mean a radical republic, with its interventionist, positive-state connotations? There was precedent for both. Liberal thought in the eighteenth century had crystallized around the idea that the right form of government guaranteed the right content, that once the machinery of the state were made perfect, natural law would take care of social and economic problems. The National Convention, however, had mocked the sacred tenets of orthodox middle-class liberal ideology and had become the leviathan state of radical democracy. After the Napoleonic interlude and the Bourbon Restoration, the advocates of the neutral state came into their own with Louis Philippe. Meanwhile, the changing composition of society brought forth the social problem in a new and acute form which demanded attention, and the Revolution of 1848 was essentially a struggle between those who believed in the neutral state and those who believed in the positive state. It was at this period that the term "Republic" was once more stigmatized as radical proletarianism, and the respectible world, abandoning faith in the laissez-faire state as adequate protection against the new monster of socialism, ran into the arms of authoritarianism on the right. The Second Empire did its work well, too well for its own good. By systematically keeping down organized labor and by carefully fostering the growth of industry, it strengthened the middle class both materially and psychologically to the point where impatience with restraints led to new demands for the neutral state. At the same time, the effect of increased industrialization on the working class had created a strong new force which could find in a positive state under popular control the only means of improving the situation of labor. Thus it was, at the end of the Second Empire, that simple opposition to the dismal regime of Louis Napoleon served to unite men of widely differing political views. When the Third Republic replaced the Empire, the Republicans inherited these schisms.

In the setting up of government under the Third Republic, the late opponents of the Empire found they faced a new enemy on the Right. The Monarchists in the National Assembly felt their chances for a restoration were good, since the Franco-

Prussian War and the Paris Commune had, to many, demonstrated the need for strong government. The Republican camp, on the other hand, contained both conservatives, laissez-faire liberals who wanted a weak state and felt safer in the hands of a moderate republic than in the hands of a reactionary monarchy representing the landed interests, and democrats, who wanted popular government and a strong state. Should the latter make their views prevail, the conservatives would turn to monarchy as the lesser of two strong state evils. If this should happen, the Republic would be doomed.

What solidarity the Republicans had came from the fact that the conservative and the democratic Republicans had in common their almost mystical concept of "republican institutions," a concept derived partly from theory, partly from experience, and taking definite form in the opposition literature of the end of the Empire. The whole idea of right laws to make right government, and of guaranteed civil rights suited the purposes of the democrats equally well as those of the conservatives. Freedom of speech, freedom of press, freedom of assembly, public education, and—above all else—universal suffrage could, from one point of view, preserve " liberty " by protecting the individual from the authoritarian state, and could, from the other point of view, pave the way for strengthening the state by making it susceptible to genuine popular control. So " republican institutions " became a means for accomplishing exactly opposite ends, and in time the oppositeness of the ends would lead to differences of opinion on the " right " interpretation of the means. Even where the Republicans seemed most in agreement, therefore, they faced potential disunion.

But the Monarchists themselves were also seriously split in 1871. The Legitimists, who claimed the throne of Henri IV for the aged Count of Chambord, sought to bestow upon him the royal prerogatives unimpaired by anything that had happened subsequent to 1789. These die-hards, who invoked Divine Right and totally rejected the blasphemous innovation of universal suffrage, dreamed of their large landed estates and yearned for the seigneury of bygone days. The Orleanists, in contrast, felt monarchy to be the government the most likely to promote a social order favorable to their vast financial and industrial holdings. To have this, they were willing that their King should accept the paraphernalia of nineteenth-century liberalism, including a parliament elected by men of means. Their candidate, the Count of Paris, was willing, moreover, to reign beneath the tricolored flag of the bourgeois revolution. The Count of Chambord was not. This proved to be the issue which fatally divided the Monarchists. But in 1871 both factions believed that nothing could prevent the smoothing out of differences between the two branches of the once reigning family, so strongly did the logic of circumstances favor a restoration. Unity between the two was essential, because neither the Legitimists nor the Orleanists had the strength to accomplish their goal alone.

Within a few years, moreover, the Republicans had not only Monarchists, but also Bonapartists and Socialists to contend with. As a political force, Bonapartism did not exist in 1871. Yet a coterie of loyal supporters had survived the fall of the Empire. Lacking both a new man on horseback and a political philosophy, they nevertheless looked to the day when the youthful Prince Imperial could be placed on his father's throne. Following in the footsteps of both Napoleons, the Bonapartists were intensely opportunistic, and before long they found in the struggle between Monarchists and Republicans the means for returning to active politics. The rapid resurgence of Bonapartism after the utter disaster of the Franco-Prussian War was one of the most startling phenomena in the early years of the Third Republic.

Marxian socialism, as a would-be threat to the Republic, appeared on the scene toward the end of the decade. Organized Marxism did not exist in France until late in the 'seventies. The attempt to start a distinctly proletarian political movement had had to wait, first of all, until the creation of a relatively large non-agricultural labor force. This had come about with the increased industrialization of France, which had started under the Empire and was continuing under the Republic. A second prerequisite was the removal of the restrictions on independent labor action that had been imposed by the Empire and strengthened by the National Assembly. Gradually these restrictions were relaxed, if not in law at least in practice, as the post-Commune fear of the workingman began to recede, and as the Republicans moved toward taking over the regime in fact. Ironically enough, every step in " republicanizing the Republic " was a step toward making an environment in which the growth of revolutionary socialism was possible.

Monarchists, Bonapartists, Socialists—three widely differing creeds, but all dedicated to the overthrow of the Republic. Each was to seek in the question of an amnesty for the Paris Commune the means for discrediting the regime. In this way the amnesty controversy was more concerned with the Third Republic than with the vanished Paris Commune. In absolute terms, therefore, because of the tenuous position of the Republicans there could be no hope of a general amnesty either until the Republic had triumphed decisively over its enemies, or until the denial of a general amnesty had come to stand in the way of consolidating the Third Republic. In reality, because of fluctuations in French politics and consequently the changing nature of the threats to the Republic, the enactment of a broad measure of amnesty in 1880 was stimulated—as will be shown—by both the security and the insecurity of the Republicans.

CHAPTER II

THE REACTIONARIES:
THE COMMUNE AS SOCIAL PLAGUE

From 1871 to 1876 the National Assembly ruled France. The question of how France could return to business as usual after the devastating experience of the Paris Commune was made infinitely more difficult by the policies which the conservative majority at Versailles pursued in the immediate post-Commune years, for the National Assembly by its fanatical hate and fear of all associated with the twin evils of republicanism and socialism laid down the main lines along which the amnesty controversy developed in France. The Assembly did this through its summary refusal to entertain any thought of leniency in dealing with those accused of participation in the Paris Commune and through its ruthless attempt to rid the country of all radical tendencies. As the Minister of Foreign Affairs, Jules Favre, wrote in his famous circular letter of June 6, 1871, " To detest [the events of the Commune] . . . and to punish them is not enough. It is necessary to seek out the germ of them and to extirpate it. The greater the evil, the more essential it is to take account of it. . . . To introduce into the laws the severities which social necessity demands and to apply these laws without weakness are novelties to which France must resign herself. For her, it is a matter of safety." [1]

Even after the National Assembly came to an end, even when government was set up under the constitution that was its handiwork, its influence was still strong in all matters relating to the Commune. This influence was evident in the

[1] *Journal officiel de la République française*, June 8, 1871, 1259:1. Henceforth this source will be cited merely as *Journal officiel*. See also " Causes et caractère de l'insurrection du 18 mars. Circulaire du ministère des affaires etrangères," *Journal des économistes* (Paris, monthly), June 1871, 431-5, where the letter is reproduced. It is interesting to note that in addition to stringent laws Favre believed that public morality must be uplifted by " sound and strong education, by a liberal economic regime, by love illumined by justice, by simplicity, by moderation, by justice."

electoral campaigns of 1876 and in the position which Gambetta now assumed toward the question of an amnesty. This influence was evident in the ineffectualness of the Radical Republicans in getting support for their amnesty bills. In addition, the influence of the National Assembly was to be found in the development of the myth of the Commune as a great socialist endeavor, in a growing determination to vindicate the Commune, and in left-wing insistence that an amnesty was a right, not a discretionary matter.

The work of the National Assembly in dealing with the problems created by the defeat of the Paris Commune falls under three main headings. In its own body it had to dispose of all proposals that an amnesty, either total or partial, be granted to the participants in the events of the Commune. From the country at large it had to eliminate all the causes—as the National Assembly saw them—of the Paris Commune. Finally, it had to defend the feeble work of its most prized organ, the Commission on Pardons.

Amnesty Bills in the National Assembly

September 13, 1871, marked the formal entry of the amnesty question into French politics. On that date the first motion for an amnesty was made and on that date began the skillful use of delaying tactics that was to prevent the enactment of a true amnesty law for almost nine years. From far on the left, where the convinced Republicans were sitting, came a motion, written by Brisson and signed by forty-eight members of the opposition. Gambetta's name was there. The former head of the recent Government of the National Defense could well afford to be favorable to a measure of political forgiveness, for his own actions since September 4, 1870, were then being investigated by a hostile assembly.[2] Thus the motion called for an amnesty, to include all "condemned or prosecuted for political crimes or lesser offenses, at Paris and in the provinces, during the past year." The only persons to be excluded were those with a

---

[2] A resolution passed by the National Assembly on June 13, 1871, established a thirty-man commission to "examine the acts of the Government of the National Defense." (See National Assembly, *Annèxes*, XX ["Enquête sur les Actes du Gouvernement de la Défense Nationale, Rapports de la commission"].)

criminal record prior to the Commune and those subsequently convicted of murder, arson, or theft.[3] In his argument, Brisson hit at the conservative majority by pointing to Spain's recent amnesty law. " Is it only in France," he asked, " that liberal governments do not feel sure enough of themselves to clear the atmosphere by forgetting about our differences? " [4] But the Assembly was unmoved. The Left's demand for immediate consideration was defeated, and the motion was sent in a routine way to one of the committees on legislation. Three months later, nothing more had been heard of the Brisson motion. The Center Left now took up the fight when the Calvinist minister Pressensé moved on December 19 to free " all who had not passed the rank of sergeant, and who are neither accused of nor convicted of any common law crime or of any established act during the so-called insurrection." Specifically excluded were those who " prior to the insurrection had been condemned to imprisonment or to more serious penalties for non-political offenses." [5] Action on this motion was prolonged during the entire life of the National Assembly.

At the end of January 1872, amnesty seemed at least to have a chance of being seriously debated. But this hope proved illusory. The report for the committee on legislation was turned in on January 31. It advised consideration of the Pressensé motion since, as La Caze said for the committee, it was up to the Assembly itself to judge if the proposed measure satisfied

[3] National Assembly, *Annales*, V, 582.
[4] *Idem.*
[5] National Assembly, *Annèxes*, VI, 243. Pressensé stressed that his proposal was " essentially different from a general amnesty." (National Assembly, *Annales*, VI, 174). Insight into Pressensé's thinking is afforded by his article, " Le 18 mars.—Paris sous la Commune," published in *Revue des deux mondes* (June 15, 1871, 561-588). His conclusion, which strikes a remarkably moderate tone, offers an interesting contrast to the Favre letter quoted above. " This is a somber hour, . . ." wrote Pressensé, " but it is also a serious, solemn, [and] truly decisive hour, when a nation—confronted by all the evils which are devouring her—must question herself, must examine her conscience, [and] must seek out the role of all that was responsible for a catastrophe which implicates more than its direct instigators."
The phrase common law crimes, which was used repeatedly in the debates on amnesty, has been employed throughout this study to differentiate ordinary crimes from so-called political crimes. Of course, it has none of the meaning of Common Law in English.

both mercy and justice.[6] There was no discussion of the report. It was adopted by voice vote, and the motion went to committee.[7]

Now the situation changed completely. Pressensé almost immediately withdrew his original motion and presented a slightly more liberalized proposal, which excluded from amnesty only the recognized leaders of the Commune, those subsequently sentenced to a year or more of prison for common law crimes, and those who had been sentenced before the Commune to over three months' imprisonment for non-political offenses. There were to be no further prosecutions except in these categories.[8] Brisson next withdrew his motion, to re-submit it as an amendment to Pressensé's new bill.[9]

Within the committee itself a serious division developed. On July 16, 1872, the majority report was presented, which demanded that all thought of amnesty be rejected. Its arguments were based on the view that military justice in the case of the Commune had not been unduly harsh, and that Parisian industry was not—as some had charged—suffering a manpower shortage.[10] A strong minority report, however, was appended. Claiming that broad clemency would not do violence either to the principle of justice or to security, the authors of this report felt that the time had come to stop the arrests which were still being made. "The minority is convinced," it read, "that the National Assembly has the right to intervene and put an end to such a vast indictment."[11] On the same day these two reports

---

[6] National Assembly, *Annèxes*, VII, 139.

[7] National Assembly, *Annales*, VII, 461.

[8] National Assembly, *Annèxes*, XIII, 134-5.

[9] *Idem.*

[10] Text of the committee's report in *ibid.*, XIII, 135-9. The scarcity of labor caused by the denial of amnesty became a frequently repeated argument. See Brisson's speech of September 13, 1871, in National Assembly, *Annales*, V, 582 ff, and Lockroy's speech of May 16, 1876, in Chamber of Deputies, *Annales*, Session ordinaire 1876, II, 55-66. A contemporary writer on conditions after the Commune supports the Brisson and Lockroy arguments: "The workshops opened up again in such a hurry that toward the end of 1871 a shortage of manpower took the place of the lack of jobs. Work benches standing idle while the goods piled up made the employers demand the first measures of appeasement for our unhappy civil discords." (Joseph-J. Barberet, *Le travail en France: monographies professionnelles* [Paris, 1886-89], I, 15.)

[11] National Assembly, *Annèxes*, XIII, 138. The division between majority and minority is not given.

were handed in, Louis Blanc asked for a debate on amnesty before adjournment. His speech was greeted with noisy threats of clôture, and his motion was voted down.[12]

The Barodet Election

Before the question of amnesty was again raised in the National Assembly, this same issue played a part in one of the most significant election campaigns waged by the Republicans during the years of the National Assembly. This was the campaign of Barodet, whose " radicalism " had caused him to be summarily revoked as the Mayor of Lyons,[13] and who now, on April 27, 1873, won a landslide victory at the Parisian polls, to sit in the National Assembly as Deputy for the Department of the Seine. The consequences of this election in the history of the Third Republic—the reactionaries' successful coup of May 24, 1873—are too well known to repeat here. For the history of the amnesty controversy, the contest was significant both for the matter-of-course way that amnesty figured in Barodet's platform as an integral item of the Republican profession of faith, and for the outstanding men who endorsed this platform of 1873. The Republicans, then fighting for their life, were unanimous with Louis Blanc in attacking a regime which had confiscated the sovereignty of the people, regarded universal suffrage as suspect, and preferred, in place of a policy of appeasement, " a relentless policy, though the country's life blood has already flowed out through so many wounds. . . ." [14] At the same time, the " Democratic Republican Congress of the Department of the Seine " pointed out that a vote for Barodet was, among other things, a vote for the integrity of universal suffrage, for the immediate dissolution of the National Assembly, for the convocation of an assembly for the exclusive purpose of drafting a constitution, for the

[12] National Assembly, *Annales*, XIII, 176-8.
[13] On radicalism at Lyons and on Barodet, see *Revue des deux mondes*, Vol. 103 (Jan.-Feb. 1873), 959 ff; Vol. 104 (Mar.-Apr. 1873), 982 ff, and Vol. 105 (May-June 1873), 219 ff.
[14] Letter of Louis Blanc, read by Nadaud at a Republican meeting at Bercy, April 24, 1873. From *La République française*, April 28, 1873, 1:4.

suppression of martial law in the forty-three departments where it was still in force, and for amnesty.[15]

Meanwhile, Barodet had issued his platform, which similarly called for the dissolution of the Versailles Assembly and " the convocation, in short order, of a special assembly, which alone can vote an amnesty and the lifting of martial law." [16] Almost immediately Gambetta's Republican Union had officially endorsed Barodet as the standard bearer of democracy, of the Republican regime, and of social peace. "Along with him, and like him," said the Republican Union, " we ask the dissolution of the existing Assembly, we demand the convocation of a new assembly [which will be] able to proclaim an amnesty, to put an end to martial law, to found the Republic. . . ." The forty-two signatures to this declaration made a roster of Republican stalwarts. Gambetta's name was there, of course, and so were those of Cazot, the future Minister of Justice; of Lepère, the future Minister of Interior; of the future Radical Republicans Naquet, Louis Blanc, Schoelcher, Laurent-Pichat, and Tolain; of Paul Bert, the future Minister of Education and Cults; and of Gent, the founder of the Republican party in the Vaucluse.[17] The list was impressive, and there was no sign that any member of the Republican bloc had mental reservations about an amnesty, or regarded it as anything more than one among the many preliminary steps to the establishment of genuine republican institutions in France. The city of Paris, for its part, responded wholeheartedly to Barodet's appeal, once more showing its deepfelt republicanism. The former Mayor of Lyons carried thirteen of the twenty arrondissements. His vote was significantly the heaviest in the XIth, the XVIIIth, and the XXth.[18] The temper of the reactionaries was such, it was said, that they could see in Barodet's victory only " revenge for the Commune." [19] In any event, Republican unity had thrown Barodet in the National Assembly's face; Republican

[15] Ibid., April 27, 1873, 1:2-3.
[16] Platform dated Lyons, April 13, 1873. Printed in *ibid.*, April 28, 1873, 1:1.
[17] Declaration signed April 21, 1873. *Idem.*
[18] *Ibid.*, April 29, 1873, 1:2.
[19] See Anon., *Du 16 mai au 2 septembre 1877. Notes à consulter* (Paris, 1877), 32. The author here was contrasting the conditions surrounding May 24, 1873, and May 16, 1877.

unity had crushed Rémusat, the hope of the Monarchists. "Very well! It must be recognized that from now on nothing can destroy this admirable unity of all democratic Republicans," [20] wrote *La République française* when the votes were counted. But it reckoned without the controversial question of amnesty for the Paris Commune, which was to be the evil bequest of the National Assembly to the "Republican Republic."

The Carron Report

Louis Blanc had tried on July 16, 1872, to get amnesty on the calendar. On December 12, 1873, eighteen months later, after Barodet had been elected, after Thiers had been ousted, Brisson made a second and equally futile attempt. A technicality of parliamentary procedure was used to postpone still further any debate on amnesty.[21] The committee, however, continued to sit, and the minority, still hoping for some measure of conciliation, drafted a bill to end all arrests and prosecutions on May 31, 1874, and to dispose of all future cases arising from the Commune by trial in the public courts, not by military justice.[22] But the majority remained unconvinced, and on May 20, 1874, Emile Carron—the new chairman of the committee—presented to the Assembly a supplementary report which endorsed without a single exception the situation as it existed.

The Carron report was a landmark in the history of the amnesty. It effectively killed all chances of further consideration of an amnesty by the National Assembly, and it became an arsenal of arguments to be used in the future against leniency toward Communards. Its very vindictiveness made it persuasive. An amnesty, as Carron saw it, was out of the question. To enact it might possibly mean the rehabilitation of the Commune, and would certainly ". . . encourage unhealthy ambitions, inspire the *déclassé* with culpable expectations, [and] revive criminal hopes everywhere. . . ." He agreed that an end must be made of the repressive measures that had followed the Commune, but

---

[20] April 29, 1873, 1:6.
[21] National Assembly, *Annales*, XXVIII, 269.
[22] National Assembly, *Annèxes*, XXXI, 436. Cases of theft, murder, and arson were specifically excluded.

added with passion, " Would to God it were vouchsafed us to wipe out the last traces of the revolt which makes this repression necessary! " There was one way, and only one way, to do this, according to Carron: not to interfere with the military tribunals. His argument was built around four points: the most guilty of all had not yet been caught and punished; the passage of time in no way mitigated the seriousness of the Commune; the record of the military courts was excellent; and the special Commission on Pardons was doing its work conscientiously and thoroughly, so that amnestying was, in fact, going on all the time. ". . . it is begun by military justice . . . [and] is completed and realized in the Commission on Pardons." [23] This was the Carron report. And it was the end of the Pressensé and the Brisson proposals. There was never any debate on the report. It was never even read in the Assembly. Buffet's dry statement, " The report will be printed and distributed," [24] ended the matter.

Purging the Country of Radicalism

During the many months when no action was being taken on the Brisson and Pressensé bills, the National Assembly was going vigorously ahead with the business of wiping out the last traces of the Commune and purging the country of radicalism. It kept all revolutionary centers under martial law and assisted in this way the operation of military justice. It held an investigation into the causes of the Commune. It outlawed the International Workingmen's Association. It stoutly defended against all outside attacks its special commission set up to handle pardons. Furthermore, in carrying out these measures, the National Assembly was hindered by no vocal public opinion, for the people of Paris were haunted by fear, and no movement for amnesty could possibly have developed in the lifetime of the National Assembly.

[23] *Ibid.*, XXXI, 436-49, *passim.*
[24] National Assembly, *Annales*, XXXI, 86.

The Work of the Military Tribunals

The importance that the majority in the National Assembly attached to the work of the military tribunals was shown by the Carron report. From the defeat of the Commune until the enactment of the amnesty law of 1880, nearly 50,000 cases went through their hands. The usual facilities of French military justice early collapsed under the magnitude of the job facing it after the Paris Commune had been defeated. In August of 1871, around 4300 cases had been handled, while over 33,000 prisoners were awaiting trial.[25] At the request of the Minister of War, the National Assembly hastily authorized the creation of a dozen or more emergency courts (the number eventually reached twenty-six),[26] and provided that " The military tribunals will continue to sit after the lifting of martial law, until the entire examination of acts committed in connection with the insurrection [has been completed]." [27] Reinforced in this way, military justice went to work. Each year brought thousands of new convictions. No one was really safe. " The workers were unceasingly under the iron rule of the courts-martial and did not dare to say anthing," wrote one observer.[28]

Even the National Assembly had to be purged. Arthur Ranc, a follower of the early, radical Gambetta in politics, had been named a member of the National Assembly in the February 1871 elections. On March 26 of that year he had been elected a member of the Commune of Paris. In less than a month he had resigned from the latter body as its aims had become increasingly revolutionary. Several members of the National Assembly, led by the rabid Bonapartist Raoul Duval, repeatedly challenged his continuing membership, but nothing could be

---

[25] *Ibid.*, IV, 486, 503. A total of 9000 cases was then in progress. These figures, as was recognized, did not accurately measure the repression. As the economist Joseph Garnier remarked, " Will we ever know the number of insurgents . . . shot after the battle, with or without judgment by military tribunals, with or without error? " (" Chronique économique," *Journal des économistes*, August 1871, 331.)

[26] National Assembly, *Annèxes*, XXXI, 439.

[27] National Assembly, *Annales*, IV, 485-7; *Annexes*, IV, 204-5.

[28] Barberet, *Monographies professionneles*, I, 15.

done until a formal charge should be brought.[29] Then, on
June 12, 1873, Buffet read a letter from General de Ladmirault,
Governor of Paris, asking for authorization to prosecute Ranc
as ". . . the only one of the members of the Commune seriously
compromised who has not yet faced charges." [30] Over the
protests of the Left, the authorization was voted, 467 to 140.[31]
Ranc promptly disappeared, and four months later was sentenced to death *in absentia*.[32] A similar demand to prosecute
one of its members was addressed to the National Assembly
in February 1874.[33] The accused man was Melvil-Bloncourt,
sitting for Guadaloupe.[34] Again the National Assembly gave
satisfaction, and in June, Melvil-Bloncourt was also condemned
to death *in absentia*.[35]

Ranc and Melvil-Bloncourt became special cases only because
they were supposed to have a sort of parliamentary immunity.
But they were only two among many summarily convicted.
After 1872, of all the cases handled by military justice, the
sharpest increase, as was to be expected, came in the numbers
condemned *in absentia*. By the time the National Assembly
went out of existence, the ratio between prisoners serving
sentence in New Caledonia for participation in the Commune
and men who had fled into exile to escape penalty was almost
exactly equal. This suggests a picture of the military courts
bringing under accusation every name remotely suspected of
sympathy with the Commune. It also explains how there came
into being one element of major importance in the future

---

[29] See for example, National Assembly, *Annales*, VI, 174, 197.

[30] *Ibid.*, XVIII, 312.

[31] *Ibid.*, XVIII, 444.

[32] André Daniel [André Lebon], *L'Année politique 1874* (Paris, 1875),
17-19.

[33] National Assembly, *Annales*, XXIX, 502. Ladmirault said that the identification of the Deputy with the man whom they had sought for a long time as
the chief of the Commune's enlistment service had just been established.
(*Annèxes*, XXIX, 217.) The vote to authorize prosecution was 522 to 64.
(*Annales*, XXX, 116.)

[34] On Melvil-Bloncourt's election and his validation, see National Assembly,
Annales, III, 137.

[35] *L'Année politique 1874*, 105.

struggle for an amnesty, namely, the body of around 3300 men who faced death or deportation if they returned to France.[36] The National Assembly was well informed of the progress of military justice, as a number of special parliamentary reports prove. That it endorsed the work of the military courts is equally well attested. Far from entertaining any thought of ending the prosecutions by an amnesty, the men of Versailles had no intention of relaxing the existing discipline. In April of 1872 Victor Hugo had written as introduction to his collection of poems, *The Terrible Year*, that " Martial law is a part of the Terrible Year, and it still reigns. . . . The moment will pass. We have the Republic; we will have liberty." [37] But

[36]   MILITARY JUSTICE AND THE COMMUNE

Disposition of Cases, 1871-1876

			Judgments				
					Convictions		
Date	Total Cases	No indict-ments	Total	Acquittals	Total	With Trial	In ab-sentia
August 1871 [a]	4262	1937	2325	INFORMATION NOT AVAILABLE			
July 1872 [b]	32905	21610	11295	2103	9192	9053	139
May 1874 [c]	49781	34112	15669	2367	13302	9877	3425
April 1876 [d]	43522	30940	12582	2443	——	10137	3313
	[46833]		[15893]		[13450]		

[a] MacMahon Report, National Assembly, *Annales*, IV, 486. Cases in progress, 9000. See also Garnier, " Chronique," *Journal des économistes*, August 1871, 331.

[b] La Caze Report, National Assembly, *Annèxes*, XIII, 139.

[c] Carron Report, *ibid.*, XXXI, 440.

[d] Paris Report, Senate, *Annèxes*, Session ordinaire 1876, I, 311-12.

Figures in brackets give the correct arithmetical totals. No documentary explanation is available for the contradictions between the May 1874 and the April 1876 figures.

[37] Victor Hugo, *L'Année terrible*, 23rd edition (Paris, 1874), fly-leaf. He was explaining the censor's suppression of several lines from the poems and the absence from the volume of several poems pertaining to the months of April, May, June and July 1871.

the day when speech and press would be free was far away. As late as July 1875, after five years of arbitrary imposition of sentences by the military courts, Buffet told his colleagues that all demands for ending martial law must be rejected until a new press law was voted.[38] There could be no better indication of the temper of the Government that this maintenance of martial law. The general witch-hunting character that marked the work of military justice could exist only in the absence of civil authority. An amnesty was patently impossible, arrests and convictions would multiply unchecked until the time when " emergency " control by the Army came to an end.

Investigation into the Causes of the Paris Commune

After the Paris Commune had been put down, the National Assembly faced a double task. It must first see to it that all who had taken part in the insurrection were punished. To do this, the National Assembly had only to give a free hand to the Army. The second task was more difficult. It must guarantee the country against another civil conflict. As a result, the National Assembly had begun its investigation of the causes of the Commune almost before the smoke of battle had cleared away.

On May 26, 1871, Haentjens made a motion to set up a commission to study the causes of the Commune.[39] Three weeks later the National Assembly authorized a special thirty-man commission under the Comte Daru to conduct such an investigation.[40] After working unceasingly for six months, the commission presented its report. This document was to exercise a profound influence not only on the lawmakers' attitude toward an amnesty for the Paris Commune, but also on their entire thinking about the general social problem. The strongly Monarchist commission attacked socialism directly and democracy by implication. Thus it found that the spread of socialism in France in recent years had led directly to the Commune, and it blamed the spread of socialism on universal suffrage, popular sovereignty, freedom of the press, and public educa-

---

[38] L'Année politique 1875, 225.
[39] National Assembly, Annales, III, 137.
[40] Ibid., III, 464.

tion.[41] Of all the dangers to be feared from socialism, the commission went on to say, none was so great as the existence of the International Workingmen's Association. France was face to face with a new barbarian invasion: " The Paris Commune has just demonstrated the insane theories, the deceptive programs which—if realized—would set humanity back many centuries." There was nothing new, however, in the theories, the report went on to say; but what was new was ". . . the organized and truly formidable army which the International puts at their service." [42] The very first recommendation of the commission, therefore, was for the suppression of the International. "It would be mad," argued the commission, " to leave society defenseless in the presence of a military weapon as formidable as the International." [43]

The recommendation of the commission to outlaw the International corresponded completely with the preconceived ideas of the Assembly's majority. And in passing a law against the dread association, the National Assembly accurately reflected conservative opinion at large. The International " caused " the Commune, as they saw it, so the International must be got rid of. To argue the relatively slight role of this society in the events of March 18 to May 28 is beside the point. Facts did not count.

Outlawing of the International

As early as June 1871, Jules Favre in a letter to the members of the diplomatic corps had written that he would be leaving out an essential element in the story of the Paris Commune if he did not " call to mind the fact that at the side of those parodies of Jacobins . . . you must place the leaders of a society . . . called the International. . . ." [44] Not long after this, on August 7, 1871, Thiers had introduced a bill making membership in the International a criminal offense.[45]

[41] National Assembly, *Annèxes*, IX, 88 ff.

[42] *Ibid.*, IX, 88. The report then gave a long history of the International. For some curious reason, the commission attacked Marx for attacking Proudhon, and in this connection incorrectly referred to *Les misères* [sic] *de la philosophie* as a chapter in *Capital* (*Annèxes*, IX, 93).

[43] *Ibid.*, IX, 117.

[44] *Journal officiel*, June 8, 1871, 1259:1.

[45] National Assembly, *Annèxes*, IV, 209.

This bill, however, did not have smooth sailing. More than one liberal-minded member of the Assembly shared the opinion that ". . . the new legal offense of affiliation with the International . . . would be the sure way to increase the danger from the International, by giving it more importance than it has, and the allure of a secret and persecuted masonry." [46]

Of all the speeches made against banning the International, the one made by Louis Blanc on March 6, 1872, contained the fullest development of the opposition point of view. His arguments also anticipated in several important respects the political creed of the future " Radical Republicans." Louis Blanc placed the blame for the Commune not on the International, but on the laissez-faire state. He took the phrase " the inevitability of poverty " from the report on Thiers' bill as his point of departure for a discussion of the evils of orthodox political economy. He quoted Turgot and J. B. Say on wage theory. He found that against such doctrines, the workingman must perforce strike back as best he could. Because of this, he contended, the proposed law against the International would be both ineffective and dangerous. It would be ineffective because it tried to suppress ideas. "[The proposed law] does not make a crime of any clearly defined overt act, . . . it does not make a crime of any specified act which is punishable only when it has been proved. What it prosecutes, what it charges against those affiliated with the International is their adherence to certain doctrines." [47] Throughout history, Louis Blanc insisted, persecution had failed to kill ideas. Did the Assembly hope, he asked, to accomplish with imprisonment, fine, and loss of French citizenship what had been impossible with the most brutal tortures? The law would be dangerous, he went on to say, because it would magnify the importance of the International, drive it underground, and stimulate class hatred. This last point was the most dangerous of all; no misunderstanding must exist between the rich and the poor, for " intimate alliance and union [between them] is the only possible guarantee of the realization of progress." [48]

[46] Joseph Garnier, " Chronique," *Journal des économistes*, August 1871, 331.
[47] National Assembly, *Annales*, VIII, 195, 196, 198-9.
[48] *Ibid.*, VIII, 199.

The majority of the Assembly was not to be swayed. On March 14 it voted to make Article 463 of the Penal Code applicable to all membership in any international organization which had as its objectives "incitement to work stoppages, [and] to the abolition of property, of the family, of the fatherland, or of religious organizations which have been recognized by the State. . . ." [49]

Effects Within France of the Law Against the International

The law of March 14, 1872, had two effects. In the first place, it made available to the Government a blanket indictment which could be used on any pretext against leftist elements. In the second place, by putting into the statutes an implied identification of the Commune with the International, the National Assembly made inevitable the development, within both anarchist and Marxist circles, of a determination to vindicate the Commune. Such a vindication could take at the outset no other form than the legal rehabilitation of the proscribed Communards. In this way, the outlawing of the International meant that the fight to win an amnesty for the Paris Commune would be looked upon, in bourgeois circles, as a fight to justify social revolution as preached by the International.

If the conservatives, moreover, needed any further proof in 1872 that the Paris Commune had been the work of the International, they had only to point to the Hague Congress of the Association,[50] which met from September 2 to September 7. Ranvier, the same man who had proclaimed the Commune in the name of the people on March 28, 1871, was elected president, and in all about eight or ten former members of the Commune were present.[51]

It was at the end of 1872 that the full impact of the law against the International began to be felt. For some time after

---

[49] Ibid., VIII, 315. Such a society, it was held, "would constitute, by the very fact of its existence, a threat to public peace."

[50] This was the congress that saw the definite break between the Marxists and the Bakuninists, with the latter, voted out of the association, holding an independent congress a few days later at Saint-Imier. Both the General Council and the Jurassian Federation, as the Bakuninists were henceforth known, continued to use the name the International.

[51] Garnier, "Chronique," Journal des économistes, September 1872, 440.

the Hague Congress, it had been possible for both Marxists
and anarchists to continue their work inside France. For
example, Engels was able to write to Sorge on December 14
that " Jurassians . . . are mining the earth in all of France and
are making progress. . . . France will be almost entirely lost
to us." [52] In addition, the several November and December
issues of the *Bulletin* of the Jurassian Federation were full of
news about French affiliates.[53] Then suddenly all publication
of information about activities in France stopped, " ' because
of the new prosecutions of which the International has just
been the object in France.' " [54] The *Bulletin*, from which this
passage comes, was referring to the large-scale arrests of collectivists made in the Midi during December 1872. The informing
and counter-informing that led to these arrests were typical of
the factional struggles between the Marxist General Council
and the anarchist Jurassians at this time. Dentraygues, Marx's
agent at Toulouse, was blamed for the arrests in his vicinity,
and Paul Brousse and Jules Guesde, who were close to the
Jurassians, allegedly put the police on Dentraygues in retalia-
tion.[55] Brousse himself was in turn denounced but got away.

These arrests did destroy the International in France, at least
for the moment. As Bakunin wrote to the exiled Communard
Pindy, " The great difficulty for your fellow countrymen is that
they have forgot how to conspire, and . . . under the present
regime, you cannot organize anything in France without conspiracy." [56] Bakunin did not exaggerate. In the Assembly's
determination to crush the International, it turned against even
the conservative press. In the spring of 1873, the *Gazette de
France* was suspended for reprinting a circular put out by the
London General Council.[57] The law invoked was, of course,
the law against the International.

[52] Quoted in James Guillaume, *L'Internationale, documents et souvenirs*
(*1864-1878*) Paris, (1905), III, 24.

[53] *Ibid.*, III, 37.

[54] *Idem.* Quoted from the minutes of the meeting of the Federal Council
of the Jurassian Federation, January 12, 1873.

[55] *Ibid.*, III, 38, 62-3 (text of letter by Guesde, dated Rome, March 29, 1873,
and published in the April 15, 1873, *Bulletin*).

[56] *Ibid.*, III 89-90. Letter dated January 11, 1873.

[57] Garnier, " Chronique,' *Journal des économistes*, April 1873, 151.

During the next year, 1873, the International regained some ground, while the politicians at Versailles fought over the ousting of Thiers, the attempt to reconcile the Count of Chambord and the Count of Paris, and the passage of the Septennate Act. But early in 1874 the dragnet was put out again, and in March the correctional court of Lyons condemned twenty-seven anarchist collectivists to a total of forty years, six months in prison, and 1,350 francs in fines, on the charge of belonging to the International. Each of the accused lost his civil rights for five years.[58]

French collectivism went into a further decline.[59] By March of 1876, when the Jurassians held a banquet at Lausanne to commemorate the Paris Commune, there were a few scattered sympathizers inside France who sent telegrams, but this was all. Twice between 1872 and 1876 it had been forcefully shown that there was little chance of organizing within France a movement sufficiently strong to bring about a rehabilitation of the Commune.

Effects of the Law Against the International on the Exiles

The consequences of the outlawing of the International were not limited to France, but profoundly affected also the lives of the exiles of the Commune. As has been shown, conservative opinion in France identified the Commune with the International. " Paris is still ablaze more than ever throughout all of Europe," the report of the National Assembly's commission investigating the causes of the Commune had said, quoting resolutions adopted by the International at Brussels, Geneva, Zurich, Milan and many other cities.[60] The various sections of the International had in fact endorsed the Commune (Bebel and Liebknecht, for example, had written, " We are and we declare ourselves to be in solidarity with the Paris Commune,")[61] without, however, claiming authorship of the event. But when the refugees from the savagery of the Versailles

---

[58] *Guillaume*, III, 170.

[59] See *ibid.*, III, 241, " The International in France, reduced to clandestine propaganda, had not progressed; the Lyons trial had intimidated a good many militants." This was the summary of the situation given at the end of 1874.

[60] National Assembly, *Annèxes*, IX, 106-8.

[61] *Idem.*

government poured into Switzerland, into Belgium, into England, they found help from the International. As the French
Embassy at London reported, the many arrivals of men compromised in the insurrection " have found in England in the
members of the International accomplices who, after having
aided them with good wishes rather, doubtlessly, than with
money, are counting on exploiting their arrival for the benefit
of their own evil designs, which they themselves are carrying
out against [existing] social institutions." [62]
    The refugees not only found help, but they also found,
because of the French Government's persistence in hunting out
and demanding the extradition of Communards, the absolute
necessity of sticking together and of expelling dissident elements
from their ranks. This was particularly true in London, where
sectarianism early made its appearance. The group known as
" The Commune," made up of followers of Blanqui, was the
most compact, cohesive group in London.[63] There was also the
" Club of Proletarians," with Joffrin, Delahaye, and Maujean
among its members.[64] All such groups were joined in the Society
of Refugees of the Commune, which administered any funds
the exiles were able to raise through subscription. In a short
time, however, the strains and tensions of exile had a telling
effect, and some refugees fell to bickering over whose fault it
was that the Commune had been defeated. This development
was the work of Vésinier, Landeck, and Lucien Geoffroy, who
called for the setting up of a jury to try (*in absentia*, of course)
the officialdom of the Commune (". . . above all, those who
had the handling of the funds of the Commune "), and so on,
an endless list.[65] Coupled with this manoeuver were gross personal assaults against Vaillant, Eudes, and Longuet. Immediately the Society of Refugees expelled the dissidents and barred
them from receiving any financial aid.[66] Significantly, the

[62] Georges Bourgin, " La lutte du gouvernement français contre la première
Internationale: Contribution à l'histoire de l'après-Commune," *loc. cit.*, 46.
    [63] Alexandre Zévaès, *Les proscrits de la Commune* (Paris, [1936?]), 15.
    [64] *La Fédération, journal révolutionnaire, socialiste, français-anglais* (London,
irregularly), January 25, 1873, 7:4.
    [65] *Ibid.*, September 28, 1872, 4:1-2. Resolution adopted at meeting of July 1,
1872.
    [66] *Ibid.*, March 18, 1875, 1:1 (reprint of article from the August 31, 1872
issue), and September 28, 1872, 4:3.

trouble-makers were not able to split the main body of exiles. Their newspaper, *La Fédération*, had to fold up for lack of resources, and their attempt to form a " Universal Federalist International Workingmen's Association "—based on the repudiation of all the acts of the true International—was a failure.[67] The majority of the London exiles maintained their solidarity, while Landeck, a voice in the wilderness, wailed " No amnesty! . . . No amnesty for those who would again compromise the people by their divisions and their malice! . . . No amnesty . . . for all the leaders of the vanquished Revolution! . . . for the inept leaders who lost the Revolution." [68]

In Switzerland, meanwhile, committees to aid the exiles had been formed wherever the International existed.[69] Closest relations were maintained between the exiles and the Jurassian Federation. There were two good reasons for this. Many Communards took refuge in Switzerland. Moreover, the anarchist sections felt the ideological bias of the Commune to have been an expression of their own views. On March 14, 1872 —the same day, ironically enough, when the National Assembly voted the law against the International—the Swiss exiles were joined by Elisée Réclus, who had just had his sentence of deportation commuted to ten years of banishment, after eighteen months of being dragged from one French prison to another.[70] In a very short time, Elisée Réclus emerged as the moral leader of the French exiles in Switzerland, and furthermore, because he was so justly celebrated, he became an important figure in the amnesty controversy. With unwavering simiplicity, he refused to think of himself apart from the totality of the proscribed men of the Commune. As early as October 20, 1871, while still in France, he had written to his wife, ". . . I wish to be only as free as my comrades, without any conditions,

---

[67] See *ibid.*, September 28, 1872, 1:1 (Lucien Geoffroy, "Project for a socialist federation"), 3:1; and January 25, 1873, 2:2-3:1, 6:4.

[68] *Ibid.*, September 28, 1872, 2:1-2.

[69] Guillaume, II, 155.

[70] Max Nettlau, *Elisée Réclus, Anarchist und Gelehrter (1830-1905)* (*Beiträge zur Geschichte des Sozialismus, Syndikalismus, und Anarchismus*, Band IV), (Berlin, 1928), 168. See 160 ff for description of the eighteen months' imprisonment.

and without my wounded honor's being compromised. . . . I will not be indebted to generosity for my freedom." [71]

The Exiles and the Deportees

With the passage of time, the exiles of the Commune were able to make some sort of living in their new circumstances. As was natural, then, with the emergency period past, all eyes turned toward the men who had not evaded military justice. In the spring of 1874, the Jurassian Federation opened a permanent subscription for the men who had been deported to New Caledonia. Elisée Réclus had the job of getting the money to them,[72] and when he was no longer able to do this, Pindy found a way of sending it through a friend in London.[73] A similar subscription for the deportees was also set up in London in 1874, handled by a committee consisting of Joffrin, Langevin, Landrin, Vichard, and Maujean. In three years, they collected— with the help of money sent from refugees in Belgium, Switzerland, and America—a total sum of about 6,000 francs.[74]

Collection of funds was at best only a very limited measure of help for the men at New Caledonia. Not only were the resources of the exiles very slim, but also financial aid in itself would not bring the deportees back to France. Under existing circumstances, however, little else could be done, while this working together to make less wretched the lives of those more unfortunate than themselves tended to bind the exiles more closely together and to give them a common purpose.

With active work in the land of the National Assembly impossible, the exiles tried to keep alive their cause by calling attention to the living dead at Noumea. For the first four months of 1874, for example, the *Bulletin* of the Jurassian Federation contained practically nothing but letters from the

[71] *Ibid.,* 165. Also on Elisée Réclus, see Guillaume, II, 89, letter of Bakunin to Pindy, January 11, 1873.

[72] Guillaume, III, 191.

[73] *Ibid.,* III, 253-54. The Jurassian Federal Council had followed Pindy's proposal by voting for the establishment of permanent subscriptions in all sections, with the funds to be sent to London monthly. From the Italian section, Cafiero sent a hundred francs.

[74] *Le Travailleur, Revue socialiste-révolutionnaire* (Geneva, monthly), May 1877, 29-30.

deportees telling of the barbarous treatment they were getting.[75] The death of Verdure,[76] the agonies of Paschal Grousset, who had been condemned to hard labor [77]—details such as these from the letters made the sufferings of the deportees seem personal and real. Already a kind of halo was beginning to form around them. Thus, when the death sentence of Marshal Bazaine, the ill-fated commander at Sedan,[78] was commuted to life imprisonment, the *Bulletin* pointed out that " Bazaine is going to end his days beneath the orange trees on the island of Sainte-Marguerite, while the defeated men of the Commune suffer agonies in New Caledonia." [79] Similarly, when the radical journalist Henri Rochefort, " a mediocre figure," made his sensational escape from the penal colony and was greeted " like a Messiah " on his return to Europe, James Guillaume, Bakunin's young disciple, dismissed him with contempt: ". . . we turn our eyes," he wrote, " to the prisons of New Caledonia, where so many obscure and devoted victims are suffering in silence, [men] who will never go seeking for fame to cry their names in history, but for whom we guard in the depths of our hearts the deepest sympathy." [80]

It was in September of 1875 that a group of the exiles in Switzerland, hoping—as they said—" to reawaken the conscience of the French proletariat," published a collection of the letters of the political deportees. The preface, believed to have been writtn by Elisée Réclus, told of conditions in New Caledonia and exulted, ". . . we are proud that we—we ourselves—are as one with these men." [81]

Scarcely four years had passed since the defeat of the Commune, and during these years the Commune as a symbol had

[75] Guillaume, III, 170.

[76] Member of the Commune from the XIth arrondissement.

[77] Letter printed in the October 12, 1873, issue of the *Bulletin* of the Jurassian Federation; from Guillaume, III, 159. Grousset had been in charge of external relations for the Commune (see National Assembly, *Annales*, II, 369). He escaped from New Caledonia with Henri Rochefort (see Henri Avenel, *Histoire de la presse française* [Paris, 1900], 700).

[78] Bazaine had been tried and sentenced to death on December 10, 1873.

[79] Guillaume, III, 159.

[80] *Ibid.*, III, 191, reprinted from the June 29, 1874, issue of the *Bulletin*.

[81] *Ibid.*, III, 289. Preface reprinted from copy that appeared in Number 24 of the *Bulletin*. Guillaume thinks Réclus wrote the preface, but does not remember with certainty.

acquired a moral unity which the Commune in fact had never had. By 1875 a cult of the Commune was in the making. It had a martyrology—the stories of suffering at New Caledonia.[82] It imposed an obligation—solidarity among all the victims of Versailles. Here were the tap roots of the emotionalism and inflexibility that marked the future struggle for an amnesty. In addition, this cult grew out of the work of the National Assembly, with its blanket proscription of the International and its nightmarish ferreting out of the refugees of the Commune.

The Commission on Pardons

So far as most of the members of the National Assembly were concerned in 1875, the question of an amnesty for the Paris Commune could never become a controversial issue in French politics, for the simple reason that, as they saw it, there was no need for an amnesty. While they admitted the possibility of some injustice, they believed that the machinery which had been set up to handle pardons would take care of all deserving cases. To go father was to them unthinkable. Thus it was that the Communards' growing emphasis on their identity as a group was matched by an equally strong belief in conservative circles that only by dealing with each Communard individually was it possible to consider some measure of leniency. An amnesty, or political forgiveness applying to all indiscriminately, would leave France defenseless against a second Commune. Pardon, on the other hand, provided ample safeguards. In this light, the National Assembly found the record of its maligned Commission on Pardons eminently satisfactory.

Set up on June 17, 1871, the Commission on Pardons was a fifteen-man body, without whose concurrence the Chief of the Executive Power could not pardon Communards. The fiction that the right to pardon belonged to the executive was thereby preserved, but exercise of the right was entrusted to a parlia-

---

[82] Of interest in connection with this point is the volume published at Leipzig in 1876 by the printers' co-operative: Paschal Grousset und Fr. Jourde, *Die Märtyrer der Commune in Neu-Caledonien*, the proceeds of the sale of which were for the benefit of the deported Communards and their families.

mentary agent.[83] From the very beginning, the Commission—regarded as the tool of reaction—was under attack. The Republican press, the only leftist press in 1871, began in November to print articles ". . . containing in the coarsest form the most violent insults and . . . the most odious threats . . ." against the Commission, and tried ". . . to arouse the citizens' distrust and hatred of the representatives of the nation." This was Dufaure's characterization of the opposition press when he asked the Assembly for the right to prosecute.[84] His window-dressing emphasis on the representative nature of the Assembly found an echo in the committee's favorable report on Dufaure's request. "Of all the duties which the confidence of the country has imposed on you," the lawmakers were told, " none is more important and more difficult than that with which your Commission on Pardons has been charged." [85] But subsequent trial by jury brought acquittal of the offending papers.[86] This in itself was noteworthy. Granting the complexity of the issues involved—Republicanism versus Monarchism, the freedom of the press, parliamentary immunity—these cases of early 1872 stand out as the first tangible suggestion that public opinion did not wholly endorse the policies of the Government in dealing with the defunct Commune.

Nevertheless, the Commission on Pardons continued its plodding, cautious work. By May 1874 it had reviewed nearly 6000 appeals and rejected 4000 of them. In all, only 350 of the condemned had got full pardon; the rest were merely reductions of sentences.[87] By the time the Commission's man-

---

[83] Jules Simon used this point some years later in his apology for Thiers. " The Commune reproached the President with not having used his pardoning power; but he did not have the right to pardon, ...only the right to consent to pardon." (*Thiers, Guizot, et Rémusat* [Paris, 1885], Preface, 67.)

[84] National Assembly, *Annales*, VI, 44.

[85] National Assembly, *Annèxes*, VI, 287.

[86] Avenel, *Histoire de la presse française*, 668. The fact alone of a jury trial indicated, in the light of French trial procedure, the seriousness of the action against these papers.

[87] National Assembly, *Annèxes*, XXXI, 439. It is difficult to reconcile the figures given here (cases reviewed, 5969; combined total, pardons and reduction of penalties, 1969) for May 1874 with Simon's statement of the situation in May 1873, when Thiers went out of office (cases reviewed, 6501; combined total, pardons and reductions of penalties, 2570). *Thiers, Guizot, et Rémusat*, Preface, 68. The most usual reduction of penalty was from " deportation to a fortress " to " simple deportation."

date expired, along with that of the National Assembly, it had handled almost 8200 requests and had granted either pardon or reduction of sentence in thirty-eight per cent of these cases.[88] The number of Communards at New Caledonia had been reduced from 4643 [89] to 3537 by April 1876.[90]

The record of the Commission on Pardons, while not imposing, did not seem bad, and the Assembly, by its failure to bring the Pressensé bill to a vote, showed its agreement with Carron that ". . . amnesty is being accomplished . . . by the Commission on Pardons." [91] But this reliance on the pardoning power to end the social schism created by the Commune was a policy destined to cause even greater discord. Once public opinion had been aroused, pardon could not be held equivalent to amnesty. Pardon removed the penalty, but the stigma of the conviction remained. The National Assembly, however, had found a simple but rigid formula—to deny amnesty in the name of pardon. And to the very end, the minds of both conservatives and middle-of-the-roaders were closed to all thought of any other solution to the amnesty problem.

The End of the National Assembly

The National Assembly went out of existence on December 31, 1875. By July of that year it had written the last of the new constitutional laws. As France prepared to hold new legislative elections, the deep animosities within the National Assembly were taken to the people. The transparent intent of the Assembly's majority to keep the door open for a restoration had driven the men who were above all else Republicans into a bitter intransigeance.

In the fall session of 1875, a last minute attempt was made to get an amnesty bill passed by the National Assembly. The Commission on Pardons handed in its report on December 20. That very day, Naquet read a bill to " grant a full and complete amnesty " to the authors of " all political crimes and lesser offenses committed since September 4, 1870," and in addition,

---

[88] Or, in 3140 cases. National Assembly, *Annèxes*, XLIV, 502.
[89] Total condemnations to deportation. *Ibid.*, XLIV, 48.
[90] Senate, *Annèxes*, Session ordinaire 1876, I, 312.
[91] National Assembly, *Annèxes*, XXI, 440.

to have reviewed within six months the trials of all condemned for common law crimes in connection with political crimes.[92] He had scarcely begun to read when the Assembly was in an uproar. The noise from the Right drowned out the speaker. When Naquet left the tribune, all the members of the Left were out of their seats milling around him. Périn, in favor of an amnesty, was demanding immediate consideration of the bill. Langlois, opposed to an amnesty, was denouncing the bill as out of order. From the President's chair, the Duc d'Audiffret-Pasquier imperiously but vainly called for quiet. Finally the Assembly became sufficiently calm to vote Naquet's bill out of order and return to the calendar.[93] This would have been the end of the matter if the Duc d'Auriffret-Pasquier, as President of the National Assembly, had not felt impelled to add his weight against any amnesty. The next day he commented at length on the minutes of the stormy session. If he but knew, he said, who had been causing all the disturbance, he would not hesitate to take severe measures. It was his duty, he affirmed, " to protest with greatest energy against the words pronounced, which are an unspeakable outrage against the heroism of those who died in the defense of law and society." [94] Prolonged and enthusiastic applause greeted this *ex cathedra* pronouncement.

The events of December 20 and 21 showed unmistakably that hostility to an amnesty was stronger in 1875 than it had been in 1871. For almost its entire lifetime the National Assembly had been plagued by the opposition's demands for an amnesty. The majority, by 1875, regarded the matter as over and done with. And now, when tempers were short and all eyes on the electorate, Naquet had dared bring the question up again. Amnesty lost whatever character it may once have had as a genuine measure of social conciliation. Bound up in parliamentary politics, it became the prized possession of all who

[92] National Assembly, *Annales*, XLIV, 27. Co-authors of the bill were Bouchet, Esquiros, Madier de Montjau, and Ollivier Ordinaire. The argument was that an amnesty must be voted at that time, since the Commission on Pardons would expire with the end of the National Assembly, and therefore, for at least three months, there would be no machinery to handle petitions for redress.
[93] *Ibid.*, XLIV, 30-4.
[94] *Ibid.*, XLIV, 51.

wanted to overthrow the Government. This connotation made sober judgment impossible and further postponed the day—if ever—when an amnesty for the Paris Commune could be realized.

The Elections of 1876

With the parliamentary elections of 1876, the amnesty question and partisan politics began their long and intimate association. French voters at that time had a chance to register their opinion of the National Assembly, and Republican politicians had a hope of ending their minority impotence of the past five years. Inevitably, the more radical Republicans found in the campaigns of January and February a means of taking the amnesty question to the people. An amnesty for the Paris Commune, however, was not a major issue in the elections. The matter of winning endorsement for the Republican form of government was of much greater concern. Furthermore, belief in republican institutions served to unite men of widely divergent views on practically every social and economic problem of the times. Thus, as the Republicans prepared to take over the Republic, the amnesty question might be a disastrous threat to Republican unity.

The Senatorial Elections

On January 30, the senatorial electoral colleges of France gave a clear majority to the Monarchists. Those Republicans elected were overwhelmingly conservative, with the Radicals able to claim but fifteen seats in the Senate.[95] Only at Paris had an attempt been made to elect men committed to a speedy amnesty. Naquet, for example, had talked of the need for drafting a Radical *cahier* that would serve for both the senatorial and the legislative elections. One point he had proposed was an investigation of the acts of the commanding generals in those departments under martial law since 1871.[96] Next,

---

[95] *L'Année politique 1876*, 28. And eight of these Radical Senators were life Senators, named by the outgoing National Assembly.

[96] *Le Journal des débats* (Paris, daily), January 12, 1876, 2:2. (The *Débats* in the 1870's reflected the conservative Republican point of view, especially that of Thiers).

Victor Hugo, after being named delegate of the Paris Municipal Council by a large majority,[97] had published in pamphlet form a letter to the other senatorial electors of the country. In this brochure the romantic poet-politician characterized the city of Paris as martyred for her patriotism. When the Prussians had reached Paris, he wrote, " They thought they would encounter Sodom. They found Sparta." For her heroic resistance, however, the only thanks Paris got had been affronts and insults. Her " diadem as the capital of France " had been snatched away. But now, in 1876, Paris was asking " Nothing for herself, everything for the country." She was asking for " the end of abuses by the accession of truth, the end of monarchy by the federation of the people, . . . the end of the civil war by an amnesty. . . ." Then Victor Hugo called upon the electors to " Create . . . a Republic to be desired, a Republic without martial law, without muzzles, without exiles, without political prisons, without a military yoke, without a clerical yoke, a Republic of truth and liberty." [98]

Equally active during the period of the senatorial elections was Laurent-Pichat, who had himself just been named a life Senator by the outgoing National Assembly, and whose powerful speeches in the campaign meetings over which he presided gave rise to the " Laurent-Pichat program," a platform categorically demanding an amnesty and the suppression of martial law.[99] Thus the January 17 meeting of the Radical Republican members of the Seine's electoral college, in discussing the drawing up of a platform which all candidates must endorse, followed point by point Laurent-Pichat's program. At this meeting, it should be noted, not only the regular Radical politicians were present, but also two men who were put forth as labor candidates, Godfrin and Malarmé.[100]

---

[97] Paris, Conseil municipal, *Procès-verbaux*, 1876, 10-11. Victor Hugo got 53 out of 73 votes. His nearest opponents got 7 votes apiece. For a popular account of the meeting, see *Le Journal des débats*, January 17, 1876, 1:3-6. Clemenceau had presided. Spuller, Gambetta's man, had been named alternate delegate.

[98] Victor Hugo, *Lettre de Victor Hugo, le délégué de Paris, aux délégués des 36,000 communes de France.* ([Paris?], 1876), 13-15.

[99] Edgar Bourloton, *Dictionnaire des parlementaires français* (Paris, 1889), III, 633.

[100] *Le Journal des débats*, January 18, 1876, 1:3.

Gambetta's Role

The final decision on the question of a Republican platform came at a meeting of the full electoral college held four days before the election. On this occasion, Gambetta argued vigorously and successfully both against electing radicals and against adopting a program for the Seine's Senators. He told the electors that " the triumph of extremists at Paris would perhaps cost the Republican party twenty nominations in the provinces." He was afraid, as he explained, that a too-radical platform would be made into a red herring by the enemies of the constitution.[101]

After Gambetta's strong stand against what he termed a " decalogue," the meeting was spent in questioning the candidates. Godfrin, one of the labor candidates, had withdrawn from the race. Nothing more was heard of the candidate Malarmé. But another labor candidate, Coutant, now stoutly upheld his " socialism " against mere political considerations. Victor Hugo, when questioned on amnesty, urged " conciliation by mercy." But in answer to the same questions, the candidate Béclard replied that " an amnesty was desirable, even necessary some day or other, but that the question was its opportuneness; and that in any event, it must apply only to political crimes. . . , not to common law crimes." [102]

As early as 1876, therefore, the moderates were arriving at their standard approach to the amnesty question. Béclard's views were but an endorsement of Gambetta's own pleas for a middle-of-the-road course. Moreover, the electoral college listened well, and after the votes were counted, the Radicals had to be content with the election of only seven candidates.[103]

In the provinces, no one at all endorsed amnesty during the senatorial campaign. Staunch Republicans everywhere made a point of repudiating any desire for it. Jules Favre, speaking in his home town of Lyons, coined an oft-to-be-repeated phrase

---

[101] *L' Année politique 1876*, 16-17. Meeting of January 26.
[102] Summary of meeting from *Le Journal des débats*, January 27, 1876, 1:4-6.
[103] *L'Année politique 1876*, 23. Louis Blanc, one of the unsuccessful Radical candidates, had not, because of illness, attended the important January 26 meeting (*Le Journal des débats*, January 27, 1876, 1:4).

with his pronouncement, "Pardon for those who deserve it, but not for murderers and arsonists!"[104]

Thus after the senatorial elections of 1876, most of the Republicans who formed the minority were at least committed to the constitution, but they were equally strongly committed against any amnesty.

The Elections to the Chamber

Gambetta's increased cautiousness, evident in the senatorial elections, set the tone of the legislative elections as well. Hence at the very opening of the campaign for election to the Chamber, the appearance of a "new" political party on the scene was signalized. The French people, said an article in Les Droits de l'homme which was believed to have been written by Henri Rochefort, thought there were only Legitimists, Orleanists, Bonapartists, and Republicans, but they were wrong—there were also the Opportunists. An Opportunist, it continued, was " that tender-hearted candidate who, deeply touched by the evils of the civil war and full of solicitude for the families it has deprived of their means of support, declares that he is the partisan of an amnesty, but that he reserves to himself the right to vote it ' at the opportune time.' . . . At the opportune time is a term of parliamentary argot that means Never!"[105]

The Radical Republicans, meanwhile, were more optimistic about their chances for the Chamber, and the majority of Radical electoral programs emphasized the pressing need for a general amnesty.[106] In Paris and in the suburbs, the candi-

[104] Ibid., 11-12. Quoted from Le Temps of January 27, 1876. Something of the political temper of Lyons is revealed in the following press notice. " A manifesto has been addressed to the Senatorial electors by the worthies of the ' Lyonnaise democracy.' We are not reprinting this manifesto here, because—without its being absolutely actionable—it seems to us dangerous in a department which had much better be kept in order than stirred up." (Le Journal des débats, January 18, 1876, 3:2.)

Jules Favre, however, was elected by 183 out of 334 Senatorial votes. (Le Journal des débats, January 28, 1876, 2:1.)

[105] Les Droits de l'homme, February 11, 1876, 1:2-3.

[106] L'Année politique 1876, 105. In connection with electoral platforms, see " Un programme de néo-socialistes," Journal des économistes, February 1876, 320-7, and Le Journal des débats, February 6, 1876, 2:2-4. Said to have originated in a Parisian electoral committee, the program reprinted in these two publications called for ". . . immediate amnesty for those unfortunate ones

dates demanding amnesty were of widely differing types. There were the known politicians: Louis Blanc, Barodet, Brisson, author of the first amnesty motion, Clemenceau, president of the Municipal Council, Talandier, prominent Radical member of the Council, Benjamin Raspail, son of a famous radical and himself a political exile under the Empire, Lockroy, once arrested on suspicion of sympathy with the Commune,[107] and Floquet, the first president of the League of Republican Union for the Rights of Paris. These were the best known candidates. There was also a newcomer to the political scene, Emile Acollas,[108] whom the Commune had named Professor of Law, even though he had been absent in Switzerland at the time.

The campaign for seats in the Chamber was vigorous. Victor Hugo, Senator, spoke eloquently for his friend Louis Blanc,[109] whose illness made it impossible for him to campaign in person. Barodet got " frenetic applause " when he demanded " a full, entire and immediate amnesty." [110] Quentin, a candidate endorsed by Louis Blanc, demanded a total amnesty "without . . . distinction between common law and political offenses" at a meeting in Saint-Denis. Pressensé, father of the limited amnesty bill and Quentin's opponent, answered that no amnesty could cover common law crimes " if it is to be given to those who deserve it." [111]

But it was Acollas who really built his campaign around an amnesty. The platform on which he ran had been drafted by a meeting of four hundred voters of the VIth arrondissement and proclaimed " A full and complete amnesty for all convic-

who are still paying the consequences of the civil war. The French Republic is as able to bear the burden of clemency as the American Republic." A more conventional Radical platform appears in Les Droits de l'homme, February 13, 1876, 2:4, in the letter from G. Maillard, attorney, to the election committee of the Ist arrondissement, accepting their nomination and stating that as his platform he wants the " realization of necessary reforms. Among the most urgent: The amnesty; [ending of] martial law . . .; separation of Church and State. . . ."

[107] See F.-X. Raspail, De la necessité de l'amnistie (Paris, 1876), 93.

[108] L'Année politique 1876, 30, and Alexandre Zévaès, Auguste Blanqui (Paris, 1920), 103. Zévaès' reference to " the candidacy of the professor Emile Acollas, demanding amnesty for the first time," is somewhat misleading in view of the several demands for an amnesty before the Acollas campaign.

[109] L'Année politique, 1876, 29.

[110] Le Journal des débats, February 9, 1876; 1:1.

[111] Ibid., February 8, 1876, 2:2.

tions, without exception, even for those termed common law, which were handed down in connection with political events which have taken place on French territory since September 4, 1870, with—first of all—the means of subsistence guaranteed to the amnestied upon their return to France." [112] The committee which chose Acollas as candidate and ran his campaign was headed by Gabriel Deville [113] and Victor Marouck,[114] both future leaders of the nascent socialist movement in France. Acollas himself explained his views at a campaign rally held at the Gymnase Pascaud on February 8. After taking his stand for decentralized federalism, revokable mandates for elected representatives, and free association as the only means for an equitable distribution of goods, he came to the heart of his campaign—the amnesty. " Fellow citizens, I'd have finished my speech if I didn't have to tell you that, as a preliminary to the enactments of the new legislature, there is one measure which I daily would demand; it is that of an amnesty toward all the condemned men of the Commune: I would demand it, not as an act of compassion, but as a measure of conciliation, of reconciliation in the largest and best meaning of that word." [115]

Acollas' opponent, Denfert-Rochereau—a staunch Republican despite being a Colonel—would not go this far on the amnesty question. Speaking in the same hall a few days later, he told the voters of the VIth that he would accept amnesty " for those who were misguided, but not for the chiefs of the Commune," and that he favored " the partial amnesty bill of M. de Pressensé." [116] When he said this, bedlam broke loose in the meeting. There was some applause, but much indignant protest. A representative of the Acollas committee tried to get the floor but was refused the right to speak.

When the election returns were in, it was found that the campaign enthusiasm for Acollas had not translated itself into

---

[112] Les Droits de l'homme, February 11, 1876, 2:6.

[113] L'Année politique 1876, 30, refers to Deville himself as a candidate in the elections of 1876. But there is no supporting evidence for this statement. For a short biographical sketch of Deville, see Ossip, Zetkin, Charakterköpke aus der französichen Arbeiterbewegung (Berlin, 1893), 28-30.

[114] Names of the electoral committee in the VIth arrondissement are to be found in Zévaès, Les proscrits de la Commune, 47.

[115] Les Droits de l'homme, February 11, 1876, 2:4-6.

[116] Ibid., February 13, 1876, 2:6.

votes. He got only 1883 to Denfert-Rochereau's 8873. Else-where in the city of Paris, the Radical Republicans, whose demand for a full amnesty had been tied to parliamentary Republicanism, made a better showing. Louis Blanc won in the Vth [117] and XIIIth arrondissements and in the first circum-scription of Saint-Denis. Clemenceau, whom *Les Droits de l'homme* had termed an Opportunist,[118] was to sit for Mont-martre. Barodet was comfortably elected in the IVth, while Lockroy was swept in by a landslide majority in the XVIIth. Benjamin Raspail and Talandier together were to represent Sceaux. Talandier's victory, won only after ballotage, meant defeat for Béclard—the same who had shown his opportunist attitude toward an amnesty when a candidate for Senator. Floquet, who ran on the so-called Laurent-Pichat platform, carried the XIth.[119] But the outstanding Opportunist, Gambetta, met no serious opposition in the XXth, with nearly eight times the vote of his nearest rival,[120] even though it was widely rumored that he did not want an amnesty until 1880. Similarly Spuller, the editor-in-chief of *La République française*, was elected in the IIIrd after ballotage, although his acceptance of a platform which had as the first item " an amnesty, great and necessary measure of forgetfulness," was suspect because of

[117] There seems to have been some question of Acollas' running also in the Vth arrondissement. See *Les Droits de l'homme*, February 11, 1876, 2:3-4, which tells of electoral complications in that arrondissement owing to the large number of candidates, among whom were both Louis Blanc and Acollas. Acollas had written an open letter to Louis Blanc, recalling their friendly exchange of letters when the former had been in prison in 1867. He then protested that it was not fair for Louis Blanc to have declared himself a candidate in the Vth without letting Acollas know beforehand, particularly since Louis Blanc had just withdrawn from the race in the XIth so that he would not oppose Floquet, " a good Republican," as Louis Blanc had said. Acollas wanted to know what reflection this cast on his political principles.

Louis Blanc replied with astonishment, saying that he had accepted a candidacy specifically offered to him, and offered before it was certain that Acollas would run. *Les Droits de l'homme* denied that this was so, pointing out that Acollas had—in writing—engaged to run as far back as January 20.

There is no evidence that Acollas actually ran in the Vth.

[118] February 11, 1876, 3:2. In giving a list of candidates, together with their party labels, *Les Droits de l'homme* explained that " radical " meant a man of principle, while " moderate-radical " meant opportunist. Then it pointed out that Clemenceau, candidate in the XVIIIth, was a " moderate-radical."

[119] Bourloton, *Dictionnaire*, III, 14.

[120] Election returns from *Le Journal des débats*, February 21, 1876, 1:2-5.

his closeness to Gambetta.[121] Brisson, who of late had himself been drawing closer and closer to Gambetta, won a sweeping victory in the Xth.

In the provinces Gambetta and his men carried the field nearly everywhere. The Radicals put all they had into the fight, but they could point to only modest successes, such as the election of the eighty-two year old F. V. Raspail, socialist candidate for president in 1848, recently imprisoned for eulogizing Delescluze,[122] and the election of the sixty-two year old Madier de Montjau, whose campaign at Valence had been marked by demands for a full and complete amnesty. The greatest battle of all was in the first circumscription of Marseilles. Gambetta against Naquet—the compromising Republic against the Radical Republic. Louis Blanc, also a candidate, withdrew to consolidate Radical support for Naquet. But in 1876 the schism between these two Republican factions was not complete, and Naquet promised to withdraw if Gambetta were not elected elsewhere.[123] Naquet need not have concerned himself. Gambetta beat him decisively. At Lyons, the leading home of radicalism next to Paris, Millaud, a vice-president of the Republican Union, was elected.[124] Gambetta himself also won at Bordeaux and at Lille.

The overwhelming victory of the chief of the Opportunists was probably due—at least in part—to the very absence of the amnesty issue from his campaign. Gambetta, it will be remembered, had all along been afraid of frightening the provinces. In his campaign speeches—the speech at Lille, for example— he was absolutely silent on the subject, a silence which lead the partisans of an amnesty to observe that " Some time ago, M. Gambetta put the amnesty off to the time when the constitution would be revised, to the year 1880. Can M. Gambetta have decided to subject it to a new adjournment? " [125]

---

[121] *Les Droits de l'homme*, February 13, 1876, 2:2. It was pointed out that Spuller's acceptance of amnesty in this context was vague. What did he mean by amnesty? Did he want full and entire amnesty, or amnesty only for political offenses, or amnesty only by categories? Did he want immediate amnesty? And so on. These were the doubts raised.

[122] Georges Duveau, *Raspail* (Paris, 1948), 60.

[123] *Le Journal des débats*, February 14, 1876, 2:5-6, 3:1.

[124] *Ibid.*, February 21, 1876, 1:6.

[125] *Les Droits de l'homme*, February 11, 1876, 1:4.

In any event, Gambetta's tactic served him well. After the March 5 second ballot, the Republicans controlled the Chamber. Of 514 seats, they had 371. But the Radicals accounted for only 98 of these.[126] To the extent that amnesty had been an issue in the elections, the country as a whole, while showing itself Republican, had—in 1876—small interest in such a measure. Its proponents numbered only a small minority, with no voice in the making of policy. Their votes were not even necessary to insure Republican control of the Chamber, barring defections in the right wing of the Republican forces.

The Elections and the Amnesty Cause

No matter how cautious the Chamber of Deputies was, the National Assembly at least was off the scene, and the very fact of a Republican majority in the Chamber, even though a middle-of-the-road majority, made for a freer political atmosphere. This meant that the Radical Republicans could now, as a vocal minority, demand an amnesty, unmoved by the argument that they were endangering acceptance of the constitution. It also meant that with the lessening of the threat of Monarchism, the extra-parliamentary champions of an amnesty—the socialists—were now looking to the day when they would no longer be compelled to collaborate with the bourgeois Republicans in order merely to save the Republic.

The Left-Wing Press After the Elections

Even before the Chambers met, the newspaper Les Droits de l'homme, the first strongly left-wing paper to appear after the Commune, was assessing the chances a full amnesty bill might have in this new legislature. The prospects did not seem at all good. As the article " To promise and to keep [your word]" said, it was unfortunate that laws could not be voted by candidates before they were elected: if this were so, then there would be some action. An amnesty bill undoubtedly was going to be introduced, continued the article, but this would not mean anything. Let the others, the men from whom pledges of amnesty had been got like pulling teeth, bring in the bill.

---

[126] L'Année politique 1876, 45-51.

Then it would mean something. The initiative would have passed to the middle-of the-roaders who had told the Extreme Left, " We want . . . [the amnesty] the same as you do. It is your violence and your hastiness which have ruined everything." [127]

A long article by Bonnet-Duverdier, entitled " A question of opportuneness," pointed out that at that very moment the transport vessel *La Loire* was embarking with fresh victims for New Caledonia. This, he wrote, was a departure which " is going to bring despair to all the unhappy families which— for a moment—had again felt hope upon seeing an amnesty figure in first place on the platforms of all Republicans during the campaign period." That such further deportations could be made, charged Bonnet-Duverdier, showed plainly that the new Dufaure Government was confident that the amnesty question was already decided, and knew it was impossible " that on this point, the two Chambers should have an opinion different from that of the Ministry." [128]

As commentary on the political scene in March 1876, however, the most telling article was written by Gabriel Deville. " Amnesty and the Center-Left " he called it, and this angry, vicious article brought a new tenor to the amnesty controversy and was the first claim of the necessity of an amnesty as a rehabilitation of the Paris Commune. No progress, Deville wrote, could come so long as the unfortunate men of the Commune were suffering at New Caledonia—those men " whose only crime was to think differently from those who govern us, whose great wrong was not to have succeeded." In the Chamber of Deputies, the Left and the Center-Left—" those pot-bellied and stuffed-crawed bourgeois "—wanted to use pardons instead of amnesty, particularly Jean Casimir-Perier, who " condescends to give us pardon, as a *bargaining device*." But true Republicans —that is, the men of the Commune—did not, Deville insisted, need pardon, or mercy, or compassion, or pity; " They want what is just, and they want only that." These Republicans " don't ask for alms; they don't beg for amnesty. You have no call to throw it to them as you cast scraps of meat to animals

---

[127] *Les Droits de l'homme*, March 13, 1876. 1:1.
[128] *Ibid.*, March 7, 1876. 1:2-5.

in order to make them stop annoying you; they ask for it as
a measure of justice, as a right." Concerning the alleged distinction between political crimes and common law crimes, " These
distinctions have no reason for being other than to enable the
Executive to treat certain personages with greater cruelty."
Everyone must be amnestied, for there was no such thing as a
common law crime in the Commune: " The conflagrations, the
executions of hostages—all those belong to the realm of politics;
in this connection there are only political acts." Of what were
the men at New Caledonia guilty? They " have been convicted
for the misdemeanor of having convictions, for the crime of
courage. . . ." But the men of the Center Left, after having
been themselves implicated—under Thiers' inspiration—in the
brutal repression of the Commune, were now insulting the
vanquished " by contemptuously throwing in their face a pardon
or a commutation of sentence." Meanwhile, wrote Deville,
the deportees would continue to die. Soon the " hypothetical
Republicans" of the Center Left would have no one left to
receive their " large mercy." [129]

Immediately the Government struck at Deville as guilty of
" apology for criminal acts," and he went to jail for six months,
despite the fact that his attorney was Engelhard of the Paris
bar and vice-president of the Municipal Council.[130] Deville's
conviction was not important. It was to be expected. What was
important was the new picture of the Commune and of the
amnesty which he had drawn. The crime of the Commune,
as he saw it, consisted of not having been successful. The guilt
of the Communards, he insisted, was the gulf that lay between
their ideas and those of the men in power. An amnesty was
not something to be begged as a favor, but to be demanded
as an inalienable right.

The New Government

The political situation at the opening of the 1876 parliamentary session seemed to be marked by a kind of tenuous
agreement to agree by avoiding any controversial issue. The

---

[129] *Ibid.*, March 7, 1876, 2:2-3.
[130] See *ibid.*, March 14, 1876, 1:3-4, March 17, 1876, 1:3, and April 12,
1876, 3:6.

Ministry was headed by Dufaure, seventy-eight years of age and until recently an Orleanist. Toward him, the Republican majority took its cue from Gambetta: " No defiance, but no confidence." [131] At the same time, Dufaure, for his part, was at pains to avoid the amnesty question. The Ministerial address of March 14 tactfully omitted the subject. Dufaure spoke at length on topics such as public works, the building up of the Army and the Navy, the dangers of the Near Eastern Question —but there was no reference to the amnesty question. He summed up his policy by promising to be faithful to " a spirit which is at one and the same time liberal and conservative. . . ." [132] The meaning of this speech was plain. " With reference to the ending of martial law and to the amnesty, no one, I hope, will accuse the Ministerial platform of lack of clarity. It did not breathe one word on the subject." [133]

The Two Amnesty Bills

In a manifestly hopeless situation, the Extreme Left decided to act at once. On Sunday, March 12, all the Senators and Deputies in favor of an amnesty met at Victor Hugo's home to draft a bill for full amnesty. The meeting was short and everyone was in accord. It was decided to introduce the bill simultaneously in the Senate and in the Chamber.[134] These men, however, formed only a small minority. Their plans for a full amnesty bill, charged Le XIXe Siècle, were insane, for the majority Republicans were ready to make whatever concessions to mercy as were compatible with " the best interests," but they would go no further.[135]

Nevertheless, on March 21, Victor Hugo in the Senate and the elder Raspail in the Chamber introduced identical bills calling for an amnesty for " all those condemned for acts relative to the events of March, April and May 1871." [136] The large crowd in the Senate galleries hoping to hear some power-

[131] Speech of Gambetta at caucus of the Lefts, reported *ibid.*, March 15, 1876, 1:5-6.

[132] Senate, *Annales*, session ordinaire 1876, I, 52-4.

[133] *Les Droits de l'homme*, March 17, 1876, 1:5.

[134] *Ibid.*, March 14, 1876, 2:2.

[135] *Ibid.*, March 16, 1876, 3:1, quoted from *Le XIXe Siècle*.

[136] Chamber of Deputies, *Annèxes*, session ordinaire 1876, I, 171.

ful speechmaking that day was disappointed.[137] There was no debate. Victor Hugo merely read the short text, giving as the reason for an amnesty the desire to "efface all traces of the civil war," [138] and was followed by Dufaure, who demanded immediate consideration. The Government, he said, was opposed to an amnesty for those who were enemies of society, and pardon was already taking care of those who deserved leniency. As proof that many Communards were still "declared enemies of our society," he pointed to what the exiles were doing: just across the frontier, they were "using the most ingenious means of getting into France literature which slanders the French social order, its Government, [and] its representatives. . . ." Even to debate the Hugo bill would give them false hopes.[139]

So it was that the bill went immediately to committee, where it was rejected at the first meeting. One Senator, Bertauld, was reported as opposing an amnesty because such a law would reverse the judges who had condemned the Communards in the first place.[140] In any event, no further action was taken by the committee, since the Government—showing again Dufaure's fear of an open debate—stepped in to ask that the Senate put off any discussion until after the Chamber had settled the question of an amnesty for the Paris Commune.[141]

Meanwhile, the Chamber on March 21 heard Raspail urge his bill in the name of "all of France," [142] but immediately a substitute motion was offered to exclude from the amnesty anyone with a criminal record before the Commune,[143] a tactic which Sigismond Lacroix condemned in Les Droits de l'homme as a "loophole." "A partial amnesty is not an amnesty," he

---

[137] Le Temps, March 23, 1876, 3:1.
[138] Senate, Annèxes, session ordinaire 1876, I, 152. In addition to Victor Hugo, the bill had six sponsors.
[139] Senate, Annales, session ordinaire 1876, I, 141.
[140] Les Droits de l'homme, March 26, 1876, 2:2.
[141] Senate, Annales, session ordinaire 1876, I, 210-11. Paris, chairman of the committee on the Hugo bill, relayed the Government's request to the Senate on April 10. See also Les Droits de l'homme, March 26, 1876, 1:6-2:1.
[142] Chamber of Deputies, Annales, session ordinaire 1876, I, 151.
[143] Idem. Rouvier was author of the motion. There were eventually five substitute bills, each with its own formula for restricting amnesty, presented by Rouvier, Margue, Allain-Targé, Marcou, and Andrieux.

wrote; " How many are there of these timid, hesitant souls who will not dare vote against an amnesty if there is only a single bill, and who will vote for the most restricted of categories if you give them the chance? " [144]

Then the voice of the Government was raised in the Chamber of Deputies. Ricard, Minister of Interior and a Senator, stated categorically that the Ministry was against all species of amnesty, whether total or partial. His speech was repeatedly interrupted by cheers from the Right and Center, and immediate consideration of the bill was voted without delay.[145] For the record, Allain-Targé next resurrected the old Pressensé bill, and the two bills were rushed off to committee.[146]

The key to the fate of any amnesty bill in the Chamber of Deputies was Gambetta's attitude. To endorse an amnesty would be to go counter to the Government, in view of Dufaure's declaration. To go counter to the Government might mean plunging the country into a prolonged crisis in which the Republicans—or even the Republic—might well be the losers. Certainly Gambetta had up to this time taken a very ambiguous position on amnesty—never coming out for it, never coming out against it. The day when the new Chamber first convened, he had been seen in heated conversation with Lockroy, Clemenceau, and Ollivier Ordinaire—all three known advocates of a full amnesty—and had given every sign of disagreeing violently with what they were saying.[147] Up to the time of the introduction of the Radicals' full amnesty bills, Gambetta's paper, La République française, had not said one word on the subject of amnesty.[148] The unofficial chief of the Chamber's majority had no share in the Raspail bill. His signature " was conspicuous by its absence." [149] Then came the Allain-Targé maneuver of reviving the Pressensé formula for amnesty, a move which was interpreted by Gabriel Deville, who had not

[144] Les Droits de l'homme, March 23, 1876, 1:1.
[145] Chamber of Deputies, Annales, session ordinaire 1876, I, 151.
[146] Ibid., session ordinaire 1876, I, 154. On the Pressensé bill, see above, pages 69-70.
[147] Les Droits de l'homme, March 15, 1876, 3:2.
[148] Ibid., March 21, 1876, 1:1. Only Les Droits de l'homme, Le Rappel, Le Bien public, and Martin Nadaud's Le Peuple came out in favor of amnesty.
[149] Ibid., March 24, 1876, 1:4.

yet been taken off to jail, as having been master-minded by Gambetta, who—he found—had the air of "playing a three-way game." Certainly, said Deville, it was clear that Allain-Targé "doesn't want amnesty; he didn't dare own up to it frankly, [so] he took a round-about way." Furthermore, there was nothing surprising in this: "Wasn't Gambetta wanting to put off examination of the question of an amnesty until 1880?"[150] Finally, the day after the Raspail bill was introduced, *La République française* carried an editorial which could be taken as Gambetta's line on amnesty. "The interest of society," it said, "will no more be sacrificed to that of humanity, than the interest of justice will be sacrificed to that of mercy. . . . No sacrifice will be made either to prejudice or to fear; no sacrifice will be made to the detriment of law, order, and public peace."[151] But what did it mean? While the Center Left might say it meant that Gambetta was against an amnesty, and the Radicals might say he was in favor of one, the statement meant only one thing with certainty: that Gambetta in 1876 had found his own formula for dealing with the amnesty question, the formula he was to follow with only slight modification for over four years, the formula of refusing to take a stand.

What chance did amnesty have in 1876? Of the eleven men name to examine the Raspail bill, only two—Lockroy and Allain-Targé—did not reject all thought of an amnesty.[152] And once again, while the committee was deliberating, the Government intervened against an amnesty, by submitting reports which showed the Communards' view of themselves as political martyrs. Such men, it insisted, could never be allowed back to France.[153]

Interim Developments

During the two and a half weeks when the committee was preparing its report on the Raspail bill, three developments took place; small in themselves, they had bearing on the future

---

[150] *Ibid.*, March 24, 1876, 1:3-4.
[151] *Ibid.*, March 24, 1876, 1:4-5.
[152] *Ibid.*, March 27, 1876, 1:3.
[153] *L'Année politique* 1876, 109.

struggle for an amnesty for the Paris Commune. First, on March 25 came the adoption without debate of the Floquet bill ending martial law.[154] This in itself was evidence of the more liberal spirit of the Chamber as compared with the National Assembly.

Next, when the newly elected Chamber got down to the partisan business of validating its membership, Gambetta heatedly urged the validation of Deputies charged with ineligibility because of being under sentence for political crimes. His motive may be questioned. The Comte de Douville-Maillefeu, whose place was in question, belonged nominally to the Republican Left. More than that, the offense—striking a sub-prefect —for which he had lost his political rights had been committed in exasperation at the obstacles placed in his way over organizing volunteer resistance against the Prussian invader in the recent war. Gambetta, with his usual fiery manner, argued successfully that in the past, men had been elected who had actually been in prison for political crimes at the time, and that it had been held that " these men were perfectly and regularly elected." [155] He was pleading a particular case. It is doubtful that he meant to establish a binding precedent. But in future years, anti-Republican radicals who felt that the only solution to the amnesty question lay in political action were quick to recall Gambetta's words of April 6, 1876.[156]

The third development of note was the appearance of two new labor candidates in the April 9 by-elections, held after the successful candidates had chosen to sit from other constituencies. Only seven places were involved, not enough to affect the balance of parties, and the public was generally apathetic toward these contests. Nevertheless, two workingmen, Chabert and Habay, even though they lost, joined the vanguard of those who believed that the politicians must be fought on every occasion by proletarians. In the XIIIth arrondissement Habay ran second out of seven candidates, but his vote was too slim

[154] Chamber of Deputies, *Annales*, session ordinaire 1876, I, 193; *Le Temps*, March 26, 1876, 1:1; and *Les Droits de l'homme*, March 26, 1876, 1:4.

[155] Chamber of Deputies, *Annales*, session ordinaire 1876, I, 495-7.

[156] See *L'Egalité, Journal républicain socialiste* (Meaux, weekly), January 27, 1878, 4:3-5:1.

to carry him through the ballotage.[157] The election in the XVIIth, held because Lockroy had opted for Aix, was much more interesting. In the pre-election manoeuvers, Gabriel Deville, Desplanches, and Guérin, backers of Chabert, were thanking Le Rappel for having withdrawn its candidate in favor of the labor candidate,[158] and the Radical Republicans, led by Lockroy, were unanimously endorsing Charles Quentin, who in the February elections had desisted in favor of Lockroy.[159] But in the regrouping for the ballotage of April 30, Lockroy had become president and Quentin the vice-president of the committee sponsoring the campaign of Chabert. Hérédia, another candidate, had also withdrawn for Chabert. This left the fight between Chabert, who had years before been deported for his part in the June Days, and Pascal Duprat, a Gambetta man.[160] Amnesty, of course, was the campaign issue. Chabert was presented as the candidate " who wants the obliteration of our civil discords, social peace, and the triumph of the Republic through liberty." [161] But Chabert was no match for the Gambetta forces. He made a stronger fight than Habay, but like Habay he was defeated. Even so, the by-elections did strengthen the handful of Intransigeants in the Chamber. Cantagrel, who defeated Habay, was far to the left of the majority Republicans.[162]

Taken together, these three developments—the end of martial law, the validation of a Deputy under sentence for political offenses, and the two electoral campaigns in the name of the workingman—were all to be of long range significance in the amnesty controversy, both by providing an environment in which

---

[157] Les Droits de l'homme, April 12, 1876, 1:5.

[158] Ibid., March 17, 1876, 2:1.

[159] Ibid., March 22, 1876, 3:2. On Quentin as the candidate standing for full amnesty in the 3rd circumscription of Saint-Denis, see above, page 96. He had run third out of four candidates (Le Journal des débats, February 21, 1876, 1:3).

[160] There was also a conservative candidate—Després—who ran third on April 30.

[161] Les Droits de l'homme, May 1, 1876, 1:6. See also 1:4-5 and 2:3-4, same date. For more on Chabert as candidate, see Eugène Petit, " Les discussions du congrès ouvrier de Paris," Journal des économistes, November 1876, 176.

[162] Note that André Daniel (L'Année politique 1876, 132) fails to take Cantagrel into consideration when he states that Radicals were defeated all along the line in these by-elections.

an organized movement for amnesty could take shape and by suggesting techniques which could be used to combat the denial of an amnesty. For the immediate question of what the committee on the Raspail bill would do, these developments had no effect. The opponents of the bill found no reason to revise their judgment.

The Committee Report

On April 11, the elderly Leblond read to the Chamber the committee's report on the Raspail bill. Back in 1848 Leblond had voted against any amnesty for the participants in the June Days. More recently, as a procurator-general of the Third Republic, he had ruled in favor of prosecution of the leaders of the Commune. Now, in 1876, he read the report that killed the Raspail bill. To Leblond, the Paris Commune was " a great crime," and prudence made an amnesty impossible. He therefore demanded the rejection of a general amnesty on principle, and the rejection of any restricted amnesty because it infringed on the pardoning power. What was a restricted amnesty, he wanted to know, " except an amnesty which requires a particular study of each condemned man? " [163]

The moment Leblond had finished reading the report, the Bonapartist Robert Mitchell asked for debate the very next day, but Leblond argued for postponement; the Government wanted it, he said. The Chamber in turn voted for postponement. [164] There was thus no chance for action on the Raspail bill before the Easter recess. The Chamber's docile action was hailed as a triumph by the conservative Republicans. Its firm attitude toward the Leblond report and toward Robert Mitchell's motion had put an end to " the disturbances which the amnesty question and the Bonapartists' unconstitutional propaganda had seemed in danger of spreading throughout the country during . . . [the Chamber's] absence." [165] The unfavorable report on the Raspail bill, the equivalent of its defeat, was indeed a Republican triumph. Leblond was a Republican. The com-

[163] Chamber of Deputies, *Annales*, session ordinaire 1876, I, 591 ff, and *Annèxes*, session ordinaire 1876, I, 322-3.
[164] Chamber of Deputies, *Annales*, session ordinaire 1876, I, 595, 599.
[165] *Le Journal des débats*, April 13, 1876, 1:1.

mittee was Republican. " These are therefore Republicans who have formulated this opinion, that amnesty would be contrary to the interests of the Republic." [166]

The End of the 1876 Amnesty Bills

The delay in voting on the Raspail bill did in fact have little effect one way or another. It proved impossible to mobilize public opinion in favor of an amnesty. The newspapers *Les Droits de l'homme* and *Le Rappel* tried to get up a petition in favor of a full amnesty, and even called on the members of the Paris Municipal Council, " who, under all circumstances, have affirmed their sympathy for this cause." [167] But nothing came of this attempt to create popular pressure for an amnesty. In addition, Louis Blanc and Victor Hugo took the lecture platform on behalf of the full amnesty, speaking at a meeting held to raise funds for sending a delegation of French workers to the Philadelphia Centenary Exposition in the United States.[168] Their audience was enthusiastic, but represented a special group. No new converts to the amnesty cause were made. At Marseilles, Rouvier, author of one of the partial amnesty bills, organized a meeting of his constituents and explained why he was for an amnesty. There were sentimental reasons, he admitted, but the political reason was even stronger. " So long as an amnesty has not been voted, it will remain a double-edged weapon in the hands of parties hostile to the Republic. On one side, they will terrify the conservatives with the fear of a forthcoming amnesty; on the other, they will frighten the masses by pretending that the Republic is too feeble to enact an amnesty, and that only the Monarchy or the Empire is in a position to decree it." He justified his own action of introducing a partial amnesty bill by saying that " If he cannot have everything, he wants at least to obtain the most possible." When asked what the people could do to get an amnesty, he warned that petitions were dangerous, and that only the pressure

[166] *Les Droits de l'homme*, April 14, 1876, 1:6. For leftist comment on the Leblond report itself, see *ibid.*, April 13, 1876, 1:1.

[167] *Ibid.*, May 1, 1876, 1:2-3. Also on the petition, see June 21, 1876, 2:3-4.

[168] *Le Temps*, April 18, 1876, 2:6. The meeting ended with shouts of *" Vive l'amnistie! Vive Victor Hugo!"*

" which the voters' opinion will exercise on the Deputies " could have any effect. The meeting ended, significantly enough, with a vote for a full and total amnesty.[169] Once again, however, nothing had happened to change the minds of those Deputies determined to vote against the bill.

But the delay in enacting an amnesty, above all the repeated insistence that pardon was all that could be given and all that was needed, sharpened the hostility between those who wanted amnesty and those who opposed it. For the first time, the belief—to be expressed so many times in coming years—that pardon must be rejected because acceptance would mean tacit approval of the denial of an amnesty became crystallized. *Les Droits de l'homme*, in an article " Forced Pardon," pointed out the company in which those pardoned for political offenses found themselves—common thieves, murderers even; "We can expect anything." Executive pardon was a device for discrediting forever the men who received it. In consequence, " The fear of an amnesty is probably going to push the Government to ' enlarge ' its clemency still further." Then the hypothetical case of Henri Rochefort was considered. He had not died on board ship to New Caledonia, as had been hoped. He had even escaped from New Caledonia. So now it was entirely possible for the Government of MacMahon to pardon him, believing that, " Since we have not been able to rid ourselves of this insufferable being, let us at least dishonor him. He is equally dangerous outside [the country] as within: let us authorize him to return, and he will be run down forever." But such a pardon could not be accepted. " To profit from a pardon would be . . . a disloyal act, because it would have the effect of contributing to the interment of the amnesty." [170] For four years, one Government after another was to offer pardon in place of amnesty, and was thereby to foster greater and greater intransigeance among the convicted men of the Commune.

[169] *Les Droits de l'homme*, May 1, 1876, 1:6.
[170] *Ibid.*, May 1, 1876, 1:1-2. A similar question of refusal of pardon was raised with reference to Elisée Réclus. A rumor was current that the geographer had been pardoned and was going to return to France. The rumor was probably false, said *Les Droits de l'homme*, and " in any event, the convicted man would obtain the privilege of returning to France only if he should consent to sign his petition for pardon." (June 21, 1876, 2:3.)

When the Chambers returned after the Easter recess, amnesty was the first item on the calendar. Its consideration was scheduled for May 15, but began on May 16. The young Chamber had never experienced such violent debates. Lockroy urged the shortage of manpower in Paris as evidence of the need for amnesty.[171] Raspail, the dean of the Chamber, told story after story of the atrocious treatment of the Communards at New Caledonia, where—dressed as convicts, their heads shaved— these political prisoners were forbidden even to speak.[172] Again and again protests and insults from the Right interrupted him. The Bonapartist Robert Mitchell even tried unsuccessfully to get Raspail's words struck from the record. The major event of the day, however, was Clemenceau's long speech, the speech which conservatives everywhere hailed as proof that an amnesty would be the same as an endorsement of the Commune.[173] In the words of the Deputy from Montmartre, Paris had revolted because Paris was ardently Republican.[174] The refusal to vote an amnesty was keeping outside of France not only those convicted of an active part in the Commune, but also an estimated hundred thousand perfectly innocent exiles who had fled in terror from the savagery of the repression. Pardon, which many called a solution, was a farce. Most of the cases so handled had only got reduction of sentence, not freedom, and the most severe penalties of all were nearly always retained after review.[175] In his conclusion Clemenceau got to the heart of the matter—the future of the Republic. " Finally, I tell you, the true way to give confidence to those you want to reassure is—above all—to succeed in the enterprise which you have begun of founding a Republican regime in France. And if you succeed in this, . . . the men you are afraid of frightening [by voting an amnesty] will be sufficiently reassured if you tell them there is nothing to be afraid of in an amnesty. But if your policy is uncertain, hedging—if you have only a half-way success—it will come to pass that when you go before the voters in 1880 . . . , the

---

[171] Chamber of Deputies, *Annales*, session ordinaire 1876, II, 56-66.
[172] *Ibid.*, session ordinaire 1876, II, 99.
[173] See *Le Journal des débats*, May 18, 1876, 1:1.
[174] Chamber of Deputies, *Annales*, session ordinaire 1876, II, 35.
[175] *Ibid.*, session ordinaire 1876, II, 48.

parties hostile [to the Republic] will not lack arms against you, even if you have refused amnesty a hundred times." [176] It was useless. Nothing said in the Chamber that day really meant anything. It was political show; there was little or no discussion of the merits of an amnesty. Everyone's mind was made up, and the measure was fought "by vote and not by speeches," as Le Temps put it. [177] By a vote of 392 to 50, with 58 abstaining, the Raspail bill was killed. Of the fifty in favor of a full amnesty, fifteen were from the Seine's twenty-five Deputies. The balance came from around Marseilles and Lyons. Very conspicuous as taking no part in the vote were Gambetta, his loyal shadow Spuller, and Lepère, the president of the Republican Union. [178]

The Chamber rejected the Raspail bill on May 18. It then systematically disposed of the various restricted amnesty bills before it. The Senate, which had been waiting for the Chamber to act, killed the Hugo bill on May 22.

In comparison with the debates in the Chamber, the Senate's treatment of the amnesty question was tame. The report of the committee on the Hugo bill had been printed and distributed. There the Senators had read of the outstanding accomplishments of the military tribunals, of the spirit of "firmness and consideration" that had marked their work, and similar praise for the generosity of the Commission on Pardons and of the President of the Republic. [179] No amnesty was necessary, the Senate had read: only 3375 Communards remained at New Caledonia, and of these, 1504 had criminal records. Furthermore, the report continued, the National Assembly by its treatment of the several proposals presented to it seemed to have put the

[176] Ibid., session ordinaire 1876, II, 51-2.

[177] May 20, 1876, 1:1. The statement here that "no one, therefore, attacked the bill," is not entirely accurate, since Lamy spoke against it for the Catholic group. See Le Journal des débats, May 18, 1876, 1:1.

[178] Roll call vote given in Chamber of Deputies, Annales, session ordinaire 1876, II, 119-20. Note that L'Année politique 1876, 149, gives the vote as 442 against the bill, to 50 in favor of it, with 58 abstaining. The figure 442 actually represents the total number voting.

[179] The Paris report on the Hugo bill gave 5839 as the number of favorable decisions by the Commission on Pardons, whereas that body's own report, dated March 8, 1876, gave 3140 as the total of favorable decisions. (See above pages 89 and 90, fn. 88.

question of an amnesty forever outside the realm of parliamentary discussion.[180] Victor Hugo alone took the floor for his bill on May 22. He read a lengthy prepared speech in the midst of profound silence. An amnesty, he argued, ought to be voted because of justice and pity, and also because of reasons of state: "Think of the fact that at this very moment the deportees and the expatriates number in the thousands. . . . This vast absence is weakening the industry of the nation. . . ." [181] When he was through, no one at all rose to reply. A voice called out, "No one answers because there is nothing to answer." [182] Then the vote was taken. It was almost unanimously against Victor Hugo's amnesty bill.[183]

[180] Senate, *Annèxes*, session ordinaire 1876, I, 310-12.
[181] Senate, *Annales*, session ordinaire 1876, II, 94.
[182] F.-X. Raspail, *De la necessité de l'amnistie*, 30.
[183] A voice vote; no numbers are given in Senate, *Annales*, session ordinaire 1876, II, 79. *L'Année politique 1876*, 149, says twelve Senators voted for it.

Chapter III

THE OPPORTUNISTS:
THE COMMUNE AS POLITICAL PAWN

The defeat of Victor Hugo's bill in the Senate on May 22, 1876, by no means ended the Radical Republicans' determination to do what they could—a full amnesty if it were possible, a lesser measure if this were all to be had—to ameliorate the lot of those who had taken part in the Paris Commune. Thus the bitter controversy which was the bequest of the Paris Commune to French parliamentary politics exerted a mounting influence on party groupings and maneuverings. For a time, it was true, there was no renewed attempt at a general amnesty, but there was at least a move to protect the as yet unapprehended suspects from the Government, a move which was the more serious in its immediate effects than the previous abortive amnesty bills because it had the backing of the majority Republicans, and which shortly gave rise to the first open conflict between parliamentary and executive prerogatives. The outcome was the first crisis of the Third Republic, with the fall of Dufaure in December of 1876. The bequest of the Commune was also operative in the now open break between the Radical Republicans and the majority, a break paralleled by and in part caused by the ever-growing political cautiousness of Gambetta, who sensed the gathering of the reactionary storm which was to culminate in the celebrated May Sixteenth crisis of 1877.

The question of an amnesty—as a dangerous issue likely to embarass the Republicans—was now kept rigidly off the floor of the Chamber, but the extra-parliamentary demands for such a measure grew apace, particularly during Jules Simon's tenuous occupancy of the premiership. Then, with the May Sixteenth crisis, it became apparent how the Republican-sponsored demands for leniency toward the defeated Paris Commune played a major role in the reactionaries' determination to rid France of representative government. With the crisis itself, the country

115

was plunged into a political controversy of such urgency that the amnesty question took second place to the far more basic struggle over the form of France's government. Immediately after the crisis, however, there was a sharp resurgence of agitation on behalf of the Communards, with the agitation more than ever before in the service of party politics.

The Move to Stop Prosecutions

Even before the defeat of the two amnesty bills in the spring of 1876, a new element had entered the picture, and that was the question of whether, in the absence of a general amnesty, the time had come to put an end to continuing arrests and prosecutions of alleged Communards. In the deliberations of the committee on the Raspail bill, two of the committee members—Allain-Targé and Philippoteaux—had proposed amendments which would have had the effect of stopping the work of the military tribunals. The majority of the committee, while agreeing in principle, did not approve of the ways the details had been worked out, and the suggestions were ignored.[1] On the day the Raspail bill was turned down, however, another Deputy, Gatineau, asked from the floor for a motion to forbid new prosecutions in connection with the Commune. No discussion was held, no vote taken;[2] and Gatineau later, at the instance of the Government, withdrew his request until the calendar was cleared of all the pending amnesty bills.[3]

Among the restricted amnesty bills discussed on May 19, two seemed designed specifically to take care of the problem of continuing arrests. Andrieux, the future Prefect of Police, framed a bill to amnesty " The political crimes and lesser offenses relative to the events of the Commune . . . which have not, up to the present time, been the object of any conviction, either with a hearing or by default." [4] The Chamber did not even consider this bill. Next came the discussion of the Allain-Targé bill, which proposed that the ten-year limitations of

[1] Chamber of Deputies, *Annales*, session ordinaire, 1876, I, 324.

[2] *Ibid.*, session ordinaire 1876, II, 118. Gatineau, it should be noted in passing, had been counsel for *Les Droits de l'homme* in its April 11, 1876, trial for failure to post bond (*Les Droits de l'homme*, April 12, 1876, 3:1).

[3] *Ibid.*, session ordinaire 1876, II, 145.

[4] *Ibid.*, session ordinaire 1876, II, 134.

ordinary criminal law be extended to cover acts committed during the Commune in those cases where the individual had not yet been convicted.[5] It was in answer to Allain-Targé that Dufaure, the Premier, now made the promises which seven months later were to be a factor in his fall from power.

Dufaure clearly implied that if there was to be a bill stopping arrests, the Government must take the initiative. An amnesty, he repeated, was impossible. But since many persons did live in doubt and fear because of the continuation of military trials, it was " Eminently sound policy . . . to give, beginning with the day when their immunity has been acquired, . . . peace and tranquillity to that part of the population which—the victim of evil impulses, more often perverse than criminal—took part in what happened in 1871." The Government, he promised, would therefore introduce such a bill, for the whole question must be examined " with care, with solicitude, with awareness of its political import. . . ." At Dufaure's request, Allain-Targé then withdrew his bill.[6]

The Gatineau Bill

Dufaure's promise of a Government bill was not the end of the Chamber's direct interest in calling a halt to the work of military justice. On May 26, exactly one week after the Premier's speech, Gatineau introduced a bill which stated flatly that all further prosecutions were forbidden.[7] The long list of sponsors—139 in all—included men of the Extreme Left, together with many Republican Union stalwarts.[8] Even Spuller's name was there, although Gambetta's was not. All the members of the committee to examine the Gatineau bill said they were favorable to it, at least in principle. Some did feel, though, that exceptions should be made in cases of common law crimes. The committee decided, in any event, to wait until Dufaure

[5] *Ibid.*, session ordinaire 1876, II, 139. He would have excluded crimes which carried the death penalty, but would have required new trial, with jury, in such cases. The limitations, which will be found in the *Code d'instruction criminelle*, Article 637, were ten years for prosecution and twenty years for carrying out the penalty if its execution were delayed after sentencing.

[6] *Ibid.*, session ordinaire 1876, II, 144-5.

[7] Chamber of Deputies, *Annèxes*, session ordinaire 1876, II, 86.

[8] Chamber of Deputies, *Annales*, session ordinaire 1876, II, 183.

was ready to confer with it and to present the Government's bill for putting an end to further prosecutions.[9] No debate was held on the Gatineau bill until late in the fall, and by that time many changes had taken place in the political situation, and public opinion had been more aroused by the problem of the Communards' fate.

MacMahon's Letter

From the end of May on, the Republicans in the Chamber were becoming increasingly uneasy at the role being taken by President MacMahon in the matter of closing the books on the Commune. A Government bill had been promised. But the Government, unable to draft a bill that suited it, abandoned the idea.[10] MacMahon instead simply issued instructions to the Minister of War to move very circumspectly in the matter of further arrests. " I hope that we will thus succeed," he wrote, " in calming all unrest by exercising the maximum of indulgence and forgetfulness that is possible without compromising principles and paramount considerations. . . ." His concluding observation, " I think that we ought to let all the acts connected with the fatal insurrection of 1871 fall into oblivion," [11] seemed to encroach dangerously on the legislative prerogative of amnesty, although nothing, of course, had been said about the men already convicted. But no sound Republican felt that even the question of stopping prosecutions could be safely left to executive largesse.

MacMahon's letter, dated June 27, started the controversy that led directly to the crisis of December 1876. Almost immediately after the publication of the President's letter, the Radicals, convinced that the time had come for an open fight, broke from the Republican Union. The Opportunists, faced with this challenge on the Left, sensing a new drift in public opinion, and—above all—fearful for the new constitution,

[9] *Les Droits de l'homme*, June 20, 1876, 3:1.
[10] *L'Année politique 1876*, 216.
[11] The letter, dated June 27, was published in the June 28 issue of the *Journal officiel*, 4593:1-2. The same issue carried a presidential decree, dated June 24, of pardon, commutation of sentence, or reduction of penalty for 87 Communards.

moved quickly to recover for the Chamber the power they charged MacMahon had usurped.

The calendar of the Chamber called for a debate July 3 on a motion by Benjamin Raspail to interpellate the Government on MacMahon's letter and on the arrests and prosecutions which had just recently taken place for acts in connection with the Commune.[12] Gambetta meanwhile felt that the Government had indeed " taken a fatal path, where it will be equally difficult for us to stop it or to support it." But Gambetta did not want a showdown with the Government. " We must find a diversion," he wrote to Léonie Léon on July 2, "[and] I believe I've hit on one." [13] In the Chamber the very next day Gambetta got the floor—before Benjamin Raspail—to interpellate the Minister of War on a messy question of alleged dishonesty in the entrance examinations for the Ecole Polytechnique. It was a beautiful diversion, full of fireworks. The sacred name of the Republic was taken in vain (it was charged that such dishonesty could happen only under a Republican regime), and Gambetta had to clear it.[14] By the time Benjamin Raspail got the floor to speak in behalf of his interpellation, the Deputies were exhausted. They voted without debate to postpone any discussion of the interpellation until the committee report on the Gatineau bill had been submitted.[15]

The Position of the Radical Republicans

For some time the Radicals had been increasingly dissatisfied with the Republican Union. The abstention of Gambetta and his satellites from voting on the Raspail bill had been just one instance of their cautious policy. Clemenceau, Lockroy, Louis Blanc, and their followers could not stay with a group that believed that " The only worthwhile progress is that which is accomplished in time and on the basis of *solutions which present themselves.*" [16] In consequence, a meeting was called for June 30, at Louis Blanc's home, to discuss the formation of

[12] Chamber of Deputies, *Annales*, session ordinaire 1876, III, 219.
[13] " Lettres de Léon Gambetta," *Revue de Paris,* December 1, 1906, 682.
[14] Chamber of Deputies, *Annales*, session ordinaire 1876, III, 209-12.
[15] *Ibid.*, session ordinaire 1876, III, 219.
[16] Louis Blanc, *Questions d'aujourd'hui et de demain* (5ᵉ série) (Paris, 1884), 390. Quoted from speech by Lepère, President of the Republican Union.

an entirely separate parliamentary group. The fourteen Radicals who attended [17] found that the Republican Union, being in the position of trying to keep together the Extreme Left, the Left, and the Center Left, must either abandon the alliance or sacrifice principles for politics.[18] It was senseless, the Extreme Left concluded, for it to stay in a position where it was condemned in the name of party discipline always to be ignored. In breaking from the Republican Union, the Intransigeants agreed that their binding principles were to be " Never to yield to the exigencies of tactics except after having loudly proclaimed principles and having sought to make them prevail," and " To vote for the *minimum* only after having demanded and tried to get the *maximum*." [19]

Throughout the summer and fall of 1876 the Radicals conducted a vigorous campaign for a general amnesty both in and out of the Chamber. In the Chamber, for example, Benjamin Raspail made a semi-sarcastic motion that a law ending prosecutions must exclude the " true organizers and directors of the insurrection of 1871 . . . [the] *agents provocateurs*, . . . [and] those who through vengeance or in the heat of an unexampled repression—brought about the summary executions." If the goal was to get rid of the traces of the civil war, he argued, official justice must at least " cease to have two weights, two measures." If Communards were to be prosecuted, he said, let the Versaillese be prosecuted also.[20]

A more direct appeal for an amnesty was the publication on August 29 of a violent pamphlet, *On the Necessity of Amnesty*, written by Dr. François-Xavier Raspail, Benjamin Raspail's young brother. As the preface said, publication had been held up for two months while vainly waiting for Dufaure's promise of a Government bill ending prosecutions to be fulfilled. Under the circumstances, the preface went on, the only possible course was " a full and complete amnesty," and the

---

[17] Louis Blanc, Cantagrel, Madier de Montjau, Marcou, Giraud, Lockroy, Clemenceau, Georges Périn, Durand, Doumas, Duportal, Bouquet, Talandier, and Douville-Maillefeu, who had been moving to the left since his validation (see above, page 107).

[18] Louis Blanc, *Questions* . . . (5ᵉ série), 387.

[19] *Ibid.*, 389. See also 391-2: resolutions adopted.

[20] Chamber of Deputies, *Annales*, session ordinaire 1876, IV, 87-90.

purpose of this brochure was to convince the Republican majority of its necessity.[21] The author's main arguments followed three lines—the Commune as the lesser of two evils when compared to Louis Napoleon's " December Second," the relative records of the Commune and Versailles when it came to bloodshed and destruction, and the historic precedents for great amnesties. The attack on Louis Napoleon was built around scurrilous back-stairs gossip about the Second Empire. The question at issue was the contrast between the unworthy end to which the Bonaparte and the worthy end to which the Commune had seized power. With reference to the record of the Commune for violence, a short history of the Commune presented it as having been mixed good and bad, but with the Communal government itself trying to restrain extremist elements. Until the day when the Versailles troops entered Paris, the young Raspail found that " Impartial study shows that the Commune did not indulge in any sanguinary excesses." [22] Finally, to prove that an amnesty could be granted—even when the defeated cause had been undeserving of sympathy—there was the example of the American Civil War, the revolt of the Southern slave owners. " This insurrection, a monstrous outrage to civilization, was finally crushed to earth, and the vanquisher cast before the vanquished an immediate, absolute pardon: full and complete amnesty." [23] In Spain, as another example, the *Carlistas* were allowed to go peacefully back to their homes.[24] From all these arguments, the conclusion was then drawn that for France, recently victorious over the Commune, " A full and complete amnesty . . . is alone capable of opening the door to the legitimate claims of law and justice." [25]

This booklet, *On the Necessity of Amnesty*, was the strongest public appeal yet made for a general amnesty. The result was that on September 21 the author was sentenced *in absentia* to eight months in jail and a fine of 1000 francs for defending and justifying the insurrection of 1871.[26]

---

[21] F.-X. Raspail, *De la necessité de l'amnistie*, 2, 5.
[22] *Ibid.*, 94.
[23] *Ibid.*, 124-5.
[24] *Ibid.*, 125.
[25] *Ibid.*, 172.
[26] *Le Temps*, September 23, 1876, 3:4. The publisher, Dubuisson, was

The Radicals were having a hard time getting their views before the people because of the strict control of the press, a relic from the days of the National Assembly. An effort was made, however, to start an opposition journal; this was Louis Blanc's *L'Homme libre*, founded on October 27, 1876, a direct outcome of the decision taken back in June to form a separate parliamentary group. As the first issue explained, the only solution to the social problem was " accord among all men of good will and . . . the pooling of all their efforts." [27] On the amnesty question, the first issue of *L'Homme libre* called for an immediate end to the parliamentary vacation, since " The merciless M. Dufaure is neglecting to accord the pardons which he has promised; in revenge, he is slashing away at the radical press." [28] In a subsequent issue, Louis Blanc adduced as firm proof that a general amnesty could safely be enacted the workers' congress held at Paris in October of 1876. This congress, it should be pointed out, was desperately afraid of being dissolved by the police and did not even mention the subject of an amnesty; its closing shout was "*Vive la République!* " [29] Louis Blanc accordingly termed the congress an object lesson: " Since the people are quieted down to the point where they discuss with perfect calm all the questions that interest them, it is time to proclaim a general amnesty and to declare that under our Republic, which is definitely established, there are no more proscripts." [30]

sentenced to one month in jail and a fine of 500 francs. Although the sentences were by default, the terms were served, according to *La Grande encyclopédie*, article " Xavier Raspail."

The origins of this pamphlet, *De la necessité de l'amnistie*, can be referred back to March of 1876, in the debates of the 11th Bureau on naming its member to the committee on the Raspail bill. On that occasion Benjamin Raspail said that " he has before him some documents of profound seriousness on the insurrection of March 18th, on its origins and on its authors. He had put these documents in a place of security, but now that today he is covered by parliamentary inviolability, he will bring forth these documents, which will establish the role of the Bonapartist party in the insurrection of March 18th and in the events of the Commune." (*Les Droit de l'homme*, March 27, 1876, 2:2.)

[27] *L'Homme libre* (Paris, daily), October 27, 1876, 1:6.

[28] *Ibid.*, October 27, 1876, 2:6.

[29] See *Séances du congrès ouvrier de France, session de 1876* (Paris, 1877). 533.

[30] *L'Homme libre*, October 28, 1876, 2:5.

Gambetta's Tactics

With the growing outspokenness of the Left, the Republican leadership was becoming progressively more prudent. Gambetta's change from opposition chief to head of the Republican majority bloc had given him a large sense of political realities and a determination to hang on to his power. This change had been noticeable early in the year, on the eve of the legislative elections. His remark at Lille, for example, that " Progress is not forced," had been hailed by *Le Temps* as striking evidence of " the transformation of the former revolutionary party into a political party." [31] On the amnesty question, Gambetta's record was neutral.

Because of this, he was finding his constituents increasingly critical by the fall of 1876, which was illustrated by the meeting at the Salle Graffard on October 26. The electoral committee of the XXth arrondissement had organized this gathering to hear Gambetta give an account of his mandate. Upon the Deputy's entrance, the room rang with shouts of "*Vive la République!*," soon to be drowned out by shouts of "*Vive l'amnistie!*" Gambetta spoke. He said that he had never explained himself on the subject of the amnesty, but that today, the moment had come. " Along with his friends, he had thought that the hour for mercy had sounded, that a generous, intelligent policy ought not even have let the question be raised: to a great extent [such a policy] ought to have brought about the amnesty," he was quoted as saying. If this were the case, those who sat and listened to the powerful Deputy of Belleville might well have wondered why there had not been an amnesty. " Public opinion would have accepted it with satisfaction," he continued, " but some men have not understood the expediency of this measure of appeasement, [while] other have exaggerated it." So far, Gambetta had not told where he himself stood. " As for himself, he is not a partisan of the absolute degree in which they demand . . . [amnesty]. By exacting it as they have done, one would have fatally over-excited the feeling against it; that is what has happened. The reaction has tried to render the purest Republicans liable along with the worst criminals of

[31] February 10, 1876, 1:4.

the Commune." Gambetta's Republic felt it had to repudiate all kinship with the Commune. " According to him, there was only one way to prevent the propagation of this error. That was to ask for a partial amnesty, with categories and distinctions. He does not believe that it may be possible to go beyond this." [32] Gambetta was not a child at the political game. Obviously he was well aware of the lines along which the extra-parliamentary campaign for an amnesty was developing. Thus he did what the logic of the situation demanded. He denied categorically that the Commune had had any political significance, but characterized it instead as merely " a sort of convulsion of misery, famine and despair." [33]

Lively signs of indignation and outraged feelings in the audience greeted this judgment. Hippolyte Buffenoir, a left-wing journalist, leaped to his feet, and delivered a bitterly anti-Gambetta speech. But then Gambetta, to conclude the evening and to appear once again in the voters' eyes as the hero of the National Defense, issued a ringing call for unity of all Republicans in the face of " the worst recrudescence of the reactionary party since 1815." [34] And so the meeting was brought to a close, with Gambetta once more applauded by Belleville. The threat of monarchism still submerged the amnesty issue.

Whether it was only the familiar red herring, or whether Gambetta had a true gift of political prophecy, no one could say in October 1876. But October 1876 to May 1877 was only six months. In six months, then, Gambetta was to be fully vindicated. Meanwhile, it was definitely true that on October 26, 1876, Gambetta was profoundly depressed. Terming his speech at the Salle Graffard meeting as " that painful harrangue," he burst out passionately, " What a trade mine is! Before I act, I have to win the right to make reason and justice triumph in the guise of violence. I have to divert the suspicions of some, escape from the calumnies or terrors of others, and deceive them all in order to serve them better." [35]

Deceive them all in order to serve them better—if the Repub-

[32] L'Homme libre, October 29, 1876, 2:4.
[33] Le Temps, October 29, 1876, 2:6.
[34] L'Homme libre, October 29, 1876, 2:4.
[35] " Lettres de Léon Gambetta," Revue de Paris, December 1, 1906, 684-5.

lican majority could not and would not endorse an amnesty, Gambetta could and did take advantage of any half-way measures—exactly as Clemenceau had foreseen in his speech of May 16—which gave an opportunity for defying the Monarchists on the Right, while seeking to win favor with the Radicals on the Left. Such a half-way measure was the bill to stop prosecutions for alleged participation in the Commune. The outcome of this policy was the resignation of Dufaure on December 3, after he had been defeated both in the Chamber and in the Senate, although the two chambers voted on opposite sides of the question.

The Fall of Dufaure

The Gatineau bill, it will be remembered, had been introduced on May 26 and forbade any further prosecutions of alleged Communards. While the committee on legislation was studying the bill, MacMahon had published his celebrated letter to the Minister of War. The committee, under the chairmanship of Leblond, the same man whose report had effectively damned the Raspail bill, could have accepted this letter as all that needed to be done. But on the committee sat Gatineau himself and the Radical Floquet.[36]

It was at this juncture that Gambetta, still nervous about what might happen, went privately to see MacMahon and was somewhat reassured by this visit, although he remained worried about both the President and the Senate, " where storm clouds are gathering." [37] At any rate, a compromise bill was reported on July 22 by Lisbonne, instead of by Leblond, the former reporter for the committee. Under the new bill, prosecutions would cease except those for murder, arson, or theft. Such cases would be tried by jury instead of in a military court. Persons who had been condemned *in absentia* for political crimes or for the enumerated common law crimes would likewise be guaranteed a jury trial if they surrendered themselves

[36] Floquet, elected to the National Assembly in February 1871, had resigned in April 1871 in order to work exclusively for conciliation through the League of Republican Union for the Rights of Paris (National Assembly, *Annales*, II, 712).

[37] " Lettres de Léon Gambetta," *Revue de Paris*, December 1, 1906, 682.

or were seized before the ten-year limitations provisions of the Code became effective.[38]

As the Government viewed the situation, no special law ending prosecutions was necessary following MacMahon's letter. But the committee had decided, after talking with Dufaure, that such a law was eminently desirable, as " a legislative resolution which would insure more clarity, above all more permanence, to the generous declarations [made] by the executive." [39] Gambetta felt better after this. By July 29 he could write, " I feel within me and all about me the certainty of deliverance and assuagement." [40] But the fact remained that the committee report, with its references to clarity and permanence, carried an insult to MacMahon. As a result, the fall session of the Chamber opened with the Premier's roundly scolding these Deputies who did not know their place.

Dufaure's speech of November 3 showed that he regarded himself as MacMahon's Premier, and not the Chamber's. He began by agreeing with the principle of giving security to those not yet arrested in connection with the Commune. He recalled his earlier promise. But the Council of Ministers, he said, had believed it would " give the pledge which we had made an infinitely more weighty character . . . by calling upon the Presi-

[38] Chamber of Deputies, *Annèxes*, session ordinaire 1876, IV, 172.

The question of those condemned *in absentia* was to be an increasingly thorny problem in the amnesty controversy. As early as June 1876, while the committee on the Gatineau bill was deliberating, one of the men so condemned had written anonymously from Geneva, " The Deputies of the Center Left . . . ought certainly to leave alone those condemned *in absentia*, who are asking nothing of them.

" The ' recourse of presenting oneself for judgment ' by jurists in red breeches who, after five years, sentence a man to ten or twenty years in a penal colony for evading arrest, and to death on the *single* testimony of a high-minded young lady seems to them a slim recourse.

" All the Lefts from the Center to the *avant-garde*, from the moment they didn't vote an amnesty ought only to have kept quiet about the question. Fifty-two Deputies and seven Senators voted full and entire amnesty; those who were not with them are not with us, and we repulse the policy of compromise and hypocrisy followed by these pharisees of the Republic." (*Les Droits de l'homme*, June 19, 1876, 2:1-2; letter dated June 16, 1876.)

The substitution by the committee of jury trial instead of court martial was a mild concession to those sentenced *in absentia* and superseded Article 13 of the law of August 9, 1848.

[39] Chamber of Deputies, *Annèxes*, session ordinaire 1876, IV, 169-70.

[40] Lettres de Léon Gambetta," *Revue de Paris*, December 1, 1906, 683-4.

dent of the Republic, in the name of the responsibility of his Ministers . . . to be himself the instrumentality for carrying it out." [41] As proof of the Government's fidelity to the President's letter of June 26, Dufaure then cited the two—only two—new cases since that date. Against this background, he declared, the Chamber had no right to vote the proposed bill. " Gentlemen, it is impossible for the Government to give its approval to such a measure. . . . The Government has done everything that it was its duty to do." [42]

The challenge was plain. Gambetta met it with an impassioned speech for the Gatineau bill. He called for its enactment as " the true policy of wisdom and concord." The measure was eagerly awaited, he said, " not only by those who are hotheaded, . . . but also by men who are equally concerned with honor and justice, with concord and public peace." [43] The Republicans on the Left hailed these words with loud applause and repeated bravos.

Some thought, however, that the Great Tribune had gone too far in defying the Government, and a substitute bill was offered by Houvey and Bethmont of the Center Left. On the following day, the committee presented a new compromise: the ordinary ten-year limitations would apply to all cases in connection with the Commune, except for cases of murder, arson, and theft.[44] In spite of Dufaure's total opposition to any legislative meddling in the question of stopping prosecutions, the Chamber passed this provision by well over a two-thirds majority.[45] It also adopted the article taking future cases out of the jurisdiction of the military courts. But the article requiring new trials, with a jury, for those sentenced *in absentia* was defeated by forty-two votes.

The gains which were offered to the Communards by this bill were very slight in its total effect. Even the continuing arrests would go on until 1881. The significance of the November 3 and 4 debates, therefore, must be evaluated in terms of

[41] Chamber of Deputies, *Annales*, session extraordinaire 1876, I, 11.
[42] *Ibid.*, session extraordinaire 1876, I, 14.
[43] *Ibid.*, session extraordinaire 1876, I, 18.
[44] *Ibid.*, session extraordinaire 1876, I, 24.
[45] *Ibid.*, session extraordinaire 1876, I, 25. The vote was 345 to 144.

the functioning of parliamentary government under the Third Republic. The Chamber had taken a step which was specifically opposed by a Premier who regarded himself as having a prior responsibility to the President. The action of the Senate might be a decisive event in Republican history.

The Senate's nine-man committee to study the bill as it came from the Chamber was under the chairmanship of the same man—Paris—who had written the devastating report on the Hugo bill. All members of the committee agreed that the work of the repression had not ended so far as the leaders of the Commune were concerned, but they did feel that the continuing arrests of obscure figures had become simply a means of satisfying the personal grudges of informers. Here the agreement stopped. On the question of how best to terminate these arrests, five members of the committee wanted only to congratulate the President for his generous letter, and four wanted a law to embody what MacMahon had written.[46] This minority charged that there was no legal basis for the President's letter, that only the two chambers, having the right to amnesty, had the right to declare prosecutions at an end.[47] Since, however, it also believed that the Chamber of Deputies had gone too far—farther than the President's intent—the minority presented a substitute bill, phrased more closely to the President's letter. Bertauld, speaking for the minority, urged this bill as necessary for good relations with the Chamber.[48] The majority report, on the other hand, asked the rejection of both bills. The Chamber's bill, it concluded, was " a dismembered and restricted amnesty," and because of its political implications, it was " useless and dangerous." Bertauld's bill, it charged, was equally bad because " the setting up of limitations opens the door to amnesty." [49]

The mere stopping of prosecutions was the equivalent of an amnesty to the Vicomte de Meaux, the most important speaker against the Bertauld bill. As he insisted, " There it is—without going into the question of whether or not, in law,

[46] Senate, *Annales*, session extraordinaire 1876, II, 4-5.
[47] *Idem.*
[48] *Ibid.*, session extraordinaire 1876, II, 14.
[49] Senate, *Annèxes*, session extraordinaire 1876, I, 182-3.

limitations ought to be confounded with amnesty—there it is, in fact an amnesty—an indirect one, but an inevitable one to our way of thinking, stemming from the vote they are asking of you at the present moment." Praising the zeal, the action, the wisdom, and the patience of the military judges, he asked that they be allowed to finish their work. " Don't . . . , at the last minute, come to laying the hand of the legislative power on the work of the judicial authority." [50] The Vicomte de Meaux was a true spokesman for his class. To the solidly Monarchist Right of the Senate, nothing whatsoever must be allowed to interfere with the way the National Assembly had disposed of the Commune. Any gesture, no matter how slight, in the direction of letting down the bars was to them an invitation anew to the scum of Paris to massacre the Archbishop.

It was Dufaure himself who took the floor to explain the Government's position. He had changed his outlook since he had gone before the Chamber and been defeated. He now told the Senate that the Council of Ministers " could not complain if the chambers insist upon giving their adherence to the principles which have been expounded in the letter of the President of the Republic." Frankly, he said, the Government " preferred the adoption of the Bertauld amendment to its rejection." [51] This was a weak way of putting it, but the meaning was clear enough to make the defeat of the Bertauld bill, even if only by a majority of fourteen, a defeat for the Government. [52]

Sunday, December 3, was an eventful day. Dufaure announced his decision to resign. [53] At the same time, even the Center Left—the most conservative of the Republican groups—met in caucus and voted unanimously not to work with any Ministry which did not represent the majority in the Chamber. [54] The crisis which everyone had feared for many months had come.

It lasted over a week. First MacMahon called on the Duc d'Audiffret-Pasquier, the President of the Senate, to form a

[50] Senate, *Annales*, session extraordinaire 1876, II, 18-19.
[51] *Ibid.*, session extraordinaire 1876, II, 24-5.
[52] *Ibid.*, session extraordinaire 1876, II, 30, 33-4. See also *Le Journal des débats*, December 3, 1876, 1:1-2.
[53] *Journal officiel*, December 4, 1876, 8985:2.
[54] *L'Année politique 1876*, 350.

Government. He refused. Next Grévy was asked, and he also refused. Then the President tried to keep Dufaure as Premier by making Jules Simon Minister of Interior. This was unsuccessful. Finally Jules Simon himself was asked to head the Government. The crisis officially ended on December 13, when the *Journal officiel* carried the names of the new Simon Ministry.[55]

As had been expected, the crisis meant merely a change at the top of the Council. Jules Simon became Premier and also Minister of Interior. Martel, an equally moderate Republican,[56] replaced Dufaure as Minister of Justice. Otherwise the personnel of the Government remained unchanged. Nothing else could have been expected, since there was no sound majority in the Chamber. Dufaure's opposition to a law ending further prosecution of alleged Communards had been overridden by a majority of the moment. It was not an operating majority that could form a solid base for a new Government, even if the principle of ministerial responsibility had been generally accepted. Whether Jules Simon could manage to stay in power, bedeviled as he was by both the President of the Republic and groups of insurgent Republican Deputies, remained to be seen.

The new Premier's first speech, delivered on December 14, gave him his opportunity to show where he stood. He spoke in the Senate, not in the Chamber, and he made no allusion whatsoever either to an amnesty or to stopping prosecutions of alleged Communards. Instead, as he said, " I bring you no program. . . . I am profoundly Republican. I say that I am profoundly Republican and profoundly conservative. . . ." For the future, " France wants security and rest; she does not want any more agitation. . . . Gentlemen, we want to give her calm, peace, [and] security." [57]

Growing Demands for an Amnesty

Jules Simon as Premier was never allowed, from the time he took office, to forget the Commune and the fate of its con-

[55] *Journal officiel*, December 13, 1876, 9273:1-2.
[56] See *Le Journal des débats*, December 14, 1876; 1:1, on the political character of Jules Simon and Martel.
[57] Senate, *Annales*, session extraordinaire 1876, II, 80.

demned men. It was true that party discipline was successfully invoked to turn the amnesty question away from the Chamber of Deputies, but there were other avenues of expression and action which could be used to harrass the Government. The Paris Municipal Council, over the outspoken opposition of the Prefect of the Seine, voted 30,000 francs into the budget of 1877 " for aid to the families of political prisoners." [58] Next, on the occasion of the New Year, Louis Blanc's newspaper printed a major article dealing with the question of an amnesty, and said that " We couldn't let these holidays pass without thinking with emotion of the victims of our civil discords, the cessation of whose afflictions has not been dependent upon us." A few months ago, it went on, there had been hope that the old year would end with " forgetfulness, . . . concord, . . . and amnesty," but this was not to be: " The apostles of a relentless policy have not wished it." Instead of an amnesty, the victims of the repression got only " more companions in suffering "; four hundred new deportees had left the Ile d'Aix for New Caledonia on December 28. All the time, the military tribunals, still at work, " continue to seize without pity the humblest soldiers of an insurrection which almost belongs to history, and which one already sees only dimly, like a bad dream, across the span of these six long years." [59] The Radical Republican approach to the amnesty question in 1877 was that of letting by-gones be by-gones. The Commune was thus a bad dream, and an amnesty—they felt—should be enacted for humanitarian reasons.

Quite another story was the attitude of the Communards and their friends. The fear and hatred which both the majority and the Right had exhibited at every reference to the Commune was fanning, as surely as with calculated intent, the flames of hatred on the part of their victims. Henri Rochefort was now writing regularly for Les Droits de l'homme,[60] hurling insults

[58] Paris, Municipal Council, Procès-verbaux, 1876, 1308-9 (meeting of December 20, 1876).

[59] L'Homme libre, January 2, 1877, 1:1-2. For the controversy with Les Droits de l'homme which this article touched off, see L'Homme libre, January 4, 1877, 1:4-5.

[60] It is worth noting that two members of the Paris Municipal Council, Sigismond Lacrois (Sigismond Krzyzanowski) and Yves Guyot, were the founders of Les Droits de l'homme.

at MacMahon in the name of the men of March 18. He outdid even his past invective in the article " Pardon for Yourself," which brought the law down on this advanced paper, so that it disappeared from the scene in January of 1877.[61] Further evidence that the Government's implacable attitude was accomplishing the very thing it most feared was the fact that the anniversary of March 18 was celebrated in several of France's industrial cities with clandestine banquets and meetings. Outside of France, these gatherings were triumphantly hailed by the Communard exiles as a sign that " the hour is soon coming when we'll get our own back." [62]

The Chamber of Deputies under Jules Simon

In the Chamber of Deputies, on the other hand, little was said directly on the subject of an amnesty for the Paris Commune during the life of the first Simon ministry, but much was said by innuendo or allusion. The Bonapartists in particular lost no chance of sniping at the Government. Their stock was rising incredibly rapidly. From total disgrace that had resulted from the fall of the Empire, the Bonapartist party was now " erect, menacing, [and] impudent." [63] Thus it was that on January 12, Robert Mitchell and Lenglé submitted a bill for amnesty in all cases of prosecution under the forest laws, which bill they prefaced with the insinuating suggestion that the Deputies now use their constitutional power to enact an amnesty for some " worthy cause," since, " Exclusively preoccupied up to the present with the political aspect of this prerogative, the Chamber has discussed at length an amnesty for all the men convicted of crimes committed during the odious insurrection of the Commune. . . ." [64] Nothing whatsoever came of this gesture; the Minister of Finance killed the bill when he advised the committee that there was no earthly reason to consider it, " unless you should wish to enact it for the sheer pleasure of according an amnesty." [65]

[61] On the fate of *Les Droits de l'homme*, see Avenel, *Histoire de la presse française*, 720, 722; and *L'Année politique 1877*, 7-8.

[62] Jules Joffrin in *Le Travailleur, Revue socialiste-révolutionnaire*, May 1877, 29-30.

[63] Anon., *Du 16 mai au 2 septembre 1877*, 32.

[64] Chamber of Deputies, *Annexes*, session ordinaire 1877, I, 90.

[65] *Ibid.*, session ordinaire 1877, II, 439.

On the opposite side of the Chamber, the Radical Republicans for their part were far from being reconciled to the majority. On February 5, their spokesman Madier de Montjau demanded an interpellation of the Government on its domestic policy. The Republican majority, with Leblond acting as its agent, was able to force Madier de Montjau to withdraw his demand,[66] and nothing more was heard of it. Nothing, furthermore, had been said about an amnesty, although the question was one to have been raised if the interpellation had been held. The following week the Radicals Naquet, Barodet, Floquet, Clemenceau, Louis Blanc, and the others—introduced a bill to amnesty all violations of the press laws committed to date. Their argument was that since it would take time to write a new press code, such an amnesty would be a token of good faith.[67] Because the bill was not even read in the Chamber of Deputies, and because there was no committee report on it before the May Sixteenth crisis, no one had the opportunity to raise in connection with this limited amnesty the question of a broader amnesty which would cover the Commune. The solidarity of the majority Republicans in the face of the precarious situation of the Ministry proved more than enough to keep out of the parliamentary debates any topic which that majority wished to exclude, and first among these topics was the amnesty.

The May Sixteenth Crisis

No matter how pallid the Radical Republicans felt the conduct of the majority under Gambetta's inspiration to be, the fact was that as the spring of 1877 moved on, the Right was beset by an overwhelming fear of radicalism; and Bonapartists, Legitimists, and even some Orleanists agreed in equat-

[66] The Republican majority insisted upon holding the interpellation that very afternoon. As Leblond said, "When it is a question of such an interpellation, the country becomes disturbed, and it must be settled immediately." Madier de Montjau was caught unprepared. He had not expected the interpellation to be held until the coming Thursday. He therefore pleaded that he was very tired, had a raging headache, and could not conduct an interpellation that afternoon. After charging the Chamber with deliberate ill-will toward him, he withdrew his demand, "for the moment." Chamber of Deputies, *Annales*, session ordinaire 1877, I, 222-4.

[67] Chamber of Deputies, *Annèxes*, session ordinaire 1877, I, 298-9.

ing "radicalism" with Republicanism. The internal nuances of the Republican party meant nothing to the men who were appalled by the Chamber's attitude toward such matters as freedom of the press from arbitrary control, freedom of education from clerical interference, and freedom of municipalities to manage their own affairs. They agreed, in short, with the Duc de Broglie, who subsequently defined the "radical spirit" as "the spirit which seeks to make of the Republic not only a form of political government, substituting the election of the head of the State for heredity, but also the instrument and the symbol of a great social transformation . . . [*sic*], the spirit which wants the Republic to have as a necessary complement and natural consequence the suppression of all the great institutions which the past has bequeathed to us, and which are the honor of our history." [68] In this atmosphere, by the time the month of May had come, every sitting of the Chamber of Deputies verged on open riot.

The Right screamed insults and threats to the Left, and the Left replied in kind. And whatever the topic of debate, sooner or later the attacks took up the subject of the Paris Commune. For example, in the spirited debates which led to a vote of censure on May 4 against the ultramontane maneuverings of the French clergy, Leblond was describing the network of disciplined Catholic committees taking orders from a central committee at Paris. "Well," said a Deputy on the Right, "that would be like the Central Committee of the Commune!" [69] And then Gambetta, to point up his charge that patriotism was not to be found in the French clergy, cited an incident of some ten or twelve years before in which the Archbishop Darboy had been a shining exception to this rule. Gambetta continued, "Indeed, today search, examine the horizon, pass the French episcopate in review! Where is Monseigneur Darboy?"

"You killed him!" shouted Paul de Cassagnac.

"If it wasn't you, it was your friends!" screamed Le Provost de Launay.

[68] Senate, *Annales*, session ordinaire 1877, III, 125.
[69] Chamber of Deputies, *Annales*, session ordinaire 1877, III, 13.

" Your friends shot him. At least respect the memory of their victim," added Baudry d'Asson.[70]

In the debates on municipal reorganization, with the question of repealing the Imperial laws of 1852 and 1855 before the Chamber, the Bonapartist Robert Mitchell was defending the Empire as having given—if not liberty—at least order and security. " Ask Alsace and Lorraine how the Empire gave them security," suggested Tirard. Robert Mitchell repeated: The Empire had not been a regime of liberty, but at least it " never by lying promises carried the unfortunate people away to revolt and civil war." Over violent protests from the Left, he continued, " There are at this very moment, gentlemen, a certain number of Republicans at Noumea who were deported because for twenty years they had faith in you, in your liberal declarations."

" The amnesty ought to have been voted," Germain Casse observed at this juncture, while Grévy from the presidential chair vainly tried to call Robert Mitchell back to the subject of debate.

" Today, you say to these wretched men," the Bonapartist went on, " you were struck down for having believed in our word; we—better advised [than you]—we are in power for having gone back on it." [71]

The uproar that followed this allegation was nothing compared to the frenzy a few days later when Paul de Cassagnac in effect accused all the Republicans of wishing to amnesty the Commune. The nominal subject of debate was still the municipal reorganization bill. The Bonapartist speaker got rather far afield and was called down by Grévy when he referred to certain newspaper attacks on the Czar of Russia as having emanated from the Republican Party. To defend himself against Grévy's rebuke for lumping all occupants of the Republican benches together, Paul de Cassagnac sneeringly explained, " The President is labouring under a misapprehension as to my thinking: I did not mean to say that these articles emanated from a section of the Chamber . . . but from a considerable segment of the Republican Party . . . , and so considerable that

[70] *Ibid.*, session ordinaire 1877, III, 37.
[71] *Ibid.*, session ordinaire 1877, III, 59-60.

each time this portion of the Republican Party proceeds to ask mercy or pardon for murderers . . . , it is with difficulty that you others dare to repudiate it."

Throughout this statement the Left had been loudly muttering its resentment. The Right burst into applause, while several members of the Left rushed down into the hemicycle, led by Allain-Targé, shouting his indignation.

" There are indeed, Monsieur Allain-Targé," said Paul de Cassagnac, " two ways of being indignant. My indignation, sir, is not always aimed at the same things as yours. During the Commune, I was indignant at the murderers, and you [were indignant] at the hostages. . . ." [72] Following this, Allain-Targé was so excited that he had to be led back to his seat by force, and it was many minutes before the verbal fighting between Right and Left subsided enough for the Chamber to proceed with its business.

With such complete deterioration of the Chamber of Deputies into two warring camps, it was plain that the reactionary forces would not long be content merely to exchange insults with the Republicans. Their bid to rid France of the dangerous influence, as they saw it, of the Republican majority came on May 16, with the forced resignation of Jules Simon. The immediate opportunity for President MacMahon thus to coerce the Premier of the majority was supplied by the Chamber's action on a bill relating to freedom of the press. On one subject in particular all Republicans, including the Radicals, were solidly united; this was their insistence upon the repeal of the press law of 1875 which Buffet and the National Assembly had insisted on as a device for keeping down radicalism. After weeks of controversy and debate, the Chamber was called on for a specific vote to repeal certain sections of the 1875 law. It was no secret that the Premier was opposed to such an action, since—as he told the committee on the bill—he did not regard the moment opportune to relax the safeguards against insults to foreign sovereigns and also he disapproved of piece-meal handling of the problem, preferring instead that the Chamber direct its efforts to an overall reform and codification of the press laws. It was likewise no secret that MacMahon was opposed to abro-

---

[72] *Ibid.*, session ordinaire 1877, III, 108-110; quoted portions, 108-109.

gation of the 1875 law. Nevertheless the Chamber of Deputies on May 15 voted 377 to 55 for the proposed repeal.[73] The sitting had been marked, moreover, by serious attacks from the Right on Jules Simon's good faith; he was accused of dissembling his opinion so that, when not in power, he would be free to take the opposite side on the question of the press laws.[74]

The very next day after this vote, MacMahon wrote the Premier an openly insulting letter, which accused him of treachery and inability to control the Chamber. There was no choice for Jules Simon but to resign; the entire Council of Ministers followed him. A new ministry, headed by the Duc de Broglie, was appointed.

The crisis was on. The country was shocked and stunned. The Republican Deputies were in an uproar. MacMahon was accused of setting himself above the law. At once the Chamber adopted a resolution that ministerial responsibility to the parliamentary majority was the first requirement of the country's government and the aim of its constitution.[75] On the eighteenth, MacMahon adjourned the Chamber for a month.

When the new Minister of Interior, Fourtou, came to read the decree of adjournment, bedlam broke loose in the Chamber. The Left was shouting its anger and defiance, the Right was triumphantly applauding and calling the Left " indecent," and the Center vainly was pleading for calm. As Fourtou began reading the message from MacMahon, he was noisily interrupted by the Left. The Right now showed its true feelings: " Go ahead and shout ' *Vive la Commune*! ' at once," screamed Le Provost de Launay.

" It's a scandal! " came from Robert Mitchell.

" On the Left, someone just cried ' To the pillory! ' and you didn't say anything about it," complained Paul de Cassagnac to Grévy.[76]

The President's message, as finally read, further infuriated the Republicans. MacMahon justified his rejection of the prin-

[73] *Ibid.*, session ordinaire 1877, III, 288.
[74] *Ibid.*, session ordinaire 1877, III, 220, attack by Raoul Duval; see also page 219. attack by Vicomte Blin de Bourdon.
[75] *Ibid.*, session ordinaire 1877, III, 237-8. The vote was 347 to 149.
[76] *Ibid.*, session ordinaire 1877, III, 249.

ciple of ministerial responsibility on the grounds of saving France from radicalism. Twice, he said, he had tried the experiment of a Premier favored by the majority in the Chamber. Both Dufaure and Simon had been unable to prevent the enactment of measures he had regarded as dangerous. Now, the only choices remaining to him for appointing a responsible Ministry were such as to require that he " appeal to or ask the support of another faction of the Republican Party, that which believes that the Republic cannot affirm itself without having as complement and consequence the radical modification of all our great institutions—administrative, judicial, and military." To confide power to such men was unthinkable, according to MacMahon. " At whatever epoch . . . [their ideas] should prevail, they would engender nothing but disorder and the abasement of France." [77]

MacMahon hoped that during the month's adjournment the Republican Deputies would calm down and return prepared to vote the 1878 budget. No hope could have been more futile. On June 16, therefore, the Chamber—still in turmoil—was informed that the President was asking the Senate for power to dissolve the unruly lower chamber.

In the short time left to them, the Republican Deputies rushed ahead with an interpellation on the events of May 16. Again in this debate the Right countered the Left's charges of unconstitutional acts with open identification of the Republicans with radicalism, the Commune, the International, and the amnesty.

The moderate Republican Bethmont, defending the fallen Government, pointed out that, " in the country . . . , calm was profound; work was being satisfactorily carried out; orders were being placed; deliveries were being made; and you saw commerce and industry everywhere. . . ."

" We were heading straight for the Commune! " interrupted Paul de Cassagnac.[78]

Bethmont continued. The fallen ministry had headed " a Republic which each day was growing in the esteem of Europe and in the confidence of the country. . . ."

[77] *Ibid.*, session ordinaire 1877, III, 250.
[78] *Ibid.*, session ordinaire 1877, III, 261.

" With members of the International in the Government! " interrupted Cuneo d'Ornano.

Rebuked by Grévy, d'Ornano repeated, " I state that the International had one of its members in the preceding Council."[79]

Later in his speech, Bethmont was praising the unity of the Republican forces, " This union, gentlemen, is the honor of our party; it is at the same time its strength. For five years, we have been hand in hand. For what purpose? I am going to tell you."

But the Right did not wait for Bethmont's explanation. It had its own; " For the amnesty! " came shouts from the Right.

The ever-interrupting Paul de Cassagnac expanded on this, " Yes, you asked forgiveness for the Communards! "

". . . I shall reply only one word," answered Bethmont, " This one word is that M. Dufaure asked it—the amnesty—the same as we did, that he did not get it from the Senate, and that he has declared it was on this adverse vote that he left the Ministry." [80]

The next speaker after Bethmont on this memorable June 16 was Fourtou, the Minister of Interior, who gave his analysis of the situation. " The truth is therefore what I affirm, to wit: that, in the matter of the constitutional laws, a fight has been engaged in from the very first day between the conservative spirit and the revolutionary spirit, a fight in which the conservative spirit has always been defeated, and from which we have seen emerge, manifestly encouraged by the favor of the advanced factions of the majority [and] manifestly submitted to by the moderate factions—even as far as the proposals which amnestied the Paris Commune. . . ." Here, protests from the Left and the Center prevented Fourtou from finishing his sentence.[81] Nevertheless, he kept on with his speech. The parliamentary majority, he alleged, had been moving toward taking over the executive and judicial branches, and had been doing so with " the flag of social disorganization in its hand." MacMahon's act of May 16, he told the Republicans, " saved

[79] Ibid., session ordinaire 1877, III, 262.
[80] Ibid., session ordinaire 1877, III, 264.
[81] Ibid., session ordinaire 1877, III, 266.

... [the Constitution] from your hands, at the same time that he blocked the way to radicalism, which was mounting little by little, step by step, by covered paths to the assault on society." [82]

Finally came Gambetta, with a dramatic defense of the Republican regime. He deplored the fact that the ministry in power had only the support of the reactionary minority.

"You prefer the Communards! You have other connections, you do!" came from Cuneo d'Ornano at this point.

"You are the friend of all the scoundrels, all the arsonists, all the murderers of the Commune!" echoed Paul de Cassagnac.[83]

And this was the story throughout Gambetta's speech. No matter what he said, the spokesmen for the Right threw the events of 1870 and 1871 up to him. When he referred to certain men as having a bent for restoration, Paul de Cassagnac replied, "Our bent is different, sir. As for myself, I don't have the bent for cowardice, for cowardice in foreign war and in civil war." Applause from the Right encouraged the gadfly: "The man who always saved himself—before the Prussians as before the Commune!" [84] This proved a popular theme on which to heckle Gambetta. Later, when he was referring to protests against MacMahon's acts throughout the press of Europe and America, and even of Spain, "the land of *pronunciamentos*," Brierre sneered, "You are familiar with ... [Spain] since your trip to San Sebastian!" [85] Still later, when Gambetta observed that the country knew what it could expect from the return of constitutional monarchy, Paul de Cassagnac countered with, "It knows what it can expect from you: your flight in the hour of peril! Oh! we know you have nothing to fear from the civil war you are fomenting." [86]

But Gambetta ignored all these side remarks, although he did take pains to refute at length the general charge that the Republicans had amnestied the Commune. "Do you ... need again to bring back the red specter?" he asked the reactionaries.

[82] *Ibid.*, session ordinaire 1877, III, 267.
[83] *Ibid.*, session ordinaire 1877, III, 271.
[84] *Ibid.*, session ordinaire 1877, III, 275.
[85] *Ibid.*, session ordinaire 1877, III, 278.
[86] *Ibid.*, session ordinaire 1877, III, 283.

" We have the red reality," retorted Paul de Cassagnac.

Gambetta elaborated on his theme. " Do you thus have the need of evoking social peril, which you have nevertheless made us a present of ever since you've been in business? It's true that you've replaced that slogan by another, ' Social Conservation.' Very well, no matter how hard up you are politically, you have to stop saying to this country that the Republican majority has amnestied the Commune. The thing must be set aright. This majority not only has not amnestied the Commune, it has excoriated it!

" Not only has it not presented the rehabilitation of the Commune, but it has circumscribed and limited its desires for clemency to one bill which was passed here . . . and taken to the Senate by a man whose authority you evoke today with I do not know what—the word escapes me. Will you help?—hypocrisy, if you will."

To another charge—that the Republican majority had acted like the Convention of 1792, Gambetta answered categorically, " The Convention is not on trial here any more than 1789 and 1793 are, any more than reprobation or amnesty for the Commune. The real truth is that after having been voted here, a law was taken to the Senate by a man whose conservative views you praise at every turn, and whom, however, you threw from power."

This brought enthusiastic applause from the Left, while the Right indignantly shouted that the Republicans themselves had overthrown Dufaure.

Gambetta went on. " You overthrew him not on a principle of social organization, not on the occasion of a daring bill, but because he considered, in his conscience as a statesman, as a good citizen, that the moment had come to shed the light of mercy over the heads of the vanquished." [87]

Gambetta was answered on June 18 by Monsieur Paris, the Minister of Public Works, who had his own interpretation of the alleged " amnesty " the Chamber had passed. " You proposed here not mercy—mercy, after the repression, was in the hearts of all. . . ."

" In theory! " exclaimed someone on the Left.

[87] *Ibid.*, session ordinaire 1877, III, 281.

" In theory you say! " Monsieur Paris was indignant. " Be so good as to go to the reports of the Commission on Pardons, and you will see how practice accompanied theory in regard to those who merited clemency."

What the Chamber had done, he explained, was to ask for a partial amnesty and to send Dufaure before the Senate with such a bill. Here Monsieur Paris defended the action of the Senate. " The Senate closed the door to amnesty while asking that pardon be given. It did not want a partial amnesty, which did not conform to any judicial principle, to become a cause of injustice with reference to other individuals, perhaps less compromised during the Commune, who should have been able to benefit from it. [The Senate] . . . rejected the law." Thus, concluded the Minister of Public Works, it was the Chamber which had really overthrown Dufaure by sending him before the Senate to die.[88]

The Dissolution and the Election

While the Chamber talked of the so-called amnesty, the Paris Commune, and the Constitution of the Third Republic, a committee of the Senate was deliberating on MacMahon's demand for the dissolution of the unruly lower chamber. The President's message embodying this demand had used virtually the same language he had employed earlier in calling down the Deputies, specifically that a responsible ministry was impossible because it would require drawing support from the radical part of the Republican majority. He had also deplored the failure of the Republican Deputies to forget their anger during the month's adjournment and had cited the many meetings of protest, public speeches, and particularly the famous manifesto of the 363 as evidence of the necessity for dissolution.[89] The Senate committee found MacMahon's reasons compelling, and its report, submitted on June 20, recommended dissolution on the same grounds. This report reviewed at length the unfortunate experiences of the Dufaure and the Jules Simon Ministries, spoke feelingly of the dangers of radicalism, but did not in any way allude to the Paris Commune or the Chamber's "amnesty." [90]

[88] *Ibid.*, session ordinaire 1877, III, 295.
[89] Senate, *Annales*, session ordinaire 1877, III, 55-6.
[90] *Ibid.*, session ordinaire 1877, III, 95.

Nor did any Senator, Right or Left, refer to these topics during the debate that followed. The Senate stayed close to the constitutional question, with the Republicans loudly attacking the " dictatorship " of MacMahon. By the close vote of 150 to 130, the Senate consented to the dissolution of the Chamber.[91] MacMahon's degree, countersigned by Fourtou, was read to the Chamber on June 25 by Jules Grévy, its presiding officer.[92]

Each side now had three months to win its cause; more than that, three months to win survival through annihilation of the opposition. This was no mere electoral campaign. This was a contest to the death between diametrically opposed political ideologies, and the violence and bitterness that marked the pre-election period made it clear to all that there could be no co-existence between MacMahon, the symbol of authoritarianism, and Gambetta, the symbol of representative democracy. To the roads took the Republicans to carry out their pleas for saving the Republic—for preserving intact the powers of the Chamber of Deputies, that sacred repository of the national will expressed through universal suffrage. But the reactionaries had on their side not merely the personal popularity of the Marshall,[93] but also the whole apparatus of official power, which they used to the full.

The gravity of the constitutional issue pushed the question of an amnesty for the Paris Commune into the background, without, however, by any means eliminating it from the political scene. The Republicans, to be sure, kept away from the subject as much as they could. As at few other times in the past they stood united, now that they were faced with a monstrous threat to overthrow everything they believed in. No one among them was inclined in this election to voice a demand for an amnesty, recalling what had of late been the painful division of the Republicans on this issue, and giving credence to the enemy's charge of sympathy toward the Commune. Even so, it was impossible for the Republicans completely to avoid the amnesty question, which now became the property of those who would

[91] *Ibid.*, session ordinaire 1877, III, 197. For the Senate debate, see 168-195.
[92] Chamber of Deputies, *Annales*, session ordinaire 1877, III, 423.
[93] See Anon., *Du 16 mai au 2 septembre 1877*, Chapter II, *passim*, on the popularity of MacMahon.

overthrow the Republic from the Left, as well as those who would overthrow it from the Right. So strong, in fact, was the leftist attack on Gambetta on this score that there was even talk of an "occult plot" against him. "If several speakers at certain public meetings are to be believed, if the Republic is today menaced by implacable enemies: It is Gambetta's fault. If the Chamber of Deputies, dissolved June 23 [sic], did not vote the amnesty: It is Gambetta's fault," wrote one pro-Gambetta paper.[94]

The reactionaries for their part lost no opportunity for subtle or not-so-subtle insinuation that the Republicans were, after all, as good as being Communards. Consider, for example, the report of MacMahon's military review, held on July 1, which Fourtou, the Minister of Interior, had posted on the public walls of every village throughout France as an official Government communication. "The partisans of the Commune, the accomplices of the arsonists and scoundrels of 1871, whom the Marshall vanquished and crushed in the streets of Paris, were not [present] at this great military festival." That the reference here was to the Republican Deputies, who had been specifically excluded by MacMahon from any invitation to attend the review, was made explicitly clear by the text that followed: "One did not see there a single one of the 363 former radical Deputies who have as their platform the disorganization and suppression of the Army as they would like to disorganize and destroy all the rest, everything that constitutes our prosperity and our greatness. . . ."[95]

But all the reactionaries' misuse of official power, all their suppression of the opposition press, their intimidation of democratic and labor organizations everywhere, and their parading of the red spectre were unavailing. In the October elections, the Republicans won a clear-cut majority.

Still the crisis was not over. There could be no working

[94] Le Livre rouge (weekly [?], Paris [?], [?], 1877 (date missing except for year), 2:4.

[95] Chamber of Deputies, Annales, 2e législature 1877, I, 114-5. François Goguel also tells of this episode in his Histoire des institutions politiques de la France, de 1870 à 1940 (Paris, 1951-52), Fasicule I, 142-3, pointing out that its net effect was to reinforce the radicals.

On the military review itself, see Journal officiel, July 2, 1877, 4989:3.

agreement between the new Republican majority and an unrepresentative ministry—and MacMahon was not yet prepared to yield. The new Chamber, like the old, was in a state of complete chaos. The Republicans moved ahead to discredit the Government's acts during the election period, and the reactionaries continued to rant of radicalism and to see a Paris-type Commune lurking in each Republican constituency. Upon the proposal of Albert Grévy, the Chamber was debating a parliamentary investigation of illegal Government influence during the elections. The Right denounced such a move as the preparation of a list of hostages, a list of suspects. "The forthcoming Commune," elaborated Baragnon, "will have its fatal list."[96] In the same debate, Jules Ferry was defending democracy in France as having no connotation of violence, being instead based upon the law, universal suffrage, and the ballot. "And the Commune?" interrupted Laroche-Joubert.[97]

Then Fourtou himself, still Minister of Interior, took the floor against the investigation. His speech had one simple theme: the Government had had to resort to official candidacies because of the great, immediate danger of radicalism in France. His proof? Disorders and seditious shouts being raised all over France. "And very recently . . . did you not see eight thousand rioters at Montluçon shouting '*Vive la Commune! Vive 93!* Down with the police!'" he asked, and then cited numerous other instances. At Ligny, the police had been pelted with both rocks and cries of "Down with MacMahon! *Vive 93! Vive la Commune!*" The same thing had happened, he went on, to the Board of Elections in the Pyrénées-Orientales. Many people had been arrested at Rouen for these shouts. More than twenty departments, concluded Fourtou, had witnessed like outbursts;[98] under the circumstances, the Government had felt it its duty to use every device to defeat the Republicans, the harbingers of radicalism.

[96] Chamber of Deputies, *Annales*, 2ᵉ législature 1877, I, 104.
[97] *Ibid.*, 2ᵉ législature 1877, I, 147.
[98] *Ibid.*, 2ᵉ législature 1877, I, 126. Chantemille, the Republican Deputy for Montluçon vehemently denied the truth in Fourtou's report (page 132). Whether or not "*Vive la Commune!*" had actually been shouted—and Chantemille said it had not been—the significance here lies in the fact that Fourtou was equating the Commune with Republican "radicalism" of 1877 and basing his defense of arbitrary governmental acts upon this equation.

As in the old Chamber, all such allusions to the Commune infuriated the Republicans, but now, with a fresh mandate from the country, they tended to treat them less seriously. When the Republican majority had been returned, the reactionary coalition had been left beating a dead horse in its attempts to invoke a terror of the Commune. Fully aware of its new power, the Chamber went right ahead in treating the existing ministry as the arch-enemy of France, and with no difficulty carried the motion for a sweeping investigation of the recent elections.[99]

The situation was not improved on November 23, when MacMahon replaced the caretaker government of Broglie with an equally reactionary, unrepresentative group of ministers headed by General de Rochebouët. He lasted exactly three weeks. Then the Marshall, finally worn down by unremitting warfare with the Chamber and the ever-present danger of a violent outbreak, did a complete about-face, appointing as Premier Dufaure, who—now identified with the Center Left— was acceptable to the majority Republicans.[100] And so ended the crisis of what Victor Hugo termed, "this strange year, 1877." [101]

Communards, Collectivists, and the Crisis

The May Sixteenth crisis did not evoke any sympathy for the regime from the Communard exiles or from the handful of collectivists working underground in France. For them, particularly since no amnesty had been voted following the Republican victory in the elections of 1876, no distinction now existed

[99] *Ibid.*, 2ᵉ législature 1877, I, 168. The vote was 312 to 205.

[100] On December 14, Dufaure, the new President of the Council of Ministers, read a message from MacMahon to the Senate, in which the principle of ministerial responsibility was unqualifiedly accepted. The message began, " The elections of October 14 have once more affirmed the confidence of the country in republican institutions. . . . The interest of the country demands that the crisis which we are going through be appeased; it demands with no less strength that it not be renewed." (Senate, *Annales*, session extraordinaire 1877, V, 59.)

[101] Victor Hugo, *L'Histoire d'un crime. Déposition d'un temoin* (Paris, 1877), reverse of fly sheet following title page [unnumbered]. As the author explained, he had started writing this study of Louis Napoleon's *coup d'état* of December Second on December 14, 1851, but chance had caused the publication to be deferred until 1877. " In making what is happening today coincide with the telling of the events of by-gone days, did chance have a design? " he wondered. " This book is more than timely; it is urgent. I am publishing it. V. H."

between Republicans and Monarchists, unless it were that the former were the greater of two evils because the more dishonest. The workers of France were therefore warned, as soon as the crisis developed, that the Republicans of 1877—the same men as of 1871—would make pretty speeches and call them to arms " for the Constitution and the law."[102] The Republic, which the workers were now called upon to save, had accomplished less than nothing: " With reference to freedom of association, they passed the law suppressing the International or any other organization of this sort, thanks to which the workers could act together in order to free themselves."[103] This was not surprising, it was explained, since " The majority, even of those who . . . have become the Intransigeants, did not have— Monsieur Louis Blanc as their leader—enough imprecations to vomit against the defeated men . . . [of the Commune]."[104] On the specific question of an amnesty, the Republican attitude was described as being one of, " Wait, . . . the moment has not yet come. Let's play up to our enemies by refusing even to take part in the comedy of an amnesty—which, furthermore, the *Loyal Sword* would be in a big hurry to turn down."[105] Jules Joffrin, writing from London, pointed out that " Not one of those elected with the mission of demanding the amnesty, . . . none of those who had this mandate carried it out."[106]

The Chamber's debates on the crisis—particularly the Republicans' strenuous denials of having sought to amnesty the Commune—infuriated the exiles. The group in Geneva exhorted

---

[102] " Bulletin," *Le Travailleur*, May 1877, 6-7.
[103] " La République bourgeoise et ses résultats," *ibid.*, May 1877, 8.
[104] *Ibid.*, May 1877, 7. On Louis Blanc's observations on the subject of the Commune in 1871, see particularly Lissagaray, *op. cit.*, 409-10:
" ' The Parisian insurrection,' continued M. Louis Blanc, ' is legitimate in its motives and in its original goal: recovery of the municipal franchises of Paris. But the intervention of the *Central Committee* and the claim put forth to govern all other municipalities in the Republic have completely denatured its character. Finally, this insurrection—within sight of a Prussian army, which is ready to enter Paris if the Commune is victorious—is utterly condemnable and must be condemned by every true Republican. That is why the Mayors of Paris, and the Left and the Extreme Left of the Assembly did not hesitate to protest against an insurrection which the proximity of the Prussian army and other circumstances could render criminal.' "
[105] " La République bourgeoise et ses résultats," *Le Travailleur*, May 1877, 10.
[106] " Correspondence," *ibid.*, May 1877, 29.

the people of France never to forget Gambetta's words of June 16, when he had insisted that the majority had castigated, not amnestied, the Commune.[107] The duplicity of the Republicans was again played upon in a report written from Paris to the Geneva exiles. "You must be told that even those who voted congratulations to the Army after the massacres of Paris now commend *the Commune* to the young people, *all the while deploring its excesses.* They know that this is the only way they can get many votes in the cities. A declaration doesn't cost them anything. They on occasion proclaim themselves socialists if that's what they have to do." [108]

But as the day for the election drew nearer, it was increasingly apparent that the question of the Commune and its amnesty was playing only a secondary role in the campaign. It was also becoming plain that the Republic, not the Commune, was the rallying ground for the average French workingman in 1877. From Lyons, he was described as "flabby, down-trodden, without energy, having lost all awareness of himself, of his own strength, and of his true interests." [109] At Paris the outlook was equally dismal for the collectivists. "In spite of the examples we strive to give them, each day brings new defections. Poverty is making them more and more brutish; they regard Gambetta as a messiah, notwithstanding all the villainies he has committed for seven years. They still believe in him and say that it is a tactic he is justified in using in order not to scare off the timid. . . ." [110] The exiles, anxiously watching events in France from across the Swiss frontier, were forced to concede that their cause was lost. The question of the amnesty had been submerged in the fight to save the Republic. "Paris this time didn't even ask its candidates—even if only as a matter of form— where they stood on the amnesty. It is true that this would have been a veritable contradiction, since these candidates had been acclaimed even though they have already refused to vote

---

[107] "Bulletin," *ibid.*, June 1877, 3. See above, page 141, for Gambetta's speech, which was here rendered as "Give up saying that this assembly has amnestied the Commune, for it has excoriated it."

[108] "Correspondence," *ibid.*, June 1877, 19.

[109] *Ibid.*, September 1877, 26.

[110] *Ibid.*, September 1877, 25.

it, despite previous formal promises." [111] And when the elections of October 14 and October 28 were over, the Geneva exiles
grimly recognized that no amnesty would be forthcoming from
these victorious Republicans. "Monsieur Leblond [112] can sleep
in peace. In the new Assembly he won't have to go over again
his famous report on . . . [the amnesty] question, which has
been entirely buried by the will of the voters themselves." [113]
    The fact was that the workers of France had failed to respond
to the anti-Republican propaganda which had been put out by
the collectivists during the crisis. A manifesto of the Jurassian
Federation, posted in many cities on the eve of the elections,
served only to provoke hysterical outbursts from the reactionaries. [114]

The New Dufaure Ministry

The pessimism of the exiles was more than warranted as
concerned the immediate political situation. Certainly, when
the new Dufaure Council of Ministers was examined, no sharp
change in the Government's policy on the amnesty was to be
expected. Dufaure's open opposition to an amnesty was a
matter of record. He had said categorically that it was impossible. [115] As for the rest, every member with the single exception
of Gambetta's protegé Freycinet was recruited from the cautious
Center Left. Two members in particular were going to do
everything in their power to block any consideration of an
amnesty. These were Marcère, the Minister of Interior, and
Waddington, who was to succeed Dufaure as Premier. [116] It
would have been absurd to expect from the new Dufaure

---

[111] *Ibid.*, October 1877, 4.
[112] See above, page 109, for the Leblond Report on the Raspail bill of 1876.
[113] *Le Travailleur*, October 1877, 5.
[114] On the manifesto, signed by Pindy but written by Paul Brousse, who had
illegally returned to France in January 1877, see Guillaume, IV, 282. *Le Gaulois*
reprinted the placard in its October 14, 1877, issue, with the threat that "Those
citizens who vote on Sunday against the Marshal will be committing the crime
of Lèse-Patrie." (See Alexandre Zévaès, *De la semaine sanglante au Congrès
de Marseille*, 1871-1879 [Paris, 1911], 10.)
[115] See above, pages 104, for Dufaure's record on amnesty.
[116] For Dufaure's full Government, see *Journal officiel*, December 14, 1877,
8349:1-3–8350:1-2. Waddington was Minister of Foreign Affairs, and Freycinet
was Minister of Public Works.

Ministry anything but implacable opposition toward an amnesty for the Paris Commune.

Meaning of May Sixteenth for an Amnesty

Although the Republicans emerged triumphant from the prolonged May Sixteenth crisis, they were bound to shun even consideration of an amnesty for the Paris Commune at this time. For one thing, their antagonists had not been eliminated from French political life. In the Chamber of Deputies there was still a vociferous minority on the Right. The Senate, moreover, had not been even partially renewed in 1877, so the upper chamber continued to have a conservative-reactionary majority. And MacMahon remained in the Presidency. The Republicans had not won decisively enough in 1877 to wipe from their minds fear of future reactionary bids for power.

The crisis also left many Republicans self-conscious about any taint of " radicalism." In particular, the way the reactionaries had exploited the Republicans' general willingness to pursue a more or less lenient policy toward some participants in the upheaval of 1871 had left them justifiably apprehensive on this score. And always it was to be remembered that the election had been fought—and won—on the question of the Republic. There was nothing in the vote to make it susceptible to interpretation as an endorsement of an amnesty.

Nevertheless the Republican victory in the May Sixteenth crisis was essential for even any hope of an amnesty for the Paris Commune. Eclipsing all other considerations was the fact that the majority in the Chamber of Deputies had taken a long step toward establishing its power as the real government of Republican France, and this put the regime on the road to being in reality the strong, self-assured authority which, as many had long been pointing out, was the fundamental prerequisite of a general amnesty.

In collateral ways, too, the outcome of the crisis served to promote the amnesty cause. For example, the Radical Republicans, ardent champions of such a measure, were restored to the good graces of the majority and were enjoying an enhanced prestige. Among the eighteen members of the Republican steering committee set up when the new legislature met on

November 7, were six known advocates of a full and complete amnesty. In addition, the Republican majority itself was committed to the destruction of all the machinery of censorship and oppression which the reactionaries had used to stifle opposition. Freer expression of opinion would be possible, and along with it could develop a popular sentiment for an amnesty. Finally, because the Deputies were taking over the effective power in the Third Republic, the Chamber—and through it the Government—were to become increasingly sensitive to public opinion and organized pressure groups.

Viewed in retrospect, the May Sixteenth crisis may be said, in short, to have broken the force of reaction, made the Chamber of Deputies the ruler of France, and created an atmosphere in which the amnesty question could eventually become the amnesty problem.

Resurgence of the Amnesty Question

The significance of the crisis was immediately grasped by the extra-parliamentary radicals. On December 23, Jules Guesde's recently founded *L'Egalité* [117] hailed the new independence of the Chamber from the Senate and the President. The Deputies, wrote the future Socialist leader, " are no longer responsible to anyone but themselves. There they are—the masters, masters to re-open France to the Frenchmen who, six thousand leagues from their homeland, beneath the jailers' clubs, are paying for their crime of not having believed the Republic safe in the hands of men who, on two occasions, had tried to strangle it violently. . . ." [118]

In the political sphere, the General Council of the Seine passed a resolution calling for the enactment of an amnesty law, only to have it promptly annulled. [119] Not long after this,

[117] The first issue had appeared on November 18, 1877.

[118] *L'Egalité*, December 23, 1877, 1:1.

[119] *Ibid.*, December 30, 1877, 4:3. For a general study of resolutions passed by the General Councils, see the very thorough study by Joseph Pey, *Les vœux politiques des conseils généraux* (Paris, 1904). In discussing the decrees annulling acts of the General Council of the Seine, Pey observes, " most frequently, these resolutions had to do with the amnesty, with the separation of Church and State, [and] with the suppression of the budget for cults or for the embassy to the Vatican." (Page 133.) Elsewhere, he points out that in all questions of resolutions calling for amnesty, " the list of deliberations

a member of the General Council of Lyons proposed a similar resolution, but the Council hurriedly turned him down.[120]

In the sphere of propaganda, the public was now offered pamphlet copies—at ten centimes each—of the speeches of Lockroy, Clemenceau, and Georges Périn in support of the Raspail bill; and the man in the street could also get Henri Rochefort's *From Noumea to Europe* serialized in fifty install-ments, at ten centimes apiece.

Meanwhile, in the Chamber of Deputies, the amnesty ques-tion again was a political football, a device to be used by any opposition to make life miserable for any Government. In this way, the Bonapartists—who were now the chief threat to the Republic [121]—became the fathers of the next amnesty proposal. Dufaure as Premier recommended on December 15 a complete amnesty for all offenses of the press committed from May 16 to December 14, 1877.[122] As was to be expected, the committee brought in a unanimously favorable report.[123] No sooner had the debate started than the Bonapartists Lenglé, the elder Janvier de la Motte, and their colleagues demanded that the dates from May 16 to December 14, 1877, be suppressed, and that the amnesty be made to cover " all crimes, misdemeanors, and lesser offenses committed both before May 16 and since December 14, 1877," for only in this way would the true prin-ciple of amnesty—" veritable equality in matters of clemency " —be preserved. The bill as it stood, charged Lenglé, was not an amnesty, it was " a partisan measure, . . . a work of reac-tion! " [124] This brought Louis Napoleon's " crime " of Decem-ber the Second into the debate. From Right to Left and from

which were annulled is long, and one finds with difficulty a few rare motions which did escape the general slaughter." (Page 213.) The usual grounds for annulling such resolutions were that they violated the law which prohibited any political discussion on the part of the General Councils.

[120] *Le Travailleur*, January-February 1878, 2.

[121] See Anon., *Du 16 mai au 2 septembre 1877*, 32. " After May Sixteenth, there is not a single enlightened and impartial soul who does not see that the real battle is between the Republic and the Empire."

[122] Chamber of Deputies, *Annales*, 2e législature 1877, II, 224.

[123] *Ibid.*, session ordinaire 1878, I, 77-9. The only amendment suggested by the committee was that persons convicted of press law violations during the months in question could recover fines paid, if claims were filed within six months.

[124] *Ibid.*, session ordinaire 1878, I, 196-7.

Left to Right and back again the Deputies threw allegations, insinuations, and insults at each other. The uproar had only slightly quieted down when Talandier mounted the tribune to speak as one who had signed the first genuine full amnesty bill.

Here at last was the discussion of an amnesty for the Commune. As Talandier began to speak, the majority Republicans began screaming for clôture. But Talandier spoke, and he neatly called the Bonapartists' hand. His indictment of their maneuver was brief and to the point. They, he charged, only proposed this general amnesty in order to divide the Republicans. They had never wanted a general amnesty and had not voted for it when the Radical Republicans had brought in such a bill. In fact, the very reason why the Chamber of Deputies had not enacted the Radicals' amnesty bill, said Talandier, was because of the Bonapartists, who " had cast trouble into the Republic; it is because you had not suffered it to establish itself sufficiently." This was the way Talandier disposed of the Bonapartists. As for the matter of an amnesty for the Commune, he affirmed that he would work as long as he had life and vigor to make the Republicans of the Chamber see that a general amnesty " is a proof of strength as well as of wisdom and humanity." Some day, he continued, very soon it was to be hoped, there would be an amnesty, but it would be a Republican and not a Bonapartist amnesty.[125]

To counter Talandier's attack Rouher, the veritable chief of the Bonapartists, denounced anew the Dufaure bill for an amnesty for the press as an act of reprisal, while Lenglé hastily denied that he had ever intended to propose a general amnesty. He had not done so—his smirk was visible as he said this— because he knew the Chamber could not vote such a measure. " To proclaim a general amnesty, there must be a strong and firm Government."[126]

On January 24, 1878, then, the amnesty question had again put in an appearance to disrupt the functioning of the parliamentary Republic. The Bonapartists were feeling out the chinks in the Republican armor, and even though their strategy on this occasion failed to split the Republican bloc (the committee's

[125] *Ibid.*, session ordinaire 1878, I, 203.
[126] *Idem* (Lenglé's remarks), and *ibid.*, session ordinaire 1878, I, 204 (Rouher's remarks).

original bill on amnesty for the press was voted 316 to 36),[127] they carefully filed away the experience for future reference.

Here was another consequence of the May Sixteenth crisis— and one which would have bearing on the amnesty controversy —the resurgence of the Bonapartists as the new enemy on the Right, who would see in the amnesty question a useful device for undermining the country's confidence in the regime. A further consequence—and one which lay at the very heart of the amnesty controversy—was the appearance of a new and real enemy on the Left, the organized Socialists.

Until such time as the Republic had seemed to be on its feet, it had been impossible to detach the workingman from a primary allegiance to the Republic. With the defeat of the immediate threat from the reactionaries, the uneasy alliance between the more class-conscious workers and the Republican politicians, who by the very logic of their position had of necessity to defend the interests of the middle class, began to fall apart. In this reforging of loyalties, the amnesty controversy was to play a major role.

Before the May Sixteenth crisis, the Radical Republicans in the Chamber had taken the lead in demanding an amnesty bill. At that time, no other leadership was forthcoming, since French labor as a whole had barely begun to recover from the effects of 1871. But the efforts of sentimentally pro-labor politicians had been totally unsuccessful. Louis Blanc, Clemenceau, Lockroy, Raspail and the others had used logical and humanitarian arguments, had spoken in terms of an abstract social justice, and had pleaded the future of the Republic. These were feeble weapons against an entrenched order which felt its existence had been dangerously near to being swept away by the Commune. In the resurgent amnesty fight after May Sixteenth, the initiative passed to extra-parliamentary, anti-Republican radicals, who were either proletarian in origin or else claimed to speak for the proletariat.

---

[127] *Ibid.*, session ordinaire 1878, I, 215. The bill did not, however, have smooth sailing before becoming law. The Senate amended it to exclude all libel cases from the amnesty and to extend the coverage to all other press cases from the beginning of the Republic to January 1, 1878. The Chamber had to accept this version. (See Chamber of Deputies, *Annèxes*, session ordinaire 1878, V, 158-9, and *Annales*, session ordinaire 1878, V, 146-7.)

CHAPTER IV

THE SOCIALISTS:

THE COMMUNE AS PROLETARIAN LEGEND

Beginning early in 1878, it became clear that the campaign to win an amnesty for the Paris Commune was acquiring a new orientation. From the extreme left wing of the parliamentary Republicans, the initiative passed to the leaders of the nascent Socialist movement in France. This profoundly altered the atmosphere in which the question of an amnesty was debated. It was one thing for the exiled Communards to urge the French workingman to resist his exploiters, to reject the Third Republic, and to make a new revolution. It was quite another thing to have skillful organizers arranging demonstrations, making speeches in Paris, Lyons, Marseilles and other traditionally proletarian centers, and conducting vigorous political campaigns. At this juncture too, amnesty itself ceased to be the goal—if indeed it ever had been—while the fight waged for it became the strategem of a small, dedicated group which urged labor's independent political action as the first step toward the overthrow of capitalism. Marxists, anarchists, Blanquists, and vague collectivists of no particular school all worked together during the next two years to force the enactment of an amnesty which would be the vindication of the right of revolution. No narrow doctrinal partisanship, moreover, marked this new leadership of the fight for an amnesty. By the middle of the eighteen-eighties, the ideological differences within the political labor movement were to split it into a number of warring factions. But this was not generally true in the period immediately after May Sixteenth, when the revolutionary collectivists were only beginning their activities under the Third Republic. The suspicion and fear with which the Government and the majority of the Deputies looked upon any attempts of labor to improve its position in society through its own efforts meant that all advocates of independent political action must

155

seek what strength they could in working together. They were weak, their followers few. Whatever was to be achieved must be done in concert. This was particularly true in connection with the fight for an amnesty, and their collaboration was furthered by the Commune's curious quality of being all things to all ideologies.

But among the groups seeking to make political capital from the legacy of the Commune, it was the early French Marxists who formed the real inner circle, the central directorate of the new leftist leadership of the amnesty cause. The great emphasis that was placed in the early years of the Third Republic on universal suffrage as a social panacea led, quite naturally, to the birth of political aspirations on the part of more advanced workers. Toward the end of the seventies, even the orthodox trade unionists were talking of the " direct representation of the proletariat." It was the Socialists' task to turn this new current into revolutionary channels. The issue of an amnesty for the Paris Commune could be their principal instrument if they could do two things: first, arouse a strong public sentiment in favor of an amnesty, and secondly, convince the working voters that independent political action was the means to this end. By representing the Commune as having been the Parisian proletariat's great bid for social and economic emancipation, the Socialists could hope to rally all militant workers. By hammering away at the patent refusal of Republican politicians to pass an amnesty bill, they might succeed in disillusioning labor of its faith in the whole of the parliamentary process. Finally, if an amnesty should ever become a reality, the Socialists could claim credit for having forced the hand of the bourgeoisie.

During the year 1878, therefore, the Socialists began to organize their use of the amnesty question as the means to winning a mass following. They made the aged, imprisoned Blanqui a symbol of the need for an amnesty; they set up committees to harrass the Deputies; they conducted ceaseless propaganda. Above all, they began to create a veritable cult of the Commune, with themselves as its spiritual heirs.

As things stood at the beginning of 1878, it was apparent that the Socialists had a long way to go to enlist the French workingman as voter in the campaign for an amnesty, let alone in the Socialist movement. Two events in January strikingly demonstrated this—the electoral campaign of Emile Chausse and the Lyons labor congress.

The Defeat of Emile Chausse

The year 1878 opened with an electoral campaign which was later to be hailed as " the first Socialist candidacy along class lines." [1] Emile Chausse, a cabinet maker, was running against the Opportunist Ulysse Parent [2] for Municipal Councillor from the XIth arrondissement, *quartier* Sainte-Marguerite. His campaign was sponsored by the Republican Committee of Democratic-Socialist Workers, which asserted the principle that the interests of the working class in politics could not be defended except by a workingman. Chausse's platform, although it was soon to be superseded by more thoroughly revolutionary demands, was as advanced as was possible for that day. His major points called for the abolition of all franchises and monopolies, the establishment of complete municipal autonomy, election of all public officials, and a single tax on rents. The Socialist candidate of 1878 next demanded the repeal of all laws interfering with individual freedom, freedom of the press, and freedom of organization and public assembly, just as the Republicans of 1869 had demanded. Then Chausse urged, as he must, " Immediate full and complete amnesty for all sentences relative to the political happenings which have taken place up to this day, with assistance guaranteed to the amnestied upon returning to their hearths." [3] But on January 6, Emile Chausse, cabinet maker, the candidate of the Socialists and the candidate who stood for full amnesty, received only 391 votes.[4]

The Lyons Congress

Very soon after Chausse's unsuccessful campaign, a general labor congress was held at Lyons. This congress, the second

[1] See Zévaès, *De la semaine sanglante au congrès de Marseille*, 60.

[2] Elected a member of the Commune from the IXth arrondissement, Ulysse Parent resigned on April 5, in protest against the sally of April 3. Brought to trial August 7, 1871, in the first of the mass actions against the Communards, he was acquitted on September 2, 1871.

[3] *L'Egalité*, January 6, 1878, 5:2-3.

[4] *Ibid.*, January 13, 1878, 6:3-7:1.

such gathering in France after the Commune, was important not only as marking the further development of the political consciousness of the French workers but also for its attitude toward the question of an amnesty. At the earlier congress, held in Paris in 1876, there had been very little interest in the question of labor in politics. Chabert, who at that time had just been defeated in spite of his Radical Republican support in the parliamentary by-elections of 1876, had—it was true—spoken at length in favor of labor candidacies and had optimistically predicted that " The moment will come when we can emerge from the exceptional laws. Then, with freedom of public gathering, [and] liberty of the press, we will prove that we are capable of governing ourselves." [5] But the delegates had been bored and restless during his speech,[6] although there had been general agreement that labor could not be adequately represented by a professional politician. The Paris congress, moreover, had carefully avoided the amnesty question. In all, it was inevitable that the exiles of the Commune should have replied to this timorous congress of 1876 with bitter invective.[7]

The congress of 1878 was a different story, and here the influence of the May Sixteenth crisis in sharpening the political awareness of French labor may be seen.[8] At Lyons there was

[5] For Chabert's speech, see Congrès ouvrier de France, session de 1876, Séances, 286-94.

[6] See Le Temps, October 9, 1876, 2:4-5, and Eugène Petit, " Les discussions du congrès ouvrier de Paris," Journal des économistes, November 1876, 187-8.

[7] A group of exiles in London, nearly all Blanquists, expressed their contempt for this congress in a violent pamphlet entitled The trade unionists and their congress, of which the following selection is representative.

" It seems monstrous that men can be found in the city of the Revolution, five years after the battle of the Commune, on the tomb of [those who were massacred], in view of the fact of penal servitude in Noumea and full prisons, who dare to pose as representatives of the proletariat, to come in its name to apologize to the bourgeoisie, to foreswear the Revolution, to disown the Commune." (Quoted from John Labusquière, La Troisième République 1871-1900 [Histoire socialiste, 1789-1900, Jean Jaurès, editor, Vol. XII; Paris, 1909], 192)

The group signed itself " The Revolutionary Commune." Names of the individual signers may be found in Zévaès, De la semaine sanglante au congrès de Marseille, 50, fn. 1.

[8] Labor felt the impact of the May Sixteenth crisis in two ways. The first and more brutal was the actual destruction of labor organizations as a Monarchist measure of political precaution (the most notorious example, of course, being the dissolution of all workers' unions in the department of the Rhône by the Perfect Vallavielle). The second and more subtly vicious was the blatant campaign

lively interest in labor candidacies, and scorn was heaped on Gambetta's appeal for a union of the bourgeoisie and the proletariat.[9] The hundred forty delegates then voted a resolution calling for direct representation of the proletariat, but with the reservation that the labor candidate would withdraw before the second balloting to throw his support to the Republican candidate " if the Republic were in danger." [10] May Sixteenth, in short, was still a vivid memory.

This congress, not an orderly gathering at best, was almost disrupted by the unexpected introduction of the amnesty question. The Committee on Resolutions asked the congress to vote for " Full and complete amnesty for all acts connected with the Commune and for all other political acts up to May 16, 1877." The delegate Labouret was on his feet instantly. Speaking for the Committee of Organization, he objected strenuously, on the ground " that this wish is locked in the heart of every delegate, but that [such a resolution] is not within the competence of this workers' congress, which is not a political assembly." The delegate Deschamps then pointed out that this item had not been on the agenda approved in advance by the delegates, and that he for one found " amnesty out of place here." Before there could be further debate, the congress voted clôture, and Gayet, in the name of the Committee on Resolutions, withdrew the paragraph on amnesty " in the interest of future congresses." He concluded, " The amnesty is in our hearts; that is sufficient." The delegates applauded wildly and went on to vote unanimously for the thus modified report of the Committee.[11]

appeals made to the workers during the crisis. (See " Elections générales," in *Le Travailleur*, July 1877, 12-13, for a satiric version of the type of campaign speech addressed to the workers by candidates of all biases.)

[9] See Congrès ouvrier de France, deuxième session, *Séances* (Lyon, 1878), especially 281, 287-8; and Charles M. Limousin, " Le deuxième congrès d'ouvriers français," *Journal des économistes*, March 1878, 421.

[10] Congrès ouvrier, deuxième session, *Séances*, 601.

[11] *Ibid.*, 611. The resolutions voted at Lyons in 1878 were in many respects—with the exception of amnesty—similar to Emile Chausse's campaign platform, including the abolition of monopolies and the return of municipal franchises to the commune (see *ibid.*, 612). The celebrated motion in favor of collectivism, which the congress rejected by an overwhelming vote, was presented, significantly enough by Jules Dupire, who had been one of the organizers of the Paris Congress of 1876, and who later was expelled from the Socialist movement as

This was the Lyons Congress of 1878, the congress of which the Geneva exiles contemptuously pointed out that while thousands were suffering exile or worse agonies, " Their brothers, in congress assembled, declare that it would be out of place to demand their amnesty." [12] But the delegates' continuing fear of arbitrary Government action against the congress had sealed their lips on the subject of an amnesty. The progress made in the direction of independent labor action, furthermore, was totally without reference to the amnesty question. At no time was the congress's belief in such action associated with the idea of winning amnesty for the Commune. On the contrary, it was made plain that the Republic still had, in 1878, the confidence of the workers. Their resolution to support the Republican candidate on the ballotage was a sign that the Republican politicians were not yet wholly discredited in labor's eyes. Before political action could mobilize a number of workers sufficient to make amnesty a critical issue for the Republicans, the Government had to have more opportunity than it had had by January of 1878 to alienate the working class. Above all, the workers themselves had to be better organized and more aroused.

The Blanqui Campaign at Marseilles

Even while the Lyons Congress was meeting, another movement was being set on foot which was ultimately going to force the Government's hand on an amnesty. This movement, which came to a dramatic climax on June 13, 1880, consisted of putting up as candidate for virtually every vacant public function the name of a man who had himself been condemned for participation in the Commune. In this way amnesty became the focal point of labor's political action; and universal suffrage, which was the Republicans' very reason for existence, now became the rallying cry of the Socialists, for the voice of universal suffrage would speak—through a vote cast for a Blanqui, a Humbert or a Trinquet—and that vote would be a vote, pure and simple, for amnesty. By denying amnesty, the Republicans

an alleged *agent provocateur*. (See *Le Prolétaire* [Paris, weekly], February 22, 1879, 8:3; March 8, 1879, 6:3, 7:1, and 7:3.)

[12] *Le Travailleur*, February-March 1878, 12.

would deny their belief in the voice of universal suffrage. This would create an impossible situation. From January 1878 to June 1880, the main line of development in the amnesty controversy, no matter what else happened, was the carefully managed sequence of political campaigns designed to embarrass the Republic into voting an amnesty.

The pattern which took shape between January 1878 and June 1880 for winning the amnesty by ceaselessly presenting as candidates the very men who were ineligible to hold public office owing to the absence of that amnesty doubtlessly was not fully formulated at the outset. The fact that eventually such a master plan was conceived resulted inevitably from the short-sighted policies of the Government of the Third Republic on the question of the amnesty.

The first identification of the amnesty cause with Socialist politics was the campaign waged for Blanqui at Marseilles. Originally the idea of running Blanqui for a parliamentary seat was presented simply as a means of getting him out of prison. By flawless evolution, however, Blanqui was christened a Revolutionary Socialist, and he was made the symbol of the demand for a general amnesty for the Commune.

Louis Auguste Blanqui, the seventy-three year old revolutionary, was in 1878 serving life sentence in the prison of Clairvaux, having been thus sentenced in February of 1872 for " incitement to civil war." Only his poor health had spared him deportation. For nearly five decades Blanqui had been one of the most conspicuous and controversial figures in the revolutionary movement. Although his ideas had not been systematically formulated, he was known to advocate the overthrow of middle-class society by a disciplined group of conspirators, who would use force and the class struggle to establish a dictatorship. But it was not his views so much as his age and the near forty years he had spent in prison for radical activity that made Blanqui important in the years following the Paris Commune. Thus it was that he became a key figure in the drama of the amnesty.

The first candidacy of the " Man Who was Locked Up," came about because of the death of F. V. Raspail, the eighty-four year old Deputy of Bouches-du-Rhône and author of the first full amnesty bill. His funeral on January 13 brought out large crowds of the Parisian proletariat.[13] About this same time, a rumor was going around that several Republican Deputies had once again asked for Blanqui's pardon, but had been handed a formal refusal by Dufaure.[14] The earliest recorded mention of running Blanqui for Raspail's place was made at the January 20 banquet held by the group of Revolutionary Socialists associated with the paper *L'Egalité*. On that occasion, Blanqui's name was cheered, and it was pointed out that the people of Marseilles could get him out of jail by electing him Deputy.[15] A week later, these arguments were repeated in an article which Gabriel Deville wrote for *L'Egalité*.[16] By a month later, the seed had taken root, and some of the voters of the 2nd circumscription of Marseilles were reportedly planning to submit Blanqui's name to one of the nominating committees. At Paris, *L'Egalité* was jubilant and urged the election of Blanqui for humanitarian motives and for " the glory of the voters of Marseilles." [17] It is significant that the amnesty was not mentioned at all.

Three days later it was learned that the Marseilles committee had formally named as candidate Clovis Hugues, editor of *La Jeune République*. *L'Egalité* urged the voters of Marseilles nevertheless to cast their ballots for Blanqui.[18] After the first balloting, held on March 3, in which Blanqui did get a few scattered votes, Clovis Hugues was called upon to retire from the ballotage. A mass meeting held in Paris on March 4 passed a futile resolution demanding that he do so " in order to enable universal suffrage *to amnesty* the old Socialist fighter." [19] A general amnesty rather than Blanqui personally now became the rallying cry of the Socialists. " A self-styled partisan of

---

[13] *L'Egalité*, January 20, 1878, 4:1.

[14] *Ibid.*, January 20, 1878, 3:2-3.

[15] There is no indication of any talk about running Blanqui before this; and when the idea had caught on everywhere, the *L'Egalité* group was first to claim credit for it.

[16] *L'Egalité*, January 27, 1878, 4:3-5:1. Zévaès (*Auguste Blanqui, patriote et socialiste français* [Paris, 1920], 104) identifies the article as from Deville's pen.

[17] *L'Egalité*, February 24, 1878, 5:2-3.

[18] *Ibid.*, March 3, 1878, 4:1.

[19] *Ibid.*, March 10, 1878, 5:3.

amnesty, . . . [Clovis Hugues] makes his own ambitious person-
ality an obstacle to the success of the most imposing demonstration possible on behalf of this great measure of justice. . . .
If the Moderate wins, it will be M. Clovis Hugues's fault; his
inhuman obstinacy will have prevented the unopposed candidacy
of M. Blanqui from rallying the numerous votes of all those
who sincerely want an amnesty." [20]

But Clovis Hugues did not retire; neither did he win on the
second ballot.[21] With 4284, he ran second to the old Republican
Amat's 4422. Blanqui trailed with 564,[22] which was " about
the same number of votes as the first time." [23]

The identification of the Blanqui campaign with the fight
for an amnesty was next made explicitly clear when some of
the citizens of Marseilles asked MacMahon for Blanqui's
release. His sister, Madame Antoine, wrote a letter to the local
press stating emphatically that Blanqui did not want pardon—
that such was not the point of the campaign in his name. The
friends who had sponsored his candidacy, she wrote, " had,
above everything else, as the objective of this demonstration,
an appeal for a general amnesty, giving the same justice to all,
after such long years of persecution." [24]

Further Blanqui Campaigns

Despite the failure at Marseilles, the idea of running Blanqui
as a tactic in the fight for an amnesty gained in popularity.

[20] *Ibid.*, March 17, 1878, 5:2-3.

[21] Four years later, when Clovis Hugues applied for membership in the
Socialist *Parti ouvrier*, he was challenged with his refusal to withdraw in favor
of Blanqui in 1878. In extenuation, Clovis Hugues explained that " If Citizen
Blanqui had been presented by the Socialist groups, he would have retired
before him, but that his name was serving as a maneuver of the Opportunist
groups at Marseilles, and that—in spite of his veneration for Blanqui—he had
had to take into account only the question of principle."
This was accepted, and the National Executive Committee of the party in
its meeting of June 25, 1882, voted unanimously to admit him. (Parti ouvrier
socialiste français, cinquième congrès national, *Séances* [Paris, 1882], 33.) There
is no proof of Clovis Hugues's allegations. Moreover, the names of Blanqui's
Marseilles sponsors included Jean Lombard and Edouard Blanqui (see *L'Egalité*,
June 2, 1878, 7:3, telegram from " the Democratic Socialists of Marseilles " to
the Blanqui committee of the VIth arrondissement).

[22] Bourloton, III, 371.

[23] *L'Egalité*, March 24, 1878, 4:3.

[24] *Ibid.*, March 24, 1878, 4:2; reprinted from *Le Peuple* (Marseilles).

Thus, when the Deputy from the Ist arrondissement of Avignon, Demaine, was invalidated, the candidacy of Blanqui was again proposed in letters to the local newspapers.[25] Similarly, a group of voters at L'Isle-sur-la-Sorgue wrote that " of all the candidacies that can be presented, that of Blanqui is the most significant! " [26] And from Paris's XIIth arrondissement, congratulations were sent to the voters of L'Isle-sur-la-Sorgue, in line with a suggestion made by Emile Gautier.[27] The idea of a Blanqui candidacy as a demand for amnesty was spreading even to the little towns, and the Socialists were delighted. " We are happy to see that such a large number of citizens, throughout the reaches of the Republic, are taking up again the proposal which came from *L'Egalité's* initiative." [28]

Of all Blanqui's early campaigns, however, the most important was in the VIth arrondissement of Paris, to fill the place left vacant by the death of Colonel Denfert-Rochereau. At a private meeting of the voters of the VIth on Sunday May 19, the candidacy of Blanqui was unanimously adopted.[29] A committee was elected, and in the face of almost insurmountable obstacles, a campaign was made for Blanqui. As Guillet, a carpenter and a member of this committee, told of their difficulties, " Needless to say, not a single newspaper dared support this candidacy. After much trouble, we succeeded in finding several hundreds of francs to put up placards on which a Government stamp was required, since Blanqui—a prisoner under this gracious Republic—could not affix his signature." [30] In all, a little over 750 francs was raised before the end of the campaign.[31] Blanqui was presented as the candidate for full amnesty. " To vote for Auguste Blanqui . . . means to protest effectively in favor of an amnesty, so ardently desired, so long in coming," wrote

[25] *Ibid.*, April 14, 1878, 4:3.
[26] *Ibid.*, April 14, 1878, 6:2.
[27] *Ibid.*, April 28, 1878, 6:2.
[28] *Idem.*
[29] *Ibid.*, May 27, 1878, 4:2.
[30] Letter of Guillet in *Le Prolétaire*, March 1, 1879, 7:3; letter dated Paris, February 12, 1878 (this is a typographical error in *Le Prolétaire*, for the date should read February 12, 1879).
[31] *L'Egalité*, June 30, 1878, 8:3. Gabriel Deville was recorded as having personally contributed 20 francs (*ibid.*, May 27, 1878, 6:2-3).

L'Egalité,[32] and not one, it was said, of Blanqui's opponents had the nerve to come out openly against an amnesty.[33]

Since the election was not to be until July 7, there was plenty of time for expression of opinion. The " Democratic Socialists " of Marseilles, led by Jean Lombard, who was the following year to play a major part in the Socialists' success at the Marseilles Congress, wired congratulations to *L'Egalité* on the candidacy.[34] Meetings were held and collections made even in the Ist and XIth arrondissements at the end of May.[35] Next, the *L'Egalité* group organized a meeting on June 5 of voters of Paris and the suburbs at the Salle des Ecoles, rue d'Arras, to endorse the candidacy of Blanqui. Congratulations were voted to the leaders of the VIth arrondissement. Most important of all, a resolution was adopted to run Blanqui in every vacancy that developed until he should be elected.[36] On June 9, a campaign biography written by Deville, the future translator of *Capital*, went on sale in Paris under the title of *Blanqui libre*. On June 25, some of Gambetta's own constituents held a meeting at the Salle Patras, Boulevard de Belleville, and declared unanimously in favor of the resolution of the Salle des Ecoles meeting. Their own resolution pledged them to use " all their strength, morally and materially," for Blanqui's campaign in the VIth, since " Blanqui's candidacy is a striking declaration in favor of a full and immediate amnesty." [37] Three days before the election, the voters of the IIIrd arrondissement met at the Salle Diderot and pledged their support to Blanqui because, " In the face of the refusal by those who have been elected to enact a general amnesty, it is the right and the duty of the voters to amnesty piecemeal, individually, all the victims of the tricolored reaction." [38]

---

[32] *Ibid.*, May 19, 1878, 5:1-2. This paper also argued that a vote for Blanqui was a vote for the " social revolution." In subsequent issues, even more emphasis was placed on Blanqui as a " Socialist." Extracts from his writings were published to show that the *L'Egalité* group claimed him as their own. See, for example, May 27, 1878, 4:1-2.

[33] Guillet in *Le Prolétaire*, March 1, 1879, 7:3.

[34] *L'Egalité*, June 2, 1878, 7:3. On the Marseilles Congress, see below, pages 287-96.

[35] *Ibid.*, June 23, 1878, 4:3; June 30, 1878, 8:3.

[36] *Ibid.*, June 9, 1878, 5:2.

[37] *Ibid.*, June 30, 1878, 8:3.

[38] *Ibid.*, July 7, 1878, 3:3.

But resolutions did not mean votes. On July 7, Blanqui polled 618 votes—only 4½ per cent of the total—while his opponent Hérisson got 8,931.[39] That was the story. It was not yet possible in 1878 to get any substantial number of votes out for a Socialist candidate who stood for full amnesty. Neither the appeal of Socialism nor of amnesty could overcome the indifference of the voters. The Blanqui committee, undiscouraged, could only shrug its shoulders: "As for us who have supported Blanqui and his principles, we will continue to shake the guilty indolence of some men, and to unmask the bad faith of others."[40] It was only mildly heartening to learn that on the same day, in the little town of Saint-Geniès de Malgoirès, in the meridional department of Gard, twenty-five ballots had been cast for Blanqui in a write-in vote. Thus, said L'Egalité, should be a lesson for the voters of the VIth arrondissement.[41]

Blanqui's signal failure in 1878 showed both the lack of public interest in the amnesty question and the weakness of the Socialists, who had not been able to attract a following, even though they had made the amnesty cause their own. But the Blanqui campaigns were only one element in the agitation for an amnesty which was fostered during the course of 1878. With their support of Blanqui, the Socialists combined a movement to threaten reprisals against those Deputies who had not lived up to their campaign promises to vote a general amnesty, and to create a lively public sentiment in favor of the measure so as to make this threat effective. This they did by organizing many public meetings and by ceaseless publicity carried on in the columns first of L'Egalité, and then, when it disappeared, in Le Prolétaire.

The first general meeting held on the amnesty question came in February 1878, in the Salle des Ecoles, rue d'Arras. All the Deputies of Paris and the members of the General Council of the Seine were summoned to appear, but not one came to the meeting.[42] A second rally brought nearly 1500 persons together in the same hall on March 4, again to demand an amnesty. This

[39] Ibid., July 14, 1878, 6:2.
[40] Guillet in Le Prolétaire, March 1, 1879, 7:3.
[41] July 14, 1878, 2:3.
[42] Le Prolétaire, December 21, 1878, 6:1.

meeting, the one that called on Clovis Hugues to desist for Blanqui at Marseilles, also voted to put a wreath on Raspail's grave, with the inscription, " To Raspail, from the Friends of Amnesty." [43] Two weeks after this meeting came the anniversary of the Commune, March 18. Commemorative banquets were held throughout Paris—and even in the provinces. In Belleville, in Gambetta's home territory, over two hundred assembled that Monday night.[44]

These banquets, representing as they did, one more step in the glorification of the Commune, served as one more factor which was going to make the winning of an amnesty doubly difficult, by seeming to furnish proof, so far as conservative opinion was concerned, that the Commune had in fact been the work of the International. These banquets, moreover, were held openly, and the Socialists marvelled that the police had not had " the maladdress to prohibit them." [45] But almost immediately afterward, the police raided the homes of all the men who had been active organizers of the amnesty meetings and the banquets —the homes of Jules Guesde, Emile Gautier, Hippolyte Bouffenoir, Jeallot, and the others. Next, as the Government moved to crush all radicalism in the bud, several aliens who had been close to the L'Egalité group were arrested. Andrea Costa, Zanardelli, and Anna Koulichof—to mention only three—were tried and convicted of being members of the outlawed International.[46]

<hr />

[43] L'Egalité, March 10, 1878, 5:3. Presumably this was the meeting Emile Gautier referred to when he said, " This time, the Deputies had been summoned by registered letters. They replied to us with insults. No one put in an appearance except one or two municipal councillors." (Le Prolétaire, December 28, 1878, 6:1.)

[44] On the banquets, see L'Egalité, March 24, 1878, 5:1, 6:1; and Ossip Zetkin, Der Sozialismus in Frankreich seit der Pariser Kommune (Berlin, 1894), 14; Peter Kropotkin, Memoirs of a revolutionary (Boston, 1930), 406, remarks, " There were not twenty of us to carry on the movement, not two hundred openly to support it. At the first commemoration of the Commune, in March, 1878, we surely were not two hundred."

[45] L'Egalité, March 24, 1878, 5:1.

[46] See Zévaès, De la semaine sanglante au congrès de Marseille, 18, and Guillaume, IV, 321. On the trials of Costa, Zanardelli, Nabruzzi, and others, see L'Egalité, April 28, 1878, 6:2, and May 12, 1878, 1:1-3.

It is interesting to note the effect which his experience in French prisons apparently had on Andrea Costa. Writing in the summer of 1879, while in prison in Paris, Costa—who had been one of the most revolutionary of the

But repression was not able, by 1878, to kill the movement for an amnesty. At a private meeting held in Montmartre on April 2, a committee of six men, obscure figures all,[47] was named to organize a Department-wide meeting on amnesty. This committee then issued a public call for all electoral groups which had had plenary amnesty in their platforms to get in touch with the committee right away, so that it could " convoke them in time to a meeting, at which the order of business will be to summon our representatives to keep their word, given to those who voted for them." [48] Several weeks later, on May 23, about 1500 people attended the meeting held at the Salle des Ecoles, presided over by the youthful Paulard, who was rapidly emerging as one of the more active Socialists in Paris.[49] A resolution was adopted calling upon all the Deputies and Senators of the Seine " to introduce, before the end of the session, in the Chamber and in the Senate, a bill granting full amnesty to all those condemned for the communalist revolution of 1870-71." If this were not done, the resolution continued, " all the citizens here assembled formally pledge themselves to fight with every means in their power against the re-election of our present representatives, and to convoke—in every arrondissement where possible—private meetings at which the mask will be torn from this policy that makes every democrat worthy of the name feel heartsick." The concurrence in this resolution of three municipal councillors—Cottiau, Maillard, and Darlot —not present at the meeting was announced.[50] Next, a collection of nearly two hundred francs was taken up and divided

Italian Socialists—now urged his party to make a fundamental change in tactics, in the direction of evolutionary socialism. (Roberto Michels, *Le prolétariat et la bourgeoisie dans le mouvement socialiste italien, particulièrement des origines à 1906* (Paris, 1921), 141.)

[47] Rébillat, Ory, Arnaud (not Antoine Arnaud, who was still in exile in London), Leclerc, Jouanneau, and Séné.

[48] *L'Egalité*, April 21, 1878, 8:3.

[49] Paulard was one of the *L'Egalité* group. It was he who presided over the July 1880 Paris Regional Congress of the *Parti ouvrier*, when the first break between the Marxists and the moderates in the political labor movement took place. (See *Le Siècle* [Paris, daily], July 21, 1880, 1:1-2, and July 23, 1880, 2:3.)

[50] *L'Egalité*, May 27, 1878, 8:2.

equally between the Blanqui Committee of the VIth arrondissement and the London committee for aid to political prisoners.[51]

Three days later, to commemorate the defeat of the Commune, *L'Egalité* organized a banquet at the Salon des Familles,
avenue de Saint-Mandé. This was the "seventh anniversary
of the Bloody Week," and those present—around two or three
hundred—dedicated themselves to work for the condemned men
of the Commune and for Socialism.[52]

The Press

From January to May, the paper *L'Egalité* never missed an
opportunity to point out what the denial of an amnesty meant.
Through its pages the evolution of the cult of the Commune
can be traced. The Commune, first and foremost, had been
"Socialist" in its nature; all who suffered because of their
participation in it were the martyrs of the French proletariat;
and finally, the campaign to win an amnesty for the Commune
was the classic manifestation of the undying class struggle. To
show this, particularly to show that there could never be peace
between the men of the Government and the heirs of the Commune, was *L'Egalité's* aim.

The men dead and the men dying because of the heartless-
ness of the Government was an oft-repeated theme. At Neuf-
châtel, ran one report, the police prohibited fellow exiles from
attending the funeral of Charles Beslay,[53] who—elected from
the VIth arrondissement—had presided at the opening session
of the Commune. At Geneva, "death by apoplexy," instead of
an amnesty, put an end to "the long proscription" of Razoua,
commander of the *Ecole militaire* under the Commune.[54] Verdure, member of the Commune from the XIth arrondissement,
had died in New Caledonia, although it had been possible for
his daughter to have received a civic funeral in Paris, with a
speech by the Deputy Talandier.[55] And meanwhile, as *L'Egalité*
pointed out, arrests and prosecutions were going ahead.
"Messieurs the members of the military tribunals are anxious

[51] *Idem.*
[52] *Ibid.*, June 2, 1878, 7:1-3.
[53] *Ibid.*, April 7, 1878, 7:2-3.
[54] *Ibid.*, July 7, 1878, 8:2.
[55] *Ibid.*, March 31, 1878, 8:2.

to earn their fees and sit as often as possible." [56] The son of Treillard, the Commune's Director of Public Assistance, had just returned to France, according to one feature story, and had been condemned *in absentia* by a court which had dwelt with horror on the Commune's alleged burning of prisoners alive.[57] Three more cases of *in absentia* convictions were announced at the end of April.[58] And much was made of the story of how Varlin's family had had to suffer the indignity of requesting from the authorities proof that he really had been killed on May 28, 1871, so that they would no longer be hounded by officials trying to arrest the same Varlin under a contumacious conviction of November 30, 1872.[59] Nothing better could be expected, the paper implied, from a Government which was renaming a street in Nantes "Rue Thiers"; "*Rue des Massacres de mai*" would be a more suitable name, said *L'Egalité*.[60] "The Broad Mercy" of the President, charged an article with that title, was a fraud.[61]

As for the Republican politicians, it was *L'Egalité*'s opinion that they had decided that "The amnesty will have to be put off still further while the Republic republicanizes itself some more." [62] Louis Blanc himself was reported as having said that the time for an amnesty had not yet come.[63]

Thus, week after week, *L'Egalité* plugged away at the suffering of the Communards and the duplicity of the men in power. And further to emphasize the significance of the Paris Commune, *L'Egalité* appeared printed in red ink during the weeks when the red flag of the Commune had flown over Paris. "March the Eighteenth . . . to express ourselves on the subject of this date is not possible; to write what we think is forbidden," the editors lamented.[64]

[56] *Ibid.*, January 13, 1878, 8:1-2.
[57] *Idem.*
[58] *Ibid.*, April 28, 1878, 8:2-3.
[59] *Ibid.*, February 3, 1878, 8:1-3. See also Lissagaray, *Histoire de la Commune*, 432.
[60] *L'Egalité*, May 12, 1878, 1:3.
[61] *Ibid.*, June 16, 1878, 8:1.
[62] *Ibid.*, May 27, 1878, 1:1-3. Compare with the March 24 statement (3:1-3) that the amnesty "instead of drawing nearer, appears to be moving still farther away as the Republic becomes more republican."
[63] *Idem.*
[64] *Ibid.*, March 24, 1878, 5:1.

No matter what the politicians might say, for *L'Egalité* the fact remained that the Commune had been a battle of the classes. " And to want to reduce to the stature of a simple attack on the political and governmental structure of the France of 1871 a revolution which—in the wake of its defeat—has brought such universal results is to turn your back on the evidence." [65] On the eve of May 28, the first page of *L'Egalité* boldly headlined " The Bloody Decade " and wrote, " In the name of the vanquished, we must keep oblivion from surrounding the conditions of their defeat." [66]

But *L'Egalite's* strongest attack on the Government with reference to the denial of an amnesty came in connection with the national festival of June 30. Held as part of the International Exposition of 1878, the fête of June 30 was the first official merrymaking Paris had seen since the last celebration of Napoleon Day in 1869. There were dancers on every corner, concerts at the Palais Royal and the Tuileries, and parades and fireworks in the evening.[67] The Republicans regarded the day as a great success: it was " truly a festival of all "; [68] Paris had never seen a festival like it; and it was all to the credit of the regime. " Oh Republic! You are still only a little spark. Tomorrow you will be the sun! " was said to be the near-universal sentiment. The Government organized the affair well. To insure harmony it handed out two francs apiece to 45,000 needy families,[69] while the *Journal officiel* announced that for the occasion, pardons were being granted to more of the convicted Communards.[70] It seemed, therefore, that as the total effect of June 30, the Republic and the people were one—for the moment. *L'Egalité* must destroy this harmony if possible. Look at the figures on pardons, it urged its readers, and " the necessity of an amnesty will appear to you all." [71] The true Paris —the Paris of the workshops—was not, it continued, to be

[65] *Ibid.*, March 24, 1878, 2:2-3:1-3.
[66] *Ibid.*, May 27, 1878, 1:1-3.
[67] See Max S. Nordau, *Paris unter der Dritten Republik* (Leipzig, 1881), 277-292 for details of the fête.
[68] Comments on the fête from *Le Temps*, July 1-2, 1878, 1:1, 2:6, 3:1-3.
[69] *Ibid.*, July 1-2, 1878, 3:3.
[70] *Journal officiel*, June 30, 1878, 7185:3.
[71] *L'Egalité*, July 7, 1878, 4:3.

seduced by a popular festival: " It forgets neither the amnesty which has been refused after having been made necessary [in the first place], nor the capitalistic extortions of which its labor is the object and by which its poverty is caused." [72]

But *L'Egalité* went too far this time. On July 14, 1878, it was suppressed on the charge of " apologizing for acts designated as crimes " [73]—that is, for its praise of the Commune. Each time the Government, nervous about its internal security, struck at its Socialist critics, it did the very thing which would give credance to the charges *L'Egalité* had made during its brief lifetime. Far from putting an end to the extra-parliamentary campaign for an amnesty, the Government was doing its part, negative though it was, in making the Paris Commune a great proletarian legend, and thereby guaranteeing that the amnesty fight would gain momentum. The suppression of a newspaper might deprive the Socialists of one means for presenting their views on the amnesty question to the people, but it would also serve to intensify their determination to vindicate the Commune.

The next blow against radical leadership of the amnesty fight came with the imprisonment of Guesde and his associates for violating the law prohibiting meetings of unauthorized organizations. The Lyons Workers' Congress earlier in the year 1878 had voted to hold a special international labor congress at Paris that fall to receive labor delegations to the Exposition. On September 5, thirty members of the committee of organization for this international congress were arrested when they tried to meet at the Salle Petrelle.[74] Their trial before the Tenth Correctional Chamber was an extremely important event in the early history of French Marxism, for it was the first full statement of the new collectivist point of view to reach a large number of French workers, because of the attention the press paid to the trial. Indirectly, of course, whatever strengthened the Socialists at this time would also strengthen the demand for a general amnesty. For a Government intent on consolidating its position in the hearts and minds of the people, this trial, because of the notoriety it attained, was a colossal blunder. Not

---

[72] *Ibid.*, July 7, 1878, 1:2-3; article, " Le 30 juin."
[73] Zévaès, *De la semaine sanglante au congrès de Marseille*, 70.
[74] See *Le Temps*, September 8, 1878, 2:5.

only the Socialists, but the Radical Republicans as well, felt that the Government had at last over-reached itself. The day after the arrests, Lockroy called on Minister of the Interior Marcère to protest the action.[75] Other Deputies of the Extreme Left were equally disturbed, and a meeting was held at the home of Louis Blanc on the afternoon of September 10 to discuss the dissolution of the congress. It was not a question of doctrine or of the aim of the congress, but only whether there had been any infringement of the rights of citizens.[76]

The effect of the trial of the international congress on the amnesty fight was evident almost immediately. The most conspicuous development during the closing months of 1878 was the increasingly outspoken disillusionment of the friends of amnesty with any and all Republican politicians: " In view of the way they carry on against the Socialists, in view of the inertia and supineness of those who accepted the engagement to introduce a bill for a full and complete amnesty every six months until they should have attained it, we may well be permitted to doubt their good faith and their political honor." [77]

This theme was to be repeated many times in *Le Prolétaire*, a new paper, first appearing in November 1878, which subscribed to no one school of political or economic thought, and which insisted only on the thorough-going labor character of its contributors. This alone was a sign of the growing articulateness of the class-conscious French workers in the post-Commune period. Moreover, because of *Le Prolétaire's* doctrinal independence, its columns were open to a wide range of opinion on the Commune and on the amnesty question. But every writer on the subject—and there were many—agreed that there must be a full amnesty immediately, and that only the people themselves could be the agents for obtaining it.

Carrying on the work of *L'Egalité* in trying to arouse public opinion over the amnesty question, *Le Prolétaire* missed no opportunity, no matter how slight, for calling attention to what the Opportunists really represented. When news of the death

---

[75] *Idem.*, and *ibid.*, September 9, 1878, 2:5. On the sentences imposed, see *ibid.*, October 26, 1878, 3:6.

[76] *Ibid.*, September 11, 1878, 2:4.

[77] *Le Prolétaire*, December 18, 1878, 3:1. Article signed " Daniel."

of La Cécilia, commander of the Commune's Second Corps, reached France, it was pointed out that these victims of the Commune had died " from their love of the country and the Republic." [78] When the military tribunals claimed a new victim, Hadaucourt, a workman in chased bronze, *Le Prolétaire* demanded, " Will they have the rare audacity to make us witness the execution of a Communard, *eight years after the Commune?* " [79] When the Municipal Council of Saint-Etienne passed a resolution in favor of a general amnesty, this was reported with Emile Chausse's comment, " And to think that our Opportunists will only vote it when there is no longer anyone left to amnesty, as if it weren't the oppressors who will have to be pardoned for the blood and the tears they could have avoided with a little bit of humanity." [80]

Of great interest was the letter, published by *Le Prolétaire* from an unnamed Communard who was now at hard labor in New Caledonia to one of the Deputies of the Seine. The author of this moving letter explained that it would be dishonorable for him to apply for a pardon or a commutation of his sentence: " Would it be just that I, as the result of an appeal made by me and seconded by men of your character, should see this ignoble sentence withdrawn from me, while others than myself —just as Republican as I . . .—remain in chains? " The writer of this letter had grave doubts about the character of the current regime in France: " We are a Republic, yes or no. If yes, the Government must make it evident by proceeding as near as possible toward equality, especially equality in the application of the law and in the dispensation of favors." [81] The most interesting point about this letter was not its expression of solidarity with all the proscribed Communards. But it was the first such printed statement to be ascribed to one who was actually suffering in New Caledonia. For the exiles, living in Geneva or in London, to take such a stand was one thing. For the men at Canala to do so was another and more meaningful expression of this solidarity.

[78] *Ibid.*, December 7, 1878, 2:3.
[79] *Ibid.*, December 28, 1878, 7:3. See also December 18, 1878, 3:1.
[80] *Ibid.*, December 14, 1878, 4:1.
[81] *Ibid.*, January 1, 1879, 6:1-2. Letter dated Canala, August 1878.

When the Radical Deputy Georges Périn took steps to induce the Government to segregate—as the least it could do—the political prisoners at New Caledonia from the common criminals, *Le Prolétaire* was quick to point out that " There is no better way of isolating them than to open again the doors of their homes and their country to these citizens whom you hold some thousands of leagues away from here, in the name . . . of family and property." [82] And when the Government did make a gesture toward improved treatment of the Communards by separating them from the others at New Caledonia, *Le Prolétaire* asked, " Is it, therefore, that despite your prejudices you have kept some esteem for them?" If this were so, " Then why not have recourse to an amnesty? Why not restore their homeland to these exiles who, as you well know, have suffered every moral and physical torture?" But, the article continued, *Le Prolétaire* had been informed, by a man in high position, that there could be no hope for an amnesty before several months, because " Out of consideration for foreign sovereigns, . . . the Government and our lawmakers want to let all the ruckus that has been raised over the Socialists die out." Here then was another effect the trial of the international congress had on the amnesty controversy. As for this nice regard for foreign relations, *Le Prolétaire* was indignant. " That policy is unworthy of France; it is unworthy of a country which wants to break with the habits of the past in order to obey only the principles of democratic societies." [83]

When Gambetta delivered one of his hedging speeches, the readers of *Le Prolétaire* got an interpretation of it, boiled down to three main points: " 1. We must have still more patience than that which he has exhausted, which is not a little thing to say; 2. We are going to enter into a period of difficulties— *Postponement of the amnesty*; 3. M. Gambetta does not wish to be Premier, because he is certain that the Executive would make him do a somersault similar to the one his artful confederate M. Jules Simon performed." [84] As for Gambetta in general, *Le Prolétaire* had little sympathy for " the man who

[82] *Ibid.*, December 25, 1878, 4:2.
[83] *Ibid.*, December 25, 1878, 1:1, 2:1.
[84] *Ibid.*, December 28, 1878, 6:2.

denies the existence of the social question as the ostrich avoids danger by hiding his head in the sand." [85]

Finally, when the Paris Municipal Council voted 30,000 francs into the 1879 budget for aid to the families of political prisoners, *Le Prolétaire* made this a front-page item.[86]

By such continual small references, sometimes direct, sometimes oblique, to the amnesty question, *Le Prolétaire* lived up to the policy stated in its very first issue: " The newspaper *Le Prolétaire* considers it its duty to protest with energy and to demand in a loud voice an amnesty, a full and complete amnesty." The Government's policy of "large mercy," V. Pierre had written on that date, was wholly inadequate; " That is not forgetfulness; that effaces nothing." Even the idea that the pardoning power had been widely used—as Dufaure claimed—was " derisive." " Six years after the event, the number of convicted men that they've used it on is only one third of the total figure." The Republic should beware of the effect such a policy would have on the Communards, he had written: " Perhaps they will curse this Republic which seems to take delight in perpetuating the hatreds of the past; and who knows? Perhaps in a certain quarter, they'd be pleased that this should be so." But the Communards—and this had been the major theme of the article—were staunch Republicans. " The exiles, the condemned men of 1871, all know that the Republic has nothing to do with their misfortune; they all know that they owe it to those who pretend to save society

[85] *Ibid.*, December 25, 1878, 4:3.

[86] *Ibid.*, December 28, 1878, 1:3. The distribution of these municipal funds had long been a source of annoyance to the friends of an amnesty. The committee in charge of their distribution was headed by the Deputy for the XIIth arrondissement, Greppo, who, as vice-president of the Extreme Left, had voted for a full and complete amnesty. After the election of October 14, 1877, however, Greppo had drawn closer and closer to the Opportunists. (Bourloton, III, 253.) His committee had been attacked as far back as January 1878, in *L'Egalité*, with the observation that Republican politicians ought to practice what they preach. " These reflections occur to us because of the way in which the committee in charge of distribution of aid to the families of political prisoners acts; in this respect, curious things—so it seems—are happening. We've had pointed out to us, . . . as distributor of relief in a certain arrondissement of the Left Bank, a personage who in many meetings has repeatedly fought furiously against the amnesty; they tell us that he is seconded in his task by his wife, who imposes on the unhappy wives of the deportees whom she has come to aid the revolting obligation of attending Mass." (January 6, 1878, 4:2.)

by thus casting an anathema upon a part of that very society!"
For this very reason, there must be an amnesty; "Those who
are absent must be given back to their country, their families,
their friends; all the sons of the Republic must be enabled
to array themselves at her side, to support her, to make her
move ahead, and to defend her if need be." To put off the
enactment of an amnesty any longer "would be to sell short
the prosperity, the honor, and the glory of the French Republic."
The time had come: "Here it is seven years that France has
lived under a government which calls itself Republican; here
it is seven years that all French workingmen, unceasingly
inspired and sustained by love of the Republic and the fatherland, anxious to forget the troubles of the past . . . , have been
laboring without respite . . . , and above all, here it is seven
years that a majority in our deliberating assemblies has refused
to forget and lets the cruel consequences of our civil discords
weigh down a part of the population." [87]

The refusal of the elected representatives of the people to
vote an amnesty had, throughout the year 1878, been the chief
emphasis of the Socialist campaign for an amnesty. The mass
meeting of May 23 had formally resolved to fight the re-election
of men who sat in the Chamber of Deputies or the Senate and
who had failed to enact an amnesty. A second mass meeting
of this sort was held on December 15, 1878, at the Salle Diderot.
In the seven months which had elapsed between the two meetings, much had happened to destroy further any respect the
people had had for the Government. There had been the
suppression of *L'Egalité*, the trial of the international congress,
and—above all—the persistent failure of the Deputies and the
Senators even to consider an amnesty. The December meeting,
standing by the May 23 resolution, was unanimously of the
opinion that something had to be done. "The resolution
adopted by a great popular meeting must not rest a dead letter;
it must be realized; and finally, we must be logical and con-
sistent with ourselves, and we must not undo the next day what
we did the night before." With perhaps unwarranted optimism,
the speaker Aubré found that "the cause of an amnesty has
so advanced that those who rule us are afraid of it; that is

[87] *Le Prolétaire*, November 23, 1878, 2:2.

why the Government has tried to feel out the ground in order to exploit it in connection with the Senatorial elections." Certainly, it was true that the forthcoming Senatorial elections would be a determining factor in the history of the amnesty. The meeting at the Salle Diderot was well aware of this, and Emile Gautier urged on this occasion that they make the most of their opportunity, saying, " On the eve of the Senatorial elections we ought to demand an amnesty more than ever before, by every possible means." This former lawyer, who by 1878 was moving toward anarchism, had become during these past few months one of the dominant figures in the amnesty fight.[88] He had been secretary of the May 23 meeting; now, at the December meeting, he gave the opening address—an analysis of the present situation which he found " very favorable for an amnesty." Next he was the chief member of the new committee elected to carry out the resolutions of this meeting.[89]

The new committee immediately issued a proclamation which reviewed the record and the intentions of the Republican politicians and made a stirring appeal to the people themselves to act at once, to act in order to get an amnesty, to act—in short— to establish the Republic, the true Republic. Soon, wrote Gautier, it would be eight years since " Paris revolted in order to save the Republic, which was threatened to its very foundations by an unrepresentative assembly." Those who had escaped

---

[88] Emile Gautier has been termed the typical French intellectual anarchist (Max Nettlau, *Anarchisten und Sozial-revolutionäre; die historische Entwicklung des Anarchismus in den Jahren 1880-1886* [*Beiträge zur Geschichte des Sozialismus, Syndikalismus, und Anarchismus*, Band V] [Berlin, 1931], 299), and has been ranked second only to Elisée Réclus and Kropotkin as the major influence on French anarchism (Zetkin, *Die Sozialismus in Frankreich*, 42). He also has been labelled the " real apostle " of those Communards who adopted anarchism in their years of exile (Ernest Alfred Vizetelly, *The Anarchists* [New York, 1911], 65; this is a highly amusing work for both the naïveté of the author and its factual errors). Contemporary recognition of his importance was the heavy sentence—along with Kropotkin's, the heaviest sentence—imposed on him in the celebrated Lyons trials of January 1883. His importance ended, however, in 1886, when he was pardoned on condition of giving up all political activity. He then turned to writing articles for *Le Figaro* and for *Le XIXᵉ siècle* (see Anne Léo Zévaès, *Louise Michel* [Paris, 1936], 23, fn. [1]).

[89] For details of the December meeting, see *Le Prolétaire*, December 21, 1878, 6:1-2. Other members of the committee were Grégoire, Dufour, Choix, Boqueste, Caryer, Pagès, Albaret, Guibaudet, Lefebvre, Gallois, Bouillon, Abel jeune, Sage, and the later-to-be-denounced-as-*agent-provocateur* Dupire.

the slaughter, " are still groaning, at this very hour, under the inhospitable sun of exile or in the depths of the dungeons at New Caledonia! Some even are in penitentiaries, riven by the same irons as the worst malefactors." The continuation of arrests made it seem that " in proportion to the way the broad clemency [of the Government] restores certain of the former to a derisive freedom, they try immediately to fill up the gaps in the convicts' ranks." As for a genuine attempt to overthrow the Republic, the abortive May Sixteenth *coup d'état* had happened less than a year ago, but the authors of this act were free even to sit in parliament. There had been hopes that in connection with the Exposition of 1878, " which they so pretentiously called ' The International Festival of Peace and Labor,' the fatherland would be restored to those workers, victims of the civil war, who had been the glory and the honor of French industry." The amnesty could not be put off. Death would not wait, and soon there would be only corpses to receive an amnesty, continued the proclamation. But what could be expected, it then asked, from an assembly that took a year even to validate its own membership. Consequently, it announced, " This time, it is to public opinion directly that we must address ourselves, no longer to those who bear our mandate, no longer to the representative but to the represented; no longer to the servant but to the master; and we will say to the people: ' Since it is you who are sovereign, take into your hands the cause of amnesty, which your agents have not wished to be burdened with.' "

There was already backstairs talk in the Chamber of Deputies, the proclamation went on, of " throwing public opinion a bone to gnaw and, as soon as the new session opens, of introducing a partial amnesty bill." Nothing could be worse than a partial amnesty: " As though an amnesty, which is synonymous with a forgetting, could be fractional!" Moreover, " Since it was an entire party which was defeated, condemned, proscribed, so likewise the doors of the country must be opened to the entire party." The people must rise in indignation against the parliamentary treachery of a partial amnesty. " Sovereign people," the proclamation urged, " make your loud voice heard. You have the right, you have the strength; it is incumbent upon you to protest fruitfully against the iniquitous *hoax of a partial amnesty*. It behooves you to raise from one end of France to another an imposing revolt of conscience." Without an amnesty, the proclamation concluded, there could be no Republic. " The Republic does not yet seem to be irresistably established, since the most devoted of its children are away from it. The gage of its definitive triumph will be a full and complete amnesty. It's up to you, the people, who for this Republic have spilled— without counting the cost—so much blood, so much money, and so many tears, to exact it and to get it." [90]

So ended the year 1878. For the New Year, *Le Prolétaire* wished, " To our friends who are dying on the beaches of New Caledonia, . . . , the return to their country; but they can take our wish as hollow mockery. They know that there is no pity in our political Opportunists. To have compassion for the sufferings of others, there must be a heart, and these grotesque Machiavellis don't have any." [91]

So ended the year 1878. And the year 1879 began with a summons to *Le Prolétaire* for having printed the proclamation issued by the Gautier committee. In reply, *Le Prolétaire* pointed out that since the Bonapartist press could say anything and get away with it, this action was proof " that the bourgeoisie fears

[90] *Ibid.*, December 28, 1878, 6:3-7:3.
[91] *Ibid.*, January 1, 1879, 1:2-3.
This same issue reprinted a poem, " Sonnet Addressed to Those in Power," subtitled " Amnesty! " originally published in *Le Patriote de la Nièvre*.

Eight years have passed . . . these children then were young,
No evil did: For, while their fathers fought
In madness, they their mother's bosom sought,
Aghast and pale, with fear upon their tongue.
Ye Great, hard winter's here. Your babes among
Their blankets warm and soft, their prayers have brought
To end. For *these* a certain death is wrought—
Hunger and cold their requiem have sung.
Beneath your strength behold their weakness lie:
The hour for clemency to innocence
Has struck. Postpone no more. Delay they die.
'Gainst hunger, innocents have no defense!
O curdle not the blood their weak hearts lift,
Speak to your souls, think of *their* Season's gift!

(Credit for the heroic task of translating the doggerel stanzas of the poems cited in this study into equally execrable English verse goes to my husband, Louis Joughin.)

nothing so much as [amnesty], this measure of justice and humanity." [92]

One more repressive measure by the Government to destroy further the people's confidence in that Government. As Prudent Dervillers summed up the implications of this new assault on freedom of the press, " It is thus perfectly plain that to ask with dignity for the doors of France to be opened to the staunchest defenders of the Republic is a misdemeanor." The Senatorial elections would come, he wrote, and everything would be the same as before; they would have no effect on the chances for an amnesty. " Our unhappy comrades shut up in the pits of New Caledonia must not hope any longer to see their friends again; they are indeed irrevocably condemned to finish their days under the leathern whips of their keepers. Formalist Republicans of all shades will never pardon them their great love of justice." [93]

---

[92] *Ibid.*, January 4, 1879, 4:3.
[93] *Ibid.*, January 4, 1879, 1:2. Emile Chausse was the personal victim of this attack on *Le Prolétaire*. Some months later, after the trial, he went to jail for a year.

CHAPTER V

THE REPUBLICANS: THE COMMUNE AS FACT

The year 1879 brought the Republicans for the first time into full power in the Third Republic. Only then did they succeed in taking over all the branches of government. Among the very first instances in which they used this new strength was the enactment of a partial amnesty bill. Because of this Republican victory of 1879, however, the political controversy over a general amnesty for the Paris Commune assumed proportions and a significance it had never had before, fanned by the irritating half-way measure of an amnesty that was not an amnesty. The Republican triumph began with the Senatorial elections of January and reached its climax with the election of Gambetta as President of the Chamber of Deputies, political changes to which the demand for an immediate full amnesty was a contributing factor, and changes of which the labor and Socialist press took a decidedly sardonic view. But the fact was that the Republicans were now not only compelled to do something, but also—for the first time—able to do something to quiet the ever-spreading agitation for an amnesty. Until the Republic seemed to be solidly in power, any demand for an amnesty would immediately run afoul of countless fears and prejudices which were associated not so much with the question of an amnesty for the Commune as with the fear of Monarchist and Bonapartist designs against the regime and with the sentimental prejudice in favor of the men who had founded the Republic. Such fears and prejudices did not belong to the politicians alone. The man in the street, the petty bourgeois, the worker—all similarly distrusted the reactionaries and did believe that the Republic must be safeguarded, even to the extent of sacrificing immediate reforms. Up to 1879, only a very small radical avant-garde had spoken out for an amnesty at all costs. But when the Chamber of Deputies, the Senate, the President of the Republic, and the Premier were all professed Republicans, then it was impossible to put off the rising

182

demand for reform by raising the cry of the Republic in danger. The Republican answer to the situation, therefore, was the Andrieux law of 1879—a law which went as far as the conservative Republicans could be led. But even such a measure as this had to be accompanied by the most resounding assurances of detestation of the Commune; and—in most un-Republican fashion—executive discretion had to be entrusted with the bestowal of so-called amnesty. Despite all this, the majority Republicans hoped and believed that by March of 1879, they, with their new power and prestige, had succeeded in eliminating the dangerous question of an amnesty from the affairs of the Third Republic.

The Senatorial Elections

The great change in the political framework in which the fight for an amnesty was to be conducted began with the Senatorial elections of January 5, 1879. Of the seventy-five Senatorial seats to be contested, sixty-five were won by the Republicans. Forty-seven out of fifty-six reactionary Senators stood for re-election, and only fourteen of them were returned to grace the upper chamber for nine more years.[1] Among those repudiated was the Comte Daru, author of the vicious report, *Inquiry on the Insurrection of March Eighteenth*.[2] In contrast, all sixteen of the eighteen Republican Senators who ran again in 1879 were elected. Joining them were thirteen former Deputies, Republicans of course,[3] and finally, over thirty new entrants on the parliamentary scene. Among the latter was Adrien Hébrard,[4] powerful director of *Le Temps*, who was thus rewarded for the staunch support his paper had given to the moderate Republicans. In all, after the elections of January 5, the Republicans could safely count on a Senatorial majority of from forty to fifty votes. The question then in

---

[1] The Duc de Broglie, particularly detested by the Socialists' was not up for re-election in 1879. His continued presence in the Senate, coupled with the Republicans' failure to take formal action against the authors of the May Sixteenth *coup*, led to much bitter comment. See below, pages 196 and 232-3.
[2] Election returns from *Le Journal des débats*, January 6, 1879, 1:1. On the Comte Daru, see above, pages 78-9.
[3] *L'Année politique 1879*, 2-4, 357-60.
[4] See Bourloton, III, 325.

everyone's mind was what effect this would have on relations between the Chamber of Deputies and the Government, now that a Monarchist Senate could no longer be relied upon to keep the Chamber in its place.

Dufaure's Declaration

Certainly, after the Republican success in the Senatorial elections, many Republican Deputies felt that from then on the Chamber ought to be the real policy-making body, with the Ministry merely its agent. As a first step in this direction, a group of Deputies conferred with Dufaure on January 12, to acquaint him with the views of their colleagues on current questions, particularly on " changes to be made in the administrative and judicial personnel and on the amnesty for the condemned men of the Commune, as demanded by a large number of Republican Deputies." [5] On January 13, Gambetta wrote, " It's war. They'll get it, and then we shall see," [6] when his candidate was passed over and a MacMahon man put in as the new Minister of War. And a showdown fight it was going to be. Even before the Ministerial program was read at the opening of the parliamentary session, the majority Republicans had planned an interpellation on Dufaure's statement of his future policy.[7]

The Ministerial declaration of January 16 was Dufaure's undoing. Whereas he, in this document, might point with pride to the fact that since he took office on December 14, 1877, pardons had been granted to 1542 Communards, this record was totally unacceptable to those—both in and out of the Chamber of Deputies—who wanted an amnesty. Furthermore, the way Dufaure characterized the Commune, and the view he took of the whole affair as absolutely closed were designed to alienate even the more cautious Republicans, who did believe

[5] L'Année politique 1879, 6. See also Madier de Montjau in the Chamber of Deputies, in Annales, session ordinaire 1879, I, 22.

[6] See letter of January 13, 1879, in " Lettres de Léon Gambetta," Revue de Paris, January 1, 1907, 61-2.

[7] Chamber of Deputies, Annales, session ordinaire 1879, I, 11, where Sénard demanded to interpellate the Government and I, 14, where he confessed that he had promised his party to conduct the interpellation before he knew what Dufaure was going to say.

that something should be done to end the disquieting agitation that had recently developed over the question of an amnesty. As the Premier saw it, " The formidable events which ravaged the country eight years ago, and of which so many traces have happily been wiped out, have left in the public spirit a vigorous and legitimate indignation against the criminal leaders who led us, with deliberate intent, to veritable social anarchy." Of course, he went on, there had been those who " were only the blind instruments" of these criminal leaders. For them, the Government had in the past used its pardoning power lavishly, and at that very moment a new decree had been drafted " which will bring to an end this salutary mission." How was this to be accomplished? " The Commission on Pardons, after three years of study, has been able to discern among those who were sent to New Caledonia or imprisoned in France, all who, on account of their backgrounds, the nature of their errors, and their conduct in deportation, would be deserving of an act of clemency; on its recommendation, 2225 [8] condemned men have just been relieved of their sentences." In other words, after the decree, there would be no one deserving of consideration left under sentence. This meant that the 1067 still at New Caledonia [9] (Dufaure, however, did not mention the figure) were, according to the letter of the Ministerial declaration, all criminal leaders of the Commune. But there remained those

[8] In the text of Dufaure's declaration as it appears in the *Annales* of the Chamber, this figure through a typographical error is given as 2225. For an itemized list of the new pardons, correctly totalling 2245, see *Journal officiel*, January 17, 1879, 314:2-3.

[9] See *Journal officiel*, January 17, 314:2-3.

Still serving sentence after the decree of January 16	891
Pardoned on condition of residing in New Caledonia—men " whose antecedents have seemed to render their return, at least for the present, dangerous "	176
Total	1067

The 176, it was explained, were " those who had received the heaviest penalties, and whose attitude appeared undeserving of favor. Among them, nevertheless, there are a few concerning whom information is awaited from New Caledonia. On this category as on the preceding, clemency will continue to be exercised. What has been done is sufficient testimony to the principles which have not ceased to inspire the Government and which will dictate its resolutions in the future." (The Commission on Pardons referred to by Dufaure had legal continuity but different personnel from that of the National Assembly. See above, pages 88-90.)

—and the number was much greater—who had been convicted *in absentia.* Some of these, the Government recognized, " took only a secondary part in the insurrection of 1871, . . . have borne the sufferings of exile with dignity, and . . . would already have been relieved of their penalties if the existing laws had made it possible." For those in this category, Dufaure promised to present a special bill which would provide " that the power to pardon be extended to include them." [10]

How was the speech received? In the Senate, Dufaure was frequently interrupted with applause, shouts of " Hear! Hear! " and general murmurs of approval.[11] But the Republican Deputies sat in " glacial silence," while Marcère read the speech in the lower chamber, and the Republican Union at once " unanimously adjudged the . . . program unacceptable." [12]

Gambetta's Plan

The Republican Union meant the parliamentary majority, and the parliamentary majority meant Gambetta. At no time in his career had he been in more complete control of his followers, or had he played a shrewder game than he now began during these critical days at the end of January 1879. The ultimate effect of the Senatorial elections of January 5 was to give Gambetta almost dictatorial power behind the facade of a parliamentary Republic. He could keep this power, however, only so long as the country was behind him. No other single factor played so large a part in the inner history of the amnesty than this preponderant power of Gambetta. After Dufaure's Ministerial declaration, it was plain that for Gambetta to consolidate his power, Dufaure must go. " Here I am, completely determined," he wrote on January 17; " I'll cast the vote of death for the Ministry." [13]

But how was Dufaure to be got rid of? Gambetta hoped that the interpellation scheduled for January 20 would do the trick. The night before, he was certain the Government would fall the next day. As for Gambetta's own role, " It's perfectly

[10] Chamber of Deputies, *Annales,* session ordinaire 1879, I, 9. Dufaure read the declaration in the Senate; Marcère, Minister of Interior, in the Chamber.

[11] Senate, *Annales,* session ordinaire 1879, I, 19-20.

[12] *L'Année politique, 1879,* 16.

[13] " Lettres de Léon Gambetta," *Revue de Paris,* January 1, 1907, 62.

understood that I don't budge from my stall; I look, I listen, I vote." He was fully confident: " I'm going to see . . . the President of the Senate, and I'll make him privy to my views on the reconstitution of the Ministry. Several Ministers have already abandoned their commanding officer and ask only a return to grace." But the changeover could not be too sudden: " It will be necessary to change two or three of them, and to get along up to 1880 with the team thus renewed, and then we'll make a clean sweep." Gambetta was even thinking, on January 19, of the speech he would make to MacMahon if he should be asked to form a Government. He would refuse categorically, since—as he said—" I will not and cannot agree to govern in second place." [14]

The Interpellation

To everyone's enormous surprise, the interpellation did not turn out as planned. When Sénard, who had called for it, confined his adverse criticisms of the Dufaure platform to its failure to go far enough on the matter of purging the bureaucracy of reactionaries, the Radical Republicans took over the show and brutally attacked Dufaure on the question of an amnesty. The cunning old Madier de Montjau denounced the platform as " a feeble echo of . . . 1876." It was not up to the Radicals, he said, to tell the Ministry what ought to take first place on its program. " We will not speak to it of the amnesty, which it does not want, and with which its pardons have nothing in common." Of course the Radicals would not, he went on, actually say that there was a sinister influence working on the Government, but there was, after all, its record on the amnesty question, and " All this together bears witness that if, between France and the Ministry there is always a gap, this gap has become enormous since January's elections." With a final threat that Republican unity might not be preserved, Madier de Montjau sat down. [15]

Next came Floquet, who said the only question at present was whether the Government really represented the country since the elections of January 5. Many, according to Floquet,

[14] *Idem.*
[15] Chamber of Deputies, *Annales,* session ordinaire 1879, I, 20-22.

did not think so. As for the Ministerial declaration, it was " a concession made with bad humor, . . . restricted and small." It was a known fact, he said, that " the country, the majority in the Chamber thought the hour for national pacification had come, and that this hour ought to have been marked by a law of amnesty." Then, with surprising moderation, the Deputy from the XIth arrondissement conceded that the amnesty need not be complete and total. There must be an amnesty, " Which I want to be complete and full, but of which the Assembly would fix the limits." Moderation? Certainly not. Floquet was playing politics. If the Extreme Left hoped to overthrow the Dufaure Ministry, that faction must not appear too intransigeant and thereby risk forcing a rapprochement between the majority Republicans and the conservative fringe. Everything at this time must be concentrated on the sole end of getting rid of Dufaure. It was perfectly true, as Floquet recognized, that the Government had just granted a prodigious number of pardons. But it was very peculiar, very peculiar indeed, he charged, that the Government, which had never had its hands tied by the Senate, had done less than nothing in this respect until after the Senatorial elections of January 5.[16]

The Radical Republicans really had gone too far. They had in fact made the timid cautious Republicans reluctant to overthrow the Ministry, for the moment at any rate. Floquet's motion, which would have been equivalent to a censure of the Government, failed to pass by only forty-five votes. Then the Moderates' motion for confidence, presented by Jules Ferry, was adopted, by the vote of 208 to 116, but with 179 abstaining —the majority Republicans, the Monarchists, and some of the Bonapartists.[17]

The Dufaure Ministry had miraculously, against all odds, survived the interpellation of January 20. " We are beaten; the Ministry is beaten; the majority is divided; the Ministerial platform won't hold water, and I am happy . . . ," wrote Gambetta. He was happy, " Because I didn't put the tip of my finger in this mess, not finding the hour propitious for striking the decisive blow." What did he want? " I prefer to

[16] *Ibid.*, session ordinaire 1879, I, 23-25.
[17] *Ibid.*, session ordinaire 1879, I, 30.

wait," he wrote, "to let all these men be dragged into the embarrassments and difficulties of every day, to let some be deceived of their foolish expectations, others to be given the necessary sense of direction . . . , to make it possible for the Ministers to achieve the last degree of unpopularity, and to give the 'Old Soldier' the leisure to choose between his inevitable fall or obedience." As for the future of the Government, " The silence in which I have enclosed myself has allowed Dufaure—him and his little skiff—not to founder; but he has swallowed a big gulp of salt water; 221 votes out of 527 [18]— there's his majority. He won't last any longer than the length of time I give him, and that won't be long." [19]

The Government's Bill on the Commune

In these last moments thus bestowed upon it, the Government took the step the most perfectly calculated to get it into these difficulties Gambetta dreamed of. On January 28, it brought in a bill, as promised in the Ministerial declaration, to make those condemned *in absentia* eligible for pardon. Lepère, the Under-Secretary of Interior, who was in the awkward position of being also the President of the Republican Union, introduced it in the name of the Ministry. This bill, together with the Government's arguments for it, was an important indication of what conservative Frenchmen believed to be the absolute limit that anyone could go in the matter of the Communards. First, there was the record on pardons. Over 50,000 cases had been investigated in connection with the Commune, and 10,522 had led to the passing of a sentence after a hearing had been held. The National Assembly's Commission on Pardons had granted 3,000 pardons, and there had been 5,639 " acts of clemency " since 1876. This meant, said the Government, that over half of the penalties had been abolished through use of the pardoning power. But there remained the problem of those convicted *in absentia*. Here the legal technicalities were formidable. Under the law, a sentence passed *in absentia* was " a threat and

[18] Where Gambetta got these figures is not apparent, unless he was basing his calculations upon the known allegiances of those who were absent on January 20.
[19] " Lettres de Léon Gambetta," *Revue de Paris*, January 1, 1907, 63-4.

not a reality," and the person so condemned would stand trial if he were caught or voluntarily surrendered himself. Of the 3,400 convictions *in absentia*, only 923 had, by 1879, had this second "trial," and admittedly, the Communards convicted *in absentia*, wrote Dufaure, the Minister of Justice and the Premier, who was the author of the report, were afraid to present themselves for trial. Moreover, the statute of limitations prescribed twenty years in their cases. Under the law, nothing could be done for these men, since the conviction was in fact only "an indictment in the most solemn form," and executive pardon could not extend to a mere accusation. Therefore the present bill was intended to remove this obstacle to the use of pardon in cases of *in absentia* conviction. The Government, the message continued, intended for its part to use this new power which would be granted it with the maximum of caution. Some of the exiles deserved generous treatment, but as for others, there was more than one man convicted *in absentia* "who would not give up plotting intrigues, and whose return to France would be the signal for new ventures." Concerning the latter, there could be no question of leniency.

What would the Dufaure proposal mean in application? In this matter of pardon for persons convicted *in absentia*, it would mean that he who should be judged worthy of a pardon would automatically, upon receiving official notice of it, lose his legal right of demanding a trial so as to defend himself against the accusation. In general, Dufaure's scheme would mean the extension of the same policy of distrust and suspicion that had marked the Government's handling of cases of the men at New Caledonia to the men in exile. Such was the "large clemency" of the Dufaure Ministry.

There was another step toward what Dufaure liked to think of as social reconciliation which the Chamber of Deputies was now asked to vote. This involved the civil rights of the man who had been pardoned. Under the existing law, pardon did not restore the convicted man to the enjoyment of his civil rights, which the fact of his conviction deprived him of. In other words, "Pardon can eliminate sentences imposed by a judge; it cannot make those penalties disappear which are imposed by law." [20] The machinery for his recovery of these rights was very slow and hopelessly encumbered with petty formalities, and was, moreover, not available to the person convicted *in absentia* or put beyond the reach of the law by the operation of the statute of limitations. The Government, with an air of making a great concession, now asked that the pardoning power be extended to cover the legal consequences of conviction, regardless of whether it had been in the first instance with trial or *in absentia*.[21] If its power were so extended, the Government promised to use this new attribute also with greatest caution, only restoring the pardoned man to his civil rights after a long investigation of each individual case, including what he had done to make amends for his crime after he had been restored to his family.

The bill which Lepère thus introduced on January 28 was the height of deception. The time had long since passed, if indeed it had ever existed, when executive pardon could heal the social wounds left by the Commune. What was more, the seeming concessions granted by the Government were in fact worse than nothing, for they reserved to the arbitrary judgment of the Government the exercise of all measures affecting the Communards. But the very elderly Dufaure had high hopes for the bill. If enacted, it "ought to make possible, after a longer or shorter delay, complete oblivion of the past, in regard to those whose conduct had been without reproach." Each one of its provisions "will enable us in the future—for all misguided citizens, and not for the benefit of those who would still incite a spirit of hate and discord—to make disappear all traces of the crimes which every Frenchman would like to efface forever from our history." As concerned an amnesty, nothing could have been more explicit than the arguments presented for this bill: " The Government . . . thought

[20] On this " civil degradation," see *Code Penal*, Article 34. The person who had received a life sentence automatically lost the right to hold public office, to vote, to serve on a jury, to testify as witness, to wear any decorations, etc., in the event he should be pardoned.

[21] No one at this juncture raised the question of separation of powers or executive encroachment on the legislative prerogative. Probably the Dufaure Ministry was too near to falling for anyone to care.

that it was compatible with neither honor nor justice to propose a general amnesty for the Commune of 1871." [22]

Two New Amnesty Bills

No sooner had the Government's bill been introduced than Louis Blanc presented a bill granting a full amnesty for the events of March, April and May 1871. Eighty-five Republicans had signed their names to this proposal. In company with the Radical Republicans were now several Gambetta men, notably Brisson, former sponsor of a partial amnesty bill, and Spuller, whose divergence from Gambetta's leadership on the question of an amnesty had long been a matter of speculation.[23] The left-wing Republicans were in full revolt.[24] In accord with a pre-arranged scheme, at the same time Louis Blanc introduced his bill in the Chamber, Victor Hugo introduced an identical measure in the Senate. But only eighteen sponsors had been obtained in the sedate upper chamber, and there were no surprise adherents to the idea of a full amnesty. The same names as before were there—Schoelcher, Scheurer-Kestner, Peyrat, Laurent-Pichat, Tolain, and the others.[25]

Political Changes

Before there could be any debate on the Louis Blanc and Victor Hugo bills, or on the Government's bill relating to *in absentia* convictions, sweeping changes in the political organization of France had taken place which put the amnesty con-

[22] For the Government's bill, see Chamber of Deputies, *Annales*, session ordinaire 1879, I, 100, and *Annèxes*, session ordinaire 1879, I, 293-4. Lepère merely introduced the bill. He read neither it nor the Government's argument.

[23] See *L'Homme libre*, October 29, 1876, 2:4, on Spuller's speech to the voters of the IIIrd arrondissement. " The amnesty," he had said, " would have been . . . the more or less necessary inauguration of the new Republican regime. . . . In spite of the unexpected resistance which the mass of the Republican majority has opposed to this necessary act, the persistent efforts of the *radical progressive* Republicans will end by imposing it."

[24] See *Le Prolétaire*, January 18, 1879, 4:2. The Extreme Left, on January 16, the day of Dufaure's Ministerial declaration, had resolved to take back its independence and break with the majority " if the majority does not want squarely to undertake the reforms necessary for the preservation of the Republic." In addition, " M. Louis Blanc is charged to take the floor, in the name of his group, in favor of a full and complete amnesty."

[25] Senate, *Annales*, session ordinaire 1879, I, 71.

trovesy in a totally new light and which led directly to the first amnesty bill of any sort to be sponsored by the Government. All this began with the long fight which had been going on between MacMahon and the Republicans over the military high command. By January 30, affairs had come to the pass where the President had either to rule arbitrarily, as he had tried to do in the May Sixteenth crisis, or to accept the principle of parliamentary government. But since he did not, in 1879, have the Senate on his side as he had had in 1877, and since MacMahon was MacMahon with all his obstinacy and his veneration for the Army, he could follow neither course. He resigned. What the Republicans were insiting upon, he charged, was " Contrary to the interests of the Army . . . and, consequently, to those of the country." And even though the Ministry should resign in the present crisis, he knew, said MacMahon, that any other Ministry representative of the majority in the two chambers would impose the same demands. It was a graceful exit. MacMahon could claim that he had never acted " from any sentiment except those of honor and duty," and the Third Republic after all these years was to have a Republican President.[26]

By 4:30 in the afternoon of that very same day, the chambers, sitting in National Assembly, had elected as President of the Republic Jules Grévy, with only ninety-nine adverse votes.[27] Immediately afterward the Dufaure Government handed him its resignations, but Grévy asked its members to stay on as caretakers.

The Republicans were quick to follow this triumph with a second, even more important for the history of the amnesty than Grévy's election. This was the election of Gambetta himself on January 31, as the powerful President of the Chamber of Deputies. Without dispute, the " Cyclops from Cahors " was the man of the hour.[28] No other name was even considered

[26] For MacMahon's resignation, see *Journal officiel*, January 31, 1879, 675:3, 676:3–677:1; also see *Le Journal des débats*, January 31, 1879, 1:4.

[27] On the election of Grévy, see *Journal officiel*, January 31, 1879, 673:1-2, 678. General Chanzy got the 99 votes.

[28] A small element of opposition tried to make itself heard with talk of organizing a meeting in the XXth arrondissement for the purpose of electing a delegation to call on Gambetta, " charged to demand his resignation in favor

for the post. He was swept in with an imposing majority, and had only sixty-seven blank ballots casts against him.[29] And while the Republicans were holding their victory party—a "long and monotonous soirée," to Gambetta's way of thinking[30]— Dufaure was writing out his resignation.

The constitution of the new Ministry, which was the last act of official consecration of the Republicans' taking over the Republic, was announced on February 5. Waddington stayed on as Minister of Foreign Affairs and also became Premier. Le Royer, a Senator, replaced Dufaure in the Ministry of Justice. Lepère, the President of the Republican Union, was moved up to the Ministry of Agriculture and Commerce. Freycinet stayed at Public Works, as did Marcère at Interior, and Leon Say at Finance. Jules Ferry came to the Government for the first time as Minister of Public Education, and there were, of course, new Ministers of War and of Marine.[31]

The question was what the changes that had taken place between January 30 and February 5 would mean for the Republic and, specifically, what they would mean to the fight for a general amnesty. Grévy, the new President of the Third Republic, was at least a Republican and well liked by the country at large. But his Republicanism was of a thoroughly middle-of-the-road, cautious bourgeois stamp. He was, moreover, the same man who in the National Assembly on March 20, 1871, had termed the Commune, "a criminal insurrection which no plausible grievance, no specious pretext can ever extenuate," and " a factious government," and had vowed that the National Assembly " can make itself . . . respected . . . by guaranteeing the maintenance of the Republic, in spite of those who compromise it by the crimes they commit in its name."[32] Waddington, the Premier, was a colorless figure, called to this high office merely in recognition of the personal friction between Grévy

of Blanqui." (*Le Prolétaire*, February 8, 1879, 6:3.) Nothing more was heard of this, however.

[29] *Journal officiel*, February 1, 1879, 706:2-3.

[30] " Lettres de Léon Gambetta," *Revue de Paris*, January 1, 1907. Letter of January 31, 1879.

[31] The new Ministry was announced in the *Journal officiel* of February 5, 1879, 769:1-2.

[32] National Assembly, *Annales*, II, 1. This was the first meeting of the National Assembly after its transfer from Bordeaux to Versailles.

and Gambetta, and holding it only on the sufferance of the latter. In its first official message, presented on February 6, the new Waddington Ministry pledged that the Government would ". . . draw its inspiration from the real needs, from the stated wishes of the country, from a spirit of progress and pacification," and would be particularly concerned with " maintaining tranquillity, security, and confidence—France's most ardent desire and her most imperative need." [33] There was not one word on amnesty, or on any of the major subjects which were troubling the country. Finally, there was Gambetta, the President of the Chamber of Deputies, the " Great Tribune " who thus voluntarily condemned himself to silence and whose personal ambition was matched only by his record of undoubted service in the founding of the Republic. The triumph of the Republicans however, had not—for Gambetta—yet reached its climax: " From now on, I am out of this terrible campaign of the past eight years; . . . I am going to be able, . . . by keeping myself above and apart from parties, to choose my hour, my road, my means." [34] That the most powerful of the Republicans was, for the moment, going to bide his time was further reflected in his remark made to a delegation from the XXth arrondissement which called to congratulate him: " We will continue to be," he said, " judicious men, men of good sense and expediency; nothing can take the place of this prudent method." [35] When the time came for Gambetta to seat himself in the presidential chair of the Chamber, his brief speech on this occasion was a masterpiece of generalities. It could not have failed to please: " Our Republic, at last emerged victorious from the contest of parties, must enter into a constructive and creative period." Hand in hand with the Government, he continued, the Chamber of Deputies was now going to bestow upon France " the blessings of peace, the guarantees of liberty, the reforms demanded by public opinion and founded on justice." [36]

---

[33] Chamber of Deputies, *Annales*, session ordinaire 1879, II, 8; and Senate, *Annales*, session ordinaire 1879, II, 36-7. The declaration, presented in Grévy's name, was read in the Chamber by Marcère, and in the Senate by Waddington.
[34] " Lettres de Léon Gambetta," *Revue de Paris*, January 1, 1907, 65. Letter of January 31, 1879.
[35] Gabriel Hanotaux, *Histoire de la France contemporaine, 1871-1900*, Vol. IV. *La République parlementaire* (Paris, 1908), 450.
[36] Chamber of Deputies, *Annales*, session ordinaire 1879, II, 7.

But what did it mean? Only that Gambetta was master of the resounding phrase, signifying little. These three men—Gambetta, Grévy and Waddington—had in their power to determine exactly what benefits of Republican liberty it would be safe, from their point of view, a political point of view, to give France.

Le Prolétaire's *View of the Changes*

To understand the further development of the fight for an amnesty it is necessary to see how the labor and Socialist press had responded to the political changes that had taken place between January 5 and February 5. When the returns from the Senatorial elections were in, *Le Prolétaire* had hailed the new fact of a Republican majority in both chambers by urging, " Now let [the parliament] go forward, let it apply without delay, frankly and resolutely, the platform with which one has been deriding France for eight years." Next, it was asserted by implication that the Republicans could not have been victorious in 1879 if it had not been for the Commune in 1871, since, " Beyond the seas and in our jails there are men whose only crime is to have loved their country too much, to have prevented the Versailles coalition from erecting the throne of Henry V on the dead body of the Republic; to these men, their country, their freedom must be restored." The conservatives, it was further implied, and not the Communards were the enemies of the Republic, and " It is a disgrace for France, a disgrace which merits the people's distrust of her, that a Broglie should still be suffered in the Senate, while an Elisée Réclus finds the doors of his homeland closed to him! " Now was the time, *Le Prolétaire* continued, for the Republicans to show where they stood; " The time for words has passed; we must have deeds." And, " If, from now on, they don't show the will to enact all these reforms, if they still talk of putting off the settling of accounts on some specious and ridiculous pretext, we will believe that they are taking advantage of the people, that they are making sport of them." Further, if the Republicans failed to act, " We, who are independent enough not to be the slaves of any Tribune . . . , we will shout to the people: ' Look out! Your former friends have become your masters. Your interests—they are trampling them beneath their feet. . . . Glutted and satisfied, they forget . . . that you are still waiting for justice." This, as *Le Prolétaire* suggested, was the Republicans' last chance. If nothing were done, the people would be told: "Vomit them forth from your bosom in legitimate disgust, and no longer expect anything except from yourselves. . . ." [37]

Three days later, a feature article, "Amnesty!", termed the Senatorial elections a great victory, which had for all time got rid of kings and emperors in France. The first act of the new representatives of the people, hopefully asked this article, "Won't it be to proclaim the amnesty?" But a partial amnesty, it warned, would be a disaster. As *Le Prolétaire* said, "And above all, no half-way measures. No one would thank you for them, and the passions which are stored up against others will turn against you." For tranquillity's sake, the amnesty must be total, the Deputies and the Senators were told, for "If you can understand the soul of the people, you will have all of our brothers from New Caledonia land on the soil of France on the same day, and on that day, forgetting our dissentions, drunk with joy at seeing them again, we will celebrate THE FÊTE OF CIVIC PEACE." [38]

To the openly expressed view of the moderate Republicans that even the subject of an amnesty should be avoided, since it might "wound or alarm serious interests," *Le Prolétaire* exclaimed, "Serious interests! And whose are more serious than those of the people?" Why, this article went one, did the people of France want an amnesty? The answer was simple: "They want it as a gage of their tranquillity, their prosperity, their happiness in the future. They want it because they, the people, have another way of evaluating what took place before, during, and after the Commune." These moderates, these former Orleanists, were still talking about extensive use of pardons as the solution, but such a policy was worth nothing in *Le Prolétaire's* eyes: "Senators and Deputies, you will vote an amnesty; you will vote it without restrictions, for the most insignificant soldiers of the Commune as well as for the most compromised leaders!" If not, "They'll say that you

[37] *Le Prolétaire*, January 8, 1879, 1:3–2:1-2.
[38] *Ibid.*, January 11, 1879, 1:1-3–2:1.

refuse an amnesty for the men of the Commune because you fear them as competitors, because you are afraid to see them use their influence to take votes away from you." [39] In all its expressions of opinion immediately after the Senatorial elections, however, Le Prolétaire accompanied its threats and allegations with a statement of confidence, insisting that the men in the parliament would give satisfaction. " We still do not doubt either your sincerity or your good faith," [40] A. Lavy had written; and again, " You will proclaim the full amnesty—France is counting on it." [41]

This note of hope for the new assembly was even more loudly sounded after Dufaure's Ministerial declaration was read on January 16. For the declaration itself, Le Prolétaire had only contempt. Dufaure was " The friend of M. Thiers, the worshipper of his memory"; he, of course, " cannot allow an amnesty." The truth made clear by the declaration was, according to Le Prolétaire, " that this Government despises the people. It has neither confidence in nor esteem for them. It regards them as a herd that they will drive according to their will, by using pretty words and flattering its passions." Thinking as it did, the Dufaure Government could not help, as this newspaper saw it, but be " all paralyzed with fear at the idea that the leaders of the Commune could return to France." [42] A further reflection of Le Prolétaire's reception of the Ministerial declaration and its promise of a law to extend pardon to those convicted in absentia was the warning note it published, " to our friends who have taken refuge abroad since '71." In the event, it said, that the exiles should read in the Journal officiel that, " Those convicted in absentia are authorized to return to France," they should take care, and " not walk into this trap until more amply informed." [43] The Dufaure declaration as it touched on the question of the exiles brought forth, moreover, from one of those very exiles a statement printed in Le Prolétaire, of his continued rejection of even the idea of accepting a pardon. To do so, he argued, was " To justify the legality

[39] Ibid., January 15, 1879, 1:1-3–2:1.
[40] Ibid., January 8, 1879, 2:2.
[41] Ibid., January 15, 1879, 2:1.
[42] Ibid., January 18, 1879, 1:2.
[43] Ibid., January 18, 1879, 3:1.

of the terrible repression of the May Days and the convictions by the military courts." But he for one was optimistic about the future, because, "*The amnesty will soon appear as a political necessity.*"[44] *Le Prolétaire* itself was of the opinion, after the Dufaure declaration, that there would be an amnesty. "France wants it, and her will is stronger than that of the Ministers." This powerful public sentiment for an amnesty must inevitably lead to a crisis: "The chambers already feel that there can be no chance of lasting accord between the Government and a majority disposed to respect the will of its electors."[45]

But as events moved along there were signs that made it increasingly clear to the labor and Socialist leaders that the amnesty had not been automatically won because of the Republicans' victory. For one thing, the failure of the January 20 interpellation to overthrow the Government gave pause for thought. Steps were taken by a group in the XIIIth arrondissement to organize a meeting of all former campaign committees in order "to protest against the strange attitude taken by the Chamber of Deputies in its *sitting of January 20, 1879.*"[46] In addition, at a meeting held on January 26 in the Salle Regnier, Faubourg de Hem, a new petition was got up, demanding a full and complete amnesty, and the speaker of the evening, the local Councillor Delambre, ended his speech for solidarity among all workers with a strong appeal that everyone join in and "Acclaim full and complete amnesty for their comrades, who are exiled far from their native land, and whose only crime was to have believed the Republic in danger."[47] Petitions meanwhile were coming in from many places in the provinces— from Limoges, from Villefranche, from Lyons, Toulouse, and Marseilles—demanding amnesty and also the freeing of Blanqui.[48] Next, the central committee on amnesty, elected

[44] *Ibid.*, February 8, 1879, 6:1-2. The letter, signed "X . . . ," was dated Vienna, January 27, 1879.
[45] *Ibid.*, January 18, 1879, 1:3–2:1. Article entitled, "A Foundering Ministry."
[46] *Ibid.*, January 29, 1879, 2:3.
[47] *Ibid.*, February 22, 1879, 6:3–7:1.
[48] See *ibid.*, January 18, 1879, 4:2; February 22, 1879, 7:3; and March 1, 1879 7:3. It was reported on January 29, incidentally, that Clemenceau had interceded unsuccessfully with Dufaure to ask Blanqui's liberation, which caused

the previous December, scheduled a meeting for February 2, at the Salle Diderot.[49] Then came the introduction of the Louis Blanc and Victor Hugo bills on January 28, signed—as *Le Prolétaire* pointed out—by only seventeen of the Seine's Deputies. As for the others, whose names were boldly printed in the paper, " We hope that the voters will know how to remember them." [50] Before the legislative session of 1879 was quite two weeks old, therefore, whatever hopes may have been held for the easy enactment of a total amnesty proved untenable.

The election of Grévy as President of the Third Republic temporarily revived these hopes. Exulting over MacMahon's resignation, A. Lavy observed, " Finally, the executive power is in the hands of a man who merits everyone's confidence." While it was true that Grévy was a moderate, that he " certainly does not see it our way with regard to social reforms," nevertheless, A. Lavy found that " He is an honest man, and that's enough for us." Up to this time, it had been possible, according to this author, to " confine the legitimate impatience of the people by pleading the lack of accord between the branches of government," but this was no longer a valid argument: with the fact that now the Chamber, the Senate, and the President were all Republicans, " The era of the Revolution has opened." [51] But the official message of February 6, to which Grévy's name was appended, left *Le Prolétaire* no room for optimism; " It contains some pretty promises, but there's no question at all of the amnesty. Does this mean we'll wait still longer? " [52]

The Government's Amnesty Bill

The very same day, February 6, that the Waddington Government failed officially to take a stand on the amnesty question in its first policy declaration, it unofficially let it be known that the new Ministry was in fact drafting an amnesty bill. In

Le Prolétaire to observe that, after all, what could you expect from a Minister " who had him convicted, thanks to the bad faith of the Faures and the Simons." (January 29, 1879, 4:1.)

[49] *Ibid.*, January 29, 1879, 8:2.
[50] *Ibid.*, February 1, 1879, 3:1.
[51] *Ibid.*, February 1, 1879, 1:3–2:1. Article entitled, " De Profundis!!! "
[52] *Ibid.*, February 8, 1879, 4:3.

answer to Louis Blanc's demand that debate on his bill be scheduled for Tuesday, February 11, the Government intervened with the request that there be no debate whatsoever until after introduction of the Government's amnesty bill.[53] The fact that the new Republican Ministry was going ahead drawing up its own amnesty bill when Louis Blanc's full amnesty bill was already in committee was the best possible proof that only a partial amnesty—as had been rumored since last December— would be forthcoming. It remained to be seen not only how, in view of the opinion specifically hostile to any partial measures which had been generated during the past few months, the Government would present its case, but also how, in the event a partial amnesty should be enacted, the half-way measure would be received—by the Radicals, by the Socialists, by labor, by the exiles, and by the men of New Caledonia.

On February 11, 1879, the Ministry introduced in the Chamber of Deputies a restricted amnesty bill, which was the joint work of Le Royer, Minister of Justice, and Marcère, Minister of Interior. Amnesty, a legislative function under the Constitution, was made subservient to the executive attribute of pardon, for the bill provided that of the persons condemned for participation in " the insurrection of 1871," those who had been pardoned or should be pardoned within three months from the promulgation of the law would automatically be amnestied. The bill further incorporated the Dufaure measure for extending the pardoning power to those convicted *in absentia*, and finally, it declared that those cases in which the prosecution had not yet been finished should henceforth be beyond the reach of the law by the operation of the statute of limitations. Persons who had been convicted before 1871 of either a common law crime or a misdeameanor punishable with a one-year prison term were specifically excluded from any opportunity to receive amnesty, even though they might be pardoned.[54] Such then was the bill called amnesty. Viewed in terms of cold legal realities, its enactment would accomplish little beyond what the Dufaure bill had proposed. The exceptions can be noted briefly. First, it made a difference in the

[53] See *idem.* for comment.
[54] Chamber of Deputies, *Annales*, session ordinaire 1879, II, 32.

question of the civil and political rights of the pardoned individual. Whereas the Dufaure bill had asked a special dispensation to give the Government arbitrary discretion in the matter of restoring such an individual to his rights, the bill now proposed would immediately endow the convicted Communard who had been deemed worthy of a pardon with his full status as a citizen, provided he had no previous criminal record. Second, the new bill went further than the Dufaure bill toward ending the work of the military courts, by dismissing those cases arising from the Commune which had not yet come to judgment.[55] But that was all. There was nothing in the spirit of the bill to suggest any fundamental change in attitude toward the Commune.

The arguments of the Waddington Government in defense of its bill showed close kinship with the arguments used for the Dufaure bill. The aim of this partial amnesty, it was stated, was " to wipe out, so far as possible, the memories of a past which was full of trouble, and to which a new era, calmer and happier, is going to succeed." The Commune itself, " that revolt which history will never amnesty," was characterized as " one of the greatest crimes which has ever been attempted against the national sovereignty." But, the Government went on, it was time to forgive and forget with regard to " those of our fellow citizens who—misguided men rather than criminals —lent their hands, without being entirely aware of what they were doing, to this crime of *lèse-patrie*." The bill would guarantee " mercy and forgiveness " for all who deserved it, while at the same time reserving " for the leaders and the principal authors of the crime, the share of just reprobation which remains attached to the Commune." The problem, as the Government saw it, was how the distinction between the worthy and the unworthy could be preserved; but the answer

[55] This was a small gain when it is considered that the ordinary limitation was ten years and that almost eight years had elapsed since the defeat of the Commune. But the benefit might have been greater in some instances, since the years elapsed were, by law, to date from the last official act of the prosecution. (See *Code d'instruction criminelle*, Article 637. " If there have taken place, in this interval, any acts of indictment or of prosecution not followed by a judgment, the public suit and the civil suit will become unactionable only after the passage of ten years, counting from the last act. . . .")

was simple: the portion which could safely be amnestied " is determined and delimited by the acts of total pardon already granted and by those which the Head of the State can still grant." Thus it was argued, within three months after the enactment of this partial amnesty law, the only persons not to have received its benefits would be " those individuals distinguished by the atrocity of their crimes, or those personalities who proclaim themselves enemies of the society in the midst of which they desire to live, and which they wish to destroy." This second category, then, those persons " who proclaim themselves enemies of society," was excluded not for any overt act, but for its opinions. And it was the Government's designating this second category, the men excluded for political reasons, which dominated the amnesty controversy until the enactment of the final amnesty in 1880.

In view of both the restricted nature of the amnesty bill and the very language with which the Government presented it, the question arises of what effect, with reference to an amnesty, the recent Republican victories had had. Only two allusions to these political changes were to be found in the Government's case for the bill. First, while stating that it was time to put an end to the continuing prosecutions, the Government pointed out that both the Chamber of Deputies and the Council of Ministers had, as far back as 1876, taken this view, and that it was, therefore, to be hoped, that now—in 1879— the Senate would concur. Second, and as the real key to the Government's actions, the Republican triumph emerged as the *raison d'être* for the bill, since—as the Government said— " The Republic is strong enough to be merciful, even with reference to those who, at its very beginning, compromised its existence. It can, without trembling for itself, renounce the protecttions which it found in the law regarding the greatest number of those who took part in the insurrection of March 18, 1871." [56] The bill, in short, was so patently a political measure that no reasonable doubt could ever have arisen that it would not be put through in short order.

[56] Chamber of Deputies, *Annèxes*, session ordinaire 1879, II, 56.

Response to the Bill

During the six days that the committee, headed by Langlois, wrangled over the amnesty bill,[57] labor and Socialist opinion was already denouncing the half-way measure. Expressions of this opinion ranged all the way from mild—such as the thanks voted to Georges Périn, one of the staunchest advocates of full amnesty in the Chamber, by a mass meeting of the craftsmen of Limoges [58]—to scurrilous, such as the articles by Arthur Arnould, Jules Vallès, and Benoît Malon in *La Révolution française*, articles for which this paper was fined 3,000 francs.[59] *Le Prolétaire*, for its part, termed the Government's bill "the most odious appeal to the people's anger." The very meaning of Republican government was betrayed by this bill, in the opinion of A. Lavy; you, the men of the Government, he charged, "respect neither your juridical practices nor your parliamentary traditions. You confound amnesty with pardon, and make of the two a mixture as shady as your inner thoughts." Amnesty had been a legislative function, but through this "masquerade of Monarchy," "you put the Chamber at your feet, and make amnesty dependent upon the pardons which it pleases you to accord." This parody of an amnesty, he went on, "by means of which you seek to dupe the people, does not spring from the generosity of your feelings, but is explained by your insatiable ambition, by your thirst for power and popular favor." But it was a worthless effort, as Lavy wrote: "Your day is done. The people today know that between you and them, there is nothing in common." This refusal to amnesty the true Republicans, the Communards, could have disastrous consequences: "Beware! Your reign can be of short duration. The popular tide ceaselessly mounts." [60] Such was the immediate

[57] The meetings of the committee must have been far from harmonious in view of the very composition of that committee, on which Lockroy and Nadaud were a formidable minority of two. Other familiar names—familiar as opponents of a full amnesty—were Langlois himself, Andrieux, and Bethmont. Constans, the future Minister of Interior, did vote, on February 22, for the Louis Blanc full amnesty bill. For the entire committee, see Chamber of Deputies, *Annèxes*, session ordinaire 1879, II, 160, fn (*). For comments on its meetings, see *Le Prolétaire*, February 22, 1879, 4:3 ("Bulletin politique" for February 16).
[58] *Le Prolétaire*, March 15, 1879, 6:2. Meeting held February 16, 1879.
[59] See *ibid.*, March 8, 1879, 2:3, and *L'Année politique 1879*, 35-6.
[60] *Le Prolétaire*, February 15, 1879, 1:1-3-2:1-2.

reaction to the bill. The Government's fond hope that the bill
" will put an end . . . to the preoccupation of public opinion
[with the amnesty]," [61] was unfounded even before the partial
amnesty became law.

The Andrieux Report

The next act of the majority Republicans served even further
to kill any element of social reconciliation which some associated with the bill. This was the committee report, read on
February 17 by Louis Andrieux, Deputy from Lyons, whose
name was thus given to the partial amnesty law, and whose
choice of words in this report marked him as the chief villain
in the eyes of the Communards and of their protagonists inside
France. Three aspects of this notorious report need to be considered: the way Andrieux characterized both the Commune
and the Communards who were excluded from the amnesty, his
categorical rejection of any thought of a full amnesty, and his
sophistical justification for tying amnesty to the pardoning
power. As for Andrieux, he was pleased to be able to say, " for
the honor of Parliament," that there was nothing in the bill
which " contains one word which would give rise to any suppo-
sition of an intention to rehabilitate the Commune." The
Commune was for him " that insurrection which was directed—
at the risk of provoking a return attack by the enemy—against
the legitimate representatives of the national will, recently
consulted in an election." The Government's bill, continued
Andrieux, " makes it possible to leave outside of the amnesty
only those against whose return the public conscience would
protest." As for the excluded, an examination of their dossiers
would reveal that some of them had had ten, fifteen, twenty—
and even twenty-four—convictions for " theft, swindling, vice,
vagrancy, begging, bail-jumping," and so on. Others of them,
" it is true, but very few of them, will be excluded for political
motives." But who dared blame the Government, Andrieux
demanded, for denying civil and political rights to " rebels who
talk of revenge and who cast the most insolent defiance at our
laws, that is to say, at the national will in its most exact and
positive expression." These, then, were the men who could

[61] Chamber of Deputies, *Annèxes*, session ordinaire 1879, II, 56.

never be amnestied, and Andrieux skillfully identified their exclusion with the general will and the parliamentary system. Next, he similarly identified the denial of a full amnesty with the security of the Republican regime. There had been for a long time, he recognized, certain of his colleagues who " seem to have received the assignment to outstrip and perhaps to create public opinion," and who had continually demanded a full amnesty. There was, for example, Victor Hugo, whom Andrieux did not, however, refer to by name, who raised up his voice in the Senate, " to demand in the name of the innocents mercy for the guilty." While respecting the love of justice, these advocates of a full amnesty must, according to Andrieux, pay tribute " to the lofty reason, the statesmanly spirit, the enlightened patriotism of those who, without weakness, knew how to refuse an amnesty." To make his point as telling as possible, Andrieux next rattled the bones of May Sixteenth. Where would France be, in whose hands would the Republic be, he wanted to know, " If May Sixteenth and [the elections of] October 14 had been fought on the question of an amnesty? " No, a full amnesty was out of the question: the Government could not overlook " what is required by public morality, respect for law, and the security of the country." This was why everybody who up to the present had looked into the these advocates of a full amnesty must, according to Andrieux, implied—" understood the necessity of limiting the application of the amnesty.'

Finally, Andrieux presented this partial amnesty bill, this pardon-amnesty, as the crowning proof that the Republicans had at last come into their own in the Third Republic. Times had changed, he said, since the days when no amnesty at all could be considered. There was now harmony between the two chambers, and Grévy was President. Today the Ministry was strong and sure of itself. " By showing its confidence in itself, it gives confidence to the country. Therefore, its first act was to introduce in the Chamber a bill for amnesty." The committee on the bill, knowing the Chamber's confidence in the Government (this was Andrieux's statement), had even extended the coverage of the bill. Thus the partial amnesty was to extend not only to the Commune, but to all " crimes and misdemeanors relative to political events anterior or posterior to the insurrection of 1871." No risk, said Andrieux, would be run by broadening the measure in this way, for "with amnesty remaining subordinated to the pardons to be granted, the Government has the choice of excluding those it judges dangerous or unworthy." For those critics of the bill who feared it gave too large a role to arbitrary executive action, Andrieux had an answer: "But the Government, gentlemen, is a parliamentary government, and it will exercise the power which you give it under its responsibility to the chambers." While he recognized that the bill went counter to the classical doctrines regarding pardon and amnesty, Andrieux concluded that this need cause no concern; "The lawmaker, particularly when he enacts a political law, has no need whatsoever to be bound by juridical tradition. Only the constitutional laws limit his freedom." In short, the legislative branch was going to enact a "conditional amnesty," and in its so doing, "Each of the two branches of government remains in possession of its constitutional prerogatives." [62]

This was the Andrieux report, and in the subsequent controversy, it proved far more important than the actual terms of the partial amnesty law. Just as the Carron Report of 1874 had furnished the enemies of the Commune a stockpile of arguments against any measure of leniency toward the Commune, so the Andrieux Report of 1879 supplied the enemies of the Opportunist Republic with all the arguments they needed against the thought of ever being reconciled to the bourgeois Republic. The Andrieux Report, by revealing the transparency of the Government's motives for refusing a full amnesty, carried a legacy of hatred.

The Debates for the Andrieux Bill

The Chamber's debate on the partial amnesty bill lacked none of the violence or melodramatic quality of that one three years before, when the Raspail bill had been on the floor. But any parallel between the two occasions stopped there. In 1876, the question had concerned only a full amnesty bill emanating from the Extreme Left. The Government had been in no way involved, and the majority Republicans had kept quiet about

[62] Chamber of Deputies, *Annales*, session ordinaire 1879, II, 118-9.

the whole issue, letting the Bonapartists do the sniping at the Radical Republicans. In 1879, by contrast, the debate concerned a Government bill as well as a full amnesty counter-bill. Because of the fact that the Government was involved, there was now an open fight within the Republican house, and the question was more one of a collapsing party discipline than one of the regime. The Republicans, in short, once their grasp on power seemed secure, now proceeded to wash their dirty linen in public, while their enemies, who were not at this moment regarded as worth reckoning with, sat on the sidelines and enjoyed the sight.

Since the Andrieux Report had covered most of the points that could be urged for a partial amnesty and had concluded with flat rejection of the Louis Blanc full amnesty bill, the debates of February 20 and 21 were largely given over to the opponents of the ambiguous pardon-amnesty. The only noteworthy speakers in its favor were Andrieux himself and Le Royer, the Minister of Justice and co-author of the Government bill. Their arguments, while closely following the lines developed in the Andrieux Report, nevertheless went even further in revealing the true thought of the majority in 1879, for in the heat of rough and tumble debate, their remarks had more bite to them, more emphasis on what the real issues involved were. The amnesty of theory and the amnesty of practice—these were Andrieux's terms for full amnesty and partial amnesty. A full amnesty was not only impracticable, it was impossible: Andrieux was convinced that " Never, never, neither today, nor tomorrow, nor later on, will you find in a French Chamber a majority to proclaim a full and complete amnesty." [63] Both Andrieux and Le Royer, as was to be expected, made much of the character of those excluded from the partial amnesty. " Is there not," Le Royer demanded, " a danger, a peril, in bringing back those who protest against the laws of the country and who glorify crime? " [64] Andrieux went beyond this, stressing again that the bill excluded " only the habitués of the police courts and the prisons; then, those men convicted of particularly infamous crimes; and finally, some

[63] Ibid., session ordinaire 1879, II, 153.
[64] Ibid., session ordinaire 1879, II, 164.

men—a very small number, however, and an insignificant proportion—excluded because of political considerations." [65]

As Andrieux and Le Royer saw it, a full amnesty would involve not only these men themselves, but also the whole affair of the Commune itself. To Andrieux's morbidly detailed recital of the atrocities perpetrated by the Communards, Naquet indignantly jumped up to protest that the men responsible for these acts were dead. Andrieux dismissed this as irrelevant, and asked Naquet if he wanted to amnesty these crimes themselves.[66] Le Royer too minced no words; accusing Louis Blanc and Lockroy of having extenuated the Commune,[67] he showed what a full amnesty would mean to him. It would be, he said, " The very glorification of the Commune, . . . the vindication of the goals of the Commune, . . . the precise, clear, categorical declaration, sent with a crash beyond our frontiers, that the hour of revenge will come." [68]

But this revenge from the left was not the underlying fear the Republican majority had of a full amnesty. It became increasingly clear, as the debate progressed, that the Monarchist threat was calling the tune. Andrieux had already, on February 17, brought up the May Sixteenth crisis. Now he did it again. Referring to the election of October 14, 1877, he asked, " Did you wage your election campaign on the question of an amnesty?" No, he answered his own question, it had been the question of the Republic; and further, in order to show a full amnesty as a menace to the Republic, Andrieux asserted that if the dissolution had been on the question of an amnesty, and if the general elections had been fought over it, the Republican majority now present on the benches of the Chamber would not be there.[69] Andrieux had tied the denial of a full amnesty to the saving of the Republic. He had so twisted the circumstances as to make it seem that the Republican majority had a specific mandate not to enact a full amnesty, and he had conjured up the spectre of the Republic in danger from yet another Monarchist *coup d'état* if a total amnesty were voted.

[65] *Ibid.*, session ordinaire 1879, II, 155.
[66] *Idem.*
[67] *Ibid.*, session ordinaire 1879, II, 162.
[68] *Ibid.*, session ordinaire 1879, II, 164.
[69] *Ibid.*, session ordinaire 1879, II, 153.

At his words, the Extreme Left could contain itself no longer, and the sitting was disrupted for several minutes, while Gambetta vainly tried to restore order from the presidential chair. But this did not deter Andrieux, who went on to say that, " By asking for a total amnesty, and above all, in the somewhat aggressive form in which they are demanding it, we would run the risk of provoking a kind of baleful reaction, which could make us lose—and in the very near future—the benefits of eight years of patience and political sagacity." [70]

To build their case completely, the opponents of a full amnesty then had to go on and prove that the Government in office was a true mirror of the popular will and that denial of a full amnesty was a sign of strength, not weakness. According to Le Royer, " The existing Government emanates from the nation; it springs from its vitals and honors itself with this fact." [71] For Andrieux also the Government was " a government of public opinion," and for himself, " I can only . . . congratulate myself on its course." [72] The existing Government, moreover, was strong, " one of the strongest executive powers which has existed in our country," according to Le Royer.[73] This strength, Andrieux did not hesitate to point out, came from the unity of all the Republicans, a unity which " it is desirable should be maintained; this union has been our strength in the past, it will be our security in the future." Then he turned to the Extreme Left; did these men realize that in obstinately backing their full amnesty bill against the will of the Ministry, did they not understand, he wanted to know, " that by refusing to be a party to these compromises which are the essence of politics, you risk weakening our strength, which is so necessary for the realization of our hopes for the future, and for the preservation, the progress, and the development of these republican institutions which are equally dear to all of us? " [74]

This Republican unity met its crucial test in the question of subordinating legislative amnesty to executive pardon. As

[70] Ibid., session ordinaire 1879, II, 154.
[71] Ibid., session ordinaire 1879, II, 162.
[72] Ibid., session ordinaire 1879, II, 153.
[73] Ibid., session ordinaire 1879, II, 162.
[74] Ibid., session ordinaire 1879, II, 156.

Andrieux argued the following day, February 21, the Deputies were by no means abdicating their right to amnesty. In truth, " It is the Chamber which is called upon to enact the amnesty, but it grants amnesty to those who will subsequently be pardoned by the Government just as it does to those who have been liberated or pardoned in the past." [75] All fine constitutional points aside, the charge made by the Extreme Left that the Chamber was surrendering one of its prerogatives could be answered in only one way by the majority Republicans. It was thus Le Royer, the only member of the Government to take part in the debate, who put squarely the question of confidence. " Do you have confidence, yes or no, in the Government which is on this bench?" he demanded. [76] This was the dramatic moment of the debate. The Chamber was in an uproar. The majority burst into spontaneous applause; the men from the Ministerial benches rushed to shake Le Royer's hand. Then the Minister of Justice turned and left the Chamber. He had done his work and done it well. In the general confusion, he probably had not even heard Benjamin Raspail's remark, " I don't have any confidence! " and he certainly did not hear Naquet, who came to the tribune to refute Le Royer's words.

The Debates Against the Andrieux Bill

The chief speakers against the Andrieux bill were Louis Blanc himself, Lockroy, Naquet, and Clemenceau. What arguments did these Radical Republicans have to offset the tight case against a full amnesty which was so skillfully prepared by Le Royer and Andrieux? As was to be expected, they urged the eight long years that had passed since the Commune; [77] they denied that an amnesty would imply any approval of the Commune; [78] and they invoked the May Sixteenth crisis as an equally grave attack upon the Republic as the Commune had been. [79] But these were not new arguments; they had been heard

[75] *Ibid.*, session ordinaire 1879, II, 194.
[76] *Ibid.*, session ordinaire 1879, II, 167.
[77] Especially Louis Blanc. *Ibid.*, session ordinaire 1879, II, 147, 149.
[78] *Ibid.*, session ordinaire 1879, II, 178. This was from Clemenceau, whose 1876 speech for a full amnesty had been hailed as " a veritable rehabilitation of the Commune."
[79] Again Clemenceau. *Ibid.*, session ordinaire 1879, II, 183.

before whenever an amnesty had been talked about. What was new and what was significant for the history of the amnesty controversy was the Radicals' specific attack on the partial amnesty bill and their prediction of what the denial of full amnesty would mean for the future.

As has been shown, the sponsors of the Government's scheme were at pains to justify the tying of amnesty to the pardoning power. The Radical Republicans for their part made this a salient point of their attack on the Andrieux bill. Louis Blanc raised this question at the very outset of his long speech, which opened the debate on amnesty in the Chamber. The issue, as he saw it, was between the Republic and the Monarchy. In his unctious, oratorical style, " which more closely resembled some religious sermon than a speech at the tribune," [80] he denounced the pardon-amnesty as " the system of arbitrary action in forgiveness, the policy of haggling over mercy." The Ministry, he charged, was asking the Chamber to hand over its power to amnesty: " It's asking you to transfer from a domain which is your own, to a domain which belongs to it, the most beautiful of your prerogatives." Pardon, to which the amnesty would be subordinated, was—in Louis Blanc's words—a prerogative of Monarchy, while, " The clemency of Republicans is amnesty." [81] Lockroy also had his say about this " half-way measure, an amnesty which is a pardon, and a pardon which is an amnesty." Such a measure, to him, could never be regarded as an act of statesmanship, which he defined, as " an act which is open, which is loyal; it is an act made by men who look big questions in the eye, who take them by the horns, and who resolve them." [82] To Le Royer's raising the question of confidence in the Government, Clemenceau replied the next day by saying " I say to him that I have confidence in it to govern, to govern under the law, but that I have no confidence at all in its arbitrary judgments." [83]

On what other scores did the Radicals attack the partial amnesty? The backers of the Andrieux bill, it will be recalled,

[80] Bourloton, I, 338, quoted from Jules Claretie.
[81] Chamber of Deputies, *Annales*, session ordinaire 1879, II, 148.
[82] *Ibid.*, session ordinaire 1879, II, 161.
[83] *Ibid.*, session ordinaire 1879, II, 179.

had placed great emphasis upon the strength of the present Republican regime in France. They had, with an air of mutual congratulation, urged this strength as the fundamental justification for an amnesty. But the Radicals raised disquieting speculations about this alleged strength, demonstrating that the very fact of a partial amnesty represented the Government as not strong, not sure of itself. They, it must be said, shared the majority's enthusiasm for the Republican victory. Louis Blanc, dismissing the fear of a Monarchist threat, called as witness the new political conditions, characterized by " the Republic standing upright." [84] Clemenceau went further and told the Republicans that on coming to power, " You ought to have declared that the Republican Party, upon peacefully taking possession of the power which finally it had just snatched after a rousing fight of eight years from the Monarchic factions coalized against it, was strong enough to confront its enemies, whichever side they should come from." [85] Lockroy too, while terming the Government strong enough to make its opinions prevail throughout the country, warned that, "[The country] will believe you are strong, if you know how to proclaim you are strong . . . ; but the country will suspect your strength, and perhaps your political intelligence, if you let it catch sight of the avowal of a weakness which nothing justifies." [86]

This remark by Lockroy pointed to the very heart of the controversy over the amnesty, which was, in short, the question of public opinion. With the Republican regime in France yet such a young thing, each side—the opponents of a full amnesty and its advocates—felt compelled to adduce public opinion in support of its position. The real issue at stake in February 1879 was whether it could be proved that public opinion was in favor of a full amnesty. The Radicals said it was. Louis Blanc asserted that public opinion was aroused over this burning question not only in the cities but in the villages as well.[87] Lockroy invoked the rapid growth of sentiment for a full amnesty in the big cities, and observed to the Chamber, " Gentle-

---

[84] *Ibid.*, session ordinaire 1879, II, 148.
[85] *Ibid.*, session ordinaire 1879, II, 183.
[86] *Ibid.*, session ordinaire 1879, II, 157.
[87] *Ibid.*, session ordinaire 1879, II, 152.

men, I do not believe that it would be possible for a Government
to govern in opposition to the big cities, to govern in opposition
to Paris!" As for the country, Lockroy was not sure it could
be shown that the provinces opposed a full amnesty. There
were, he pointed out, full amnesty petitions emanating from
such country towns at Fontvieille and Trets; and Georges Périn
broke into the speech to call attention to the fact that fifty
rural Deputies had signed the full amnesty counter-bill.[88]
Finally, in this argument over public opinion, Clemenceau came
along and sawed off the branch that Andrieux had got himself
out on. According to the Deputy from Montmartre, the Deputy
from Lyons, in his speech of February 20, had with an excess
of parliamentary melodramatics portrayed himself as a martyr
to the Republican cause. He recognized, he had said, that in
fighting against a full amnesty he was taking an unpopular
view, and that to support it would be much easier for a Deputy
" than to serve his party usefully by sacrificing to it his popularity and perhaps his re-election." [89] Clemenceau pounced on
the instrinsic contradiction in this line of thought. The opponents of a full amnesty, he charged, were trying to make out that
a full amnesty was not endorsed by public opinion in the country
at large. Yet, he continued, Andrieux himself had said in all
sincerity that " his role was the role of a sacrifice, and that he
was gambling his popularity in speaking against the full and
complete amnesty." The only inference to be drawn from this,
according to Clemenceau, was that " the [full] amnesty must
be popular." [90]

Not only was the existing state of public opinion a major issue
in the debate for and against a total amnesty, but also the
effect of such a measure on future opinion was explored at
length by the Radicals. Their remarks dealt both with the
state of public opinion in the event of a full amnesty and with
the popular mood should this be denied. Behind the arguments
presented by Andrieux and Le Royer in behalf of a partial
amnesty lay the fear of what repercussions a full amnesty
would have. This was made abundantly plain. In short, the

[88] *Ibid.*, session ordinaire 1879, II, 157.
[89] *Ibid.*, session ordinaire 1879, II, 154.
[90] *Ibid.*, session ordinaire 1879, II, 182.

political situation of 1879 dictated that a full amnesty be regarded exclusively in terms of its effect on the Republic. As Naquet said, " The question . . . is to know whether—from the point of view of the consolidation of the Republic, to which we are all devoted at this hour, from whatever point of the horizon we have arrived there—a full amnesty is not superior to this system of restricted amnesty combined with pardon which the Government proposes to us." [91] Each side—the majority Republicans and the Radical Republicans—had its answer. For the majority in 1879, a full amnesty law might be the death warrant of the Third Republic. For the Radicals, the denial of a full amnesty might well have the same effect. The latter, therefore, tried first of all to show that the dangers alleged in the return to France of those Communards whose ideas were viewed with alarm and those who had common law convictions were without foundation and would not menace the security of the Republican regime.

What of the allegation that a full amnesty could not be enacted because certain Communards convicted of common law crimes must be screened and kept out of France? Louis Blanc devoted much of his speech to demonstrating the fallacy of accepting the verdict of the military courts as a true indication of guilt. On close examination, he claimed, many Communards who bore criminal convictions on their records were guilty of nothing except a political offense, citing the cases of Melvil-Bloncourt and Elié Réclus as examples.[92] The Commune had been, Louis Blanc pointed out, not a mere insurrection; it had assumed the proportions of a civil war. Consequently it was absurd, from his point of view, to attempt to preserve ordinary peacetime legal distinctions and to accept as just or accurate the arbitrary decisions handed down by the military courts in the heat of the moment.[93] So much for those convicted of common law crimes. As for those excluded from the partial amnesty for their ideas, Clemenceau found that it would be equally impossible, in all justice, to establish this category: " I ask how," he said, " at what sign, by what criterion you recog-

---

[91] *Ibid.*, session ordinaire 1879, II, 168.
[92] See above, page 76, on the conviction of Melvil-Bloncourt.
[93] Chamber of Deputies, *Annales*, session ordinaire 1879, II, 150-2.

nize an enemy of society." To show how ridiculous it all was, he pointed out that " There is not one among us who is not, in someone's eyes, an enemy of society." Le Royer, he continued, was an enemy of society in the eyes of the Duc de Broglie, who was himself an enemy of society in the eyes of the speaker.[94] By what warrant, then, Clemenceau implied, were the Communards to be excluded as enemies of society? The fear which the majority had of seeing the revolutionary chiefs back in France was wholly unfounded, according also to Louis Blanc, who found in the device of universal suffrage, as the true expression of Republican government, ample safeguard against future revolution. " I say," he argued, " that this fear is practically an insult to the Republic, such as we have seen emerge from the wisdom of the people, and such as the peaceful victories of universal suffrage will make it." France, the people, would not turn to violence, for under the Republic there was " a nation sure that henceforward it can make its will win out by means of the right to vote." [95] The important role that universal suffrage was to play in the amnesty controversy was thus once more brought out in the debate on the Andrieux bill. What, Louis Blanc repeated, do you fear? Are you afraid that these Communards will write inflammatory articles against the Republic? He answered his own question: " Well, yes, they will write; they will do what they are doing, and which you cannot prevent them from doing in England, in Switzerland, in Germany— everywhere. Would you pretend, perchance, to proscribe their thoughts at the same time that you proscribe their persons? You would try in vain! " [96] If, in addition, these attacks should prove justified, Louis Blanc concluded, it would be the Republicans' own fault, their failure to put through essential social reforms. Naquet, for his part, wanted to know if the Deputies who would exclude those Communards of hostile views did not believe that there were already in France men of subversive opinions? Yes, there were some, he insisted, although very few. As for their influence, " They are more dangerous," insisted

[94] Ibid., session ordinaire 1879, II, 179-80.
[95] Ibid., session ordinaire 1879, II, 148.
[96] Idem.

Naquet, "if you do not enact the amnesty, than those who would return from abroad would be if you did enact it." [97]

Naquet's remark touched on the Radicals' principal talking point for a full amnesty. Others developed this contention that the mockery of a partial amnesty, far from bringing the desired pacification of the country, would lead inevitably to a surging wave of hatred against the Government which thus opened the doors to some while keeping them closed to others. To exclude certain men of the Commune, contended Louis Blanc, was to magnify disastrously the importance of those thus excluded, for "all the more you take away from yourselves the appearance of strength in order to give it to them." [98] If all but one man were amnestied, he said, think of the enormous importance that would attach to this single individual. An amnesty, to be a true act of social appeasement, must—according to all the Radicals—be a full and complete one. Louis Blanc explained: because, he said, "It is absolutely irreconcilable with all ideas of appeasement and concord that you should accord [amnesty] to others, and thereby provoke the bitter comparisons which make hatreds eternal." [99] Clemenceau too sounded an ominous note. He and his colleagues who supported a full amnesty had been accused, he said—referring to Andrieux's speech of the day before—of being agitators. But the real authors of the public unrest that was to come were the moderate Republicans themselves, were, in short, "those who refuse to take a definitive step." [100]

The key arguments of the Radical Republicans against the Andrieux bill can be summarized as follows. The bill made the legislative branch of the government subordinate to the executive. By limiting the application of the amnesty, the Government failed to live up to the very real strength it had. Public opinion both in Paris and in the country at large was in favor of a full amnesty. The establishment of the Republican Republic, resting on the principle of universal suffrage, afforded adequate guarantees against a future armed uprising and security against dangerous ideas. Finally, the denial of a full

[97] *Ibid*, session ordinaire 1879, II, 168.
[98] *Ibid.*, session ordinaire 1879, II, 148.
[99] *Ibid.*, session ordinaire 1879, II, 147.
[100] *Ibid.*, session ordinaire 1879, II, 180.

amnesty would inevitably strengthen the enemies of the Republic by giving legitimate cause for hatred of the regime which thus proscribed certain designated enemies not for their acts but for their ideas.

Significantly enough, the Radical Republicans were not alone in their attack on the Andrieux bill. A group of moderate Republicans, led by Gatineau, found it inadmissable to put the power to amnesty in executive hands, and they proposed to amnesty outright and immediately all Communards except those convicted of arson or murder, and those with a previous criminal record. With reference to public opinion, these moderates were convinced that if the Government had had the courage to introduce a general amnesty of this sort, " France would not have been frightened by the return of the most compromised men in the insurrection." [101] But this maneuver came to nothing. So did the counter-bill proposed by Marcou, who had also signed the Louis Blanc full amnesty bill, and who now proposed in his own bill to amnesty even common law crimes provided they had been committed with political intent.[102] As Marcou argued, continued reliance on the pardoning power would destroy Republican unity. " You will be obliged," he told the Deputies, " you others who do not want to break the union which is so desired among the groups in the Assembly, you will be obliged to split yourselves, to constitute the existing Chamber into two parties, into two big parties." [103]

Nothing, however, that could be said against the Andrieux bill in February 1879 could make a full amnesty prevail in its place. Since rejection of this bill would mean in all probability the fall of the Government, the Republican majority in the Chamber of Deputies was not inclined to bring on a crisis for the sake of the Communards. The Marcou bill was defeated by a simple show of hands, as was the Gatineau amendment. And the Louis Blanc bill calling for a general amnesty was defeated by 99 to 350.[104] The Andrieux bill was, in its turn,

[101] *Ibid.*, session ordinaire 1879, II, 187. On the Gatineau amendment, see 186-8.

[102] For the Marcou bill, see *ibid.*, session ordinaire 1879, I, 101.

[103] *Ibid.*, session ordinaire 1879, II, 178.

[104] *Ibid.*, session ordinaire 1879, II, 201. These are the corrected figures. As originally announced (page 186), the vote was 105 to 363; the connotations

adopted without a hitch. The controversial first article, con-taining the provision that the amnesty should extend only to those who were pardoned, passed by 345 to 104, with the Radicals, so outspoken in their criticism, voting for it in a block.[105] The bill as a whole rallied 343 against 94.[106] Those abstaining represented largely the Bonapartist faction, although the moderate Republican Jean Casimir-Perier's name was there, as was, of course, Gambetta,'s, and also that of the Radical Douville-Maillefeu, one of the sponsors of the Louis Blanc bill.[107]

The Andrieux Bill in the Senate

The Andrieux bill got by the Senate without undue difficulty. Transmitted to the upper chamber on February 22,[108] the bill as passed by the Deputies was favorably reported out of committee by Ribière on February 27.[109] The committee recognized, the report said, that there had been at the time of the Commune a great many men who " still thrown off balance by the catas-trophes of that heroic battle which Paris had just endured, made themselves guilty of misdeameanors and of crimes having in varying degrees a political character." But the fact remained that there had been others, men " deeply perverse," who " proved only too plainly, by their common law crimes, their implacable hatred of the social order, whatever it may be." This was why the committee could never approve a full amnesty, since it believed " that pity must never, neither politically nor socially, stiffle the voice of justice." For the very sake of those who should be worthy of an act of amnesty, the report insisted, certain others must be excluded, so that the former should not " be confounded with the authors of the most horribly heinous crimes." The committee, Ribère explained, had had only one

of this figure caused quite a commotion when the Chamber was told that this was the majority that had rejected the full amnesty.

[105] The vote, ibid., session ordinaire 1879, II, 194; the names, 202-3.

[106] Ibid., session ordinaire 1879, II, 200.

[107] See names, ibid., session ordinaire 1879, II, 203-5.

[108] Senate, Annales, session ordinaire 1879, II, 147.

[109] The Senate committee on the amnesty bill had Adrien Hébrard, director of Le Temps, as secretary, a rabidly reactionary minority of one in the person of Léon Clément, and only a single advocate of a full amnesty, Combescure. For the full committee, see Senate, Annèxes, session ordinaire 1879, II, 233.

reservation about the bill as it came from the Chamber; namely, that there were persons who had been deprived of their political and civil rights before 1871 who were nevertheless eligible for the amnesty—since it was possible to lose these rights for an offense punishable with even less than a year's imprisonment; such persons would recover their civil and political rights by virtue of having taken part in the Commune, an unthinkable situation. But when Le Royer had assured the committee that this was not the Government's intention, the last objection to the bill had been swept away. As for the committee, it certainly did not believe the country would be sorry that the amnesty was not a total one, for such a measure " would profoundly trouble that sentiment of justice which is one of the best and the most positive forces of Republican governments."

No difficulty need arise, the report continued, over the delegation of legislative power to the executive branch, since the grant was for a specific purpose and for a clearly limited time, and the power, moreover, was to be confided to a Government " which possesses our entire and warranted confidence." Ribière then added, as a comment on the side, an appeal for Republican solidarity. Saying that " Questions of the first magnitude have found us and will always find us indissolubly united," he designated the amnesty law as one of those measures " which must, when the vote is taken, reunite in one common accord all the devoted friends of France and the Republic." [110] After this, debate on the Andrieux bill was scheduled as the first item on the calendar for the very next day.[111]

Unlike the debate in the Chamber of Deputies, the Senate debate on the Andrieux bill was marked not by any fight between the Radicals and the Government, but instead, by displays of bad feeling between the majority Republicans and the reactionary coalition of the Right, which came to the point where many of the latter, led by the intensely Royalist Baron de Lareinty, stalked out of the Senate chamber, to the accompaniment of gleeful Republican applause.[112]

To sample the flavor of the Senatorial debate, and to get a

---

[110] Senate, *Annales*, session ordinaire 1879, II, 180-1.
[111] *Ibid.*, session ordinaire 1879, II, 199.
[112] *Ibid.*, session ordinaire 1879, II, 218.

cross-section of the thinking of the upper chamber, three key
speeches are sufficient: that of Victor Hugo, in favor of a full
and complete amnesty; that of the militant Monarchist Fresneau,
against any kind of an amnesty whatever, and that of Le Royer,
in support of the partial amnesty.

Victor Hugo opened the debate with a brief and dignified
appeal for a full amnesty, which alone, he contended, " has
within it enough of pacification for wiping [our civil war] off
the slate. Civil wars are only finished when they are made up."
He described the Republic—" the sovereign Republic, the all-
powerful Republic "—as having triumphed over both the threat
of the Commune on the Left and the menace of " three
monarchies and the power of the Church " on the Right. The
real choice before the Senators according to Victor Hugo, was
between amnesty and pardon; the two, according to him, were
mutually irreconcilable: " Pardon is a penalty . . . amnesty is
an expunging." Yet the Government and the majority Republicans were trying to combine these opposites. As a result, in
Victor Hugo's prophetic words, " When you shall have ended,
you will find that all these unfinished bandages chafe, that
all these wounds are bleeding, that all these pains are throbbing;
[you will see] hatreds among them, hatreds against you, and
the melancholy mounting of anger. The question will go on
whimpering until it comes back again." [113]

Next came Fresneau. He was neither so brief nor so dignified
as Victor Hugo. Before he sat down, he had touched upon the
instability of the Republic, on Auguste Blanqui, on the Revolution of 1848, socialism, and—strange talk from a Monarchist—
the subordination of the legislative to the excutive power. An
amnesty he defined as " a judgment on the social condition of
a country, and on the fixity of and respect conquered by the
sovereign authority." Turning to the majority Republicans,
he observed, " If you believe that we have arrived at that point
. . . , that the authority is uncontested, that no one even among
yourselves objects to your laws and your decrees, and there is
no longer any danger of armed conspiracy—you are in a happier
position than we are—that is all! " The way Blanqui's name
had been injected into the amnesty controversy had thrown some

[113] *Ibid.*, session ordinaire 1879, II, 201-2.

light on the whole affair—at least, so Fresneau asserted for
himself. No one, he alleged, questioned Blanqui's Republicanism, although he frankly did not see how this could be,
since " this Citizen Blanqui " had behind him " thirty-six years
of prison for insurrection against all the governments which
have followed one after the other, including that of the
Republic." No one, continued Fresneau, had questioned the
Republicanism of Louis Blanc and of Tolain. Why? Fresneau's
answer was ready: " Because no one in the world can imagine
the systems [they espouse] put into operation in anything but
a Republic." The upshot of all this was a dispute between
Fresneau and Tolain on the meaning of socialism; and when
several Senators shouted that the disputants ought to keep to the
subject of the amnesty, Fresneau indignantly retorted, " We are
at the very heart of the discussion in question." Then, when he
did get back to the question of an amnesty, he alleged that
" the Ministers who brought before us this bill which I have
beneath my eyes have a strength which, I fear, is only an
illusion." Plainly Fresneau and his colleagues of the Right
did not believe that " Order has returned here to the point
where we could in full safety open the doors of France to
those who would not be long in menacing her security." [114]

Between these extremes—the demand for a full amnesty and
the rejection of any amnesty—how did Le Royer, speaking for
the Government, steer a middle course? He did his work as
thoroughly as he had done it in the Chamber, and here, in the
Senate, he quite understandably was even more emphatic concerning the strength of the Government and gave an even more
ferocious scourging to the Commune. His was without doubt
the most important speech in the Senatorial debate on the
amnesty of 1879. The Government, as the Minister of Justice
now explained, had been inspired to sponsor an amnesty bill
by two circumstances: the one, the fact that an end must be
put to the disturbances generated by the question of an amnesty;
the other, the incontestable desire for social appeasement which
did actually exist. For those who wanted a full amnesty, Le
Royer set himself next to prove that the Government was truly

strong enough to enact a full amnesty with perfect security. As proof, he alluded to the peaceful transfer of the Presidency from MacMahon to Grévy. Why, then, did the Government not sponsor a total amnesty? Le Royer had his own answer: " Because we are a Government that does not yield to impulses, a Government which draws its inspiration from the political conditions in which the country finds itself, from the circumstances and the environment." This was his first reason for denying a full amnesty. The Government, moreover, did not agree that the Commune, that " abominable insurrection," should be forgot. No, Le Royer corrected himself, the Commune had not been an insurrection, " It was a crime, the memory of which we could not consent to efface." Consequently, he went on, " The country had to remember, she had to maintain without weakness the castigation which the insurrection had incurred, and she had to maintain it with the same vigor. . . ." This was his second reason for denying a full amnesty. If other reasons were needed, Le Royer had them: there could be no " wiping out," no " forgetting " for the perpetrators of " such ferocious acts as have never been seen in earlier insurrections." There was also a second category of men who must not be forgot; these were " the organizers of the Commune . . . , the men of letters, they who drew up those inflammatory appeals, those horrible denunciations . . . , they who thought up those singular decrees, those atrocious measures taken against a population which, deeply disturbed, Gentlemen, found itself beneath the blow of an almost absolute prostration." The majority of these men had been convicted *in absentia.* They, according to Le Royer, could not be suffered to " escape expiation, while the soldiers pay for them," or to be able to " claim as a title of glory their participation in the Commune and in its organization! " Of course, Le Royer hastened to explain, he was talking about " those who loudly declare that they would return here not only to object, but morover, to take their revenge." He added, " We could not amnesty them." These were the Government's reasons for a restricted amnesty.

What were the Government's reasons for urging an amnesty for even some of the Communards? There were certain ones among the 14,000 condemned men, said Le Royer, who deserved

pity. Not to amnesty them, to keep them deprived of their civil
and political rights and under police surveillance would prevent
their returning to their normal place in society and would
condemn them to poverty. Amnesty for them was an act of
simple humanity. These were the considerations of policy underlying the partial amnesty.

Three practical aspects of the partial amnesty bill had next
to be disposed of. Le Royer repeated his earlier assurances that
the tying of amnesty to executive pardon did not infringe on
the constitutional rights of the legislative branch; he went even
further " There will never be Ministers seated on this bench
who will ask of you the violation of a constitution to which
they have consecrated their efforts and of which they are the
guardians." With reference to the laborious work of examining
all the dossiers of those who had not yet been pardoned, Le
Royer anticipated no difficulty. A team of twenty-five men who
had been at work on the dossiers had managed to cover between
thirty and fifty a day, and the Minister of War had recently
assigned ninety additional men for this job. Accepting the
probability that there had been a margin for error and perhaps
regrettable miscarriages of justice in the original convictions
handed down by the military courts, Le Royer had a way out of
this difficulty too. Working through the Ministry of Foreign
Affairs, he was going to call upon the refugees of the Commune
to appear before the local French Consul and furnish him with
details on their cases. In this way, information could be got
which conceivably might lead to the return of the convicted
men to France. Le Royer placed great confidence in this scheme,
persuaded as he was that " only those who have court records
could refuse to give our consular agents the information we
ask. . . ."

The final portion of Le Royer's speech was devoted to the
great blessings which would come to France because of the
partial amnesty law. It would be a true act of appeasement.
The Communards who were to return under its provisions were,
as Le Royer described them, worthy men who had worked hard
in exile, had succeeded in " winning esteem there," and had
even managed to accumulate a little savings. And how they
longed " to breathe this air of Paris, of which they have been

deprived for eight years!" To the Senators, Le Royer exclaimed, "If you only knew what an assuagement is going to take place in their hearts, and to what an extent their anger is going to disappear!" Once the partial amnesty became law, the whole amnesty controversy would be over and done with; in Le Royer's words, "There will be no more of these irritating questions; and, allow me to tell you, you have no need to dread a return of this question of an amnesty." Why was he so sure this was the end of the matter? With great indignation, the Minister of Justice pointed out, "How indeed! When we'll have reached the point of excluding from this measure of clemency only those guilty of common law crimes, those who steeped their hands in blood to commit thievery, those who became arsonists . . . , murderers of hostages—when we shall have limited the chastisement to those I have just spoken of and to those who persist in breathing forth their fury and in laying claim to their deeds of 1871 as an honor, I ask you, who is the patriot, who is the honest man among the eighteen signers of the bill for a full and complete amnesty who would yet say: I am going to renew the agitation, I am going to go back to this amnesty bill, I am introducing it [again]?" Certain professional "amnesty-makers" might try to keep the issue alive in the press, but "they will suffer public disdain; they will find no echo!" At the climax of his speech, Le Royer turned to Victor Hugo and declared, with full dramatic effect, that "Our glorious colleague will himself recognize that clemency has been exercised to the limits that it can be, and he will forbid himself to bring again to this tribune a request which would have as its object only the deliverance of villains, unworthy of pity, or the amnestying of deeds which—in the depths of his conscience, so very pure—he repulses with all the force of his indignation." [115]

Significantly Le Royer had not raised the question of confidence in his speech to the Senate, but when it came to voting, the Republican machine functioned smoothly. The majority Senators scarcely concealed their boredom as they voted on Victor Hugo's full amnesty bill, which was turned down with-

[115] Le Royer's speech summarized from *ibid.*, session ordinaire 1879, II, 209-16.

out any comment whatsoever.[116] In the roll-call vote on the Andrieux bill, only a few conservative Republicans kept company with the better part of the Bonapartists among the forty-six abstaining. The bill thus passed by 159 to 84.[117]

Application of the Andrieux Law

The partial amnesty law was promulgated on March 5, 1879.[118] The first pardon under its provisions was dated March 11, and affected 151 Communards,[119] including Elie and Elisée Réclus and Arthur Ranc.[120] By June 5 and the expiration of the three months provided for by the law, nearly 3400 full pardons had been granted.[121] The largest number covered by any one decree was the 661 pardoned on April 20, 1879.[122] These pardons, combined with previous measures of clemency, reduced —from a total of 14,000 convictions in connection with the Commune—the number of men still serving sentence or still in exile to around a thousand by the summer of 1879.

---

[116] Ibid., session ordinaire 1879, II, 220.

[117] Ibid., session ordinaire 1879, II, 220-22.

[118] Journal officiel, March 5, 1879, 1673:1-2.

[119] Ibid., March 12, 1879, 1941:2.

[120] See Zévaès, Auguste Blanqui, 106-7, and Le Prolétaire, March 15, 1879, 4:2.

[121] Exact total, 3347—from decrees in the Journal officiel.

[122] Journal officiel, April 21, 1879, 3434:1.